Fatal
Half Measures

Books by Yevgeny Yevtushenko

POETRY

The Collected Poems 1952–1990
The Poetry of Yevgeny Yevtushenko
A Dove in Santiago: *A Novella in Verse*
Almost at the End
Bratsk Station and Other New Poems
From Desire to Desire
Ivan the Terrible and Ivan the Fool
Kazan University and Other New Poems
Poems Chosen by the Author
Stolen Apples
The Face Behind the Face
The New Russian Poets 1953–1966: *An Anthology*
Selected Poems
Poems
Early Poems

FICTION

Wild Berries
Ardabiola

NONFICTION

A Precocious Autobiography
Fatal Half Measures: *The Culture of Democracy in the Soviet Union*

PHOTOGRAPHY

Divided Twins: *Alaska and Siberia*
Invisible Threads
Shadows and Faces

Fatal Half Measures

The Culture of Democracy in the Soviet Union

YEVGENY YEVTUSHENKO

Edited and Translated by
Antonina W. Bouis

LITTLE, BROWN AND COMPANY
Boston   Toronto   London

First Edition

"Half Measures" from *The Collected Poems 1952–1990* by Yevgeny
Yevtushenko. Copyright © 1991 by Henry Holt and Company, Inc.
Reprinted by permission of Henry Holt and Company, Inc.

"Cradle of Glasnost" from *Early Poems* by Yevgeny Yevtushenko.
Copyright © 1989 by Marion Boyars Publishers Ltd. Reprinted with
permission of Marion Boyars Publishers Ltd, New York, London.

"Tolerance" was previously published in part in a different translation in *Time*
magazine, June 27, 1988, under the title "We Humiliate Ourselves."

Excerpt from *Divided Twins: Alaska and Siberia* by Yevgeny Yevtushenko. Copyright © 1988 by Yevgeny Yevtushenko. Reprinted by
permission of the publisher, Viking Penguin, a division of Penguin Books
USA Inc.

Grateful acknowledgment is made to APA Publishing, Singapore, for
permission to reprint "The Lotus Floats to the Horizon."

Library of Congress Cataloging-in-Publication Data
Yevtushenko, Yevgeny Aleksandrovich, 1933–
    Fatal half measures : the culture of democracy in the Soviet Union
    / by Yevgeny Yevtushenko; edited and translated by Antonina W.
Bouis.
      p. cm.
    Translated from the Russian.
    ISBN 0-316-96883-8
    1. Soviet Union — Politics and government — 1985– 2. Perestroĭka.
3. Perestroĭka — Poetry. 4. Yevtushenko, Yevgeny Aleksandrovich,
1933– — Political and social views. I. Bouis, Antonina W.
II. Title.
DK288.Y48 1991
947.085'4 — dc20   90-48295

10 9 8 7 6 5 4 3 2 1

RRD VA

Published simultaneously in Canada
by Little, Brown & Company (Canada) Limited

Printed in the United States of America

Half Measures

Half measures
            can kill
when,
        chafing at the bit in terror,
we twitch our ears,
                    all lathered in foam,
on the brink of precipices,
because we can't jump halfway across.
Blind is the one
            who only half sees
                        the chasm.
Don't half recoil,
            lost in broad daylight,
half rebel,
        half suppressor
of the half insurrection
                    you gave birth to!
With every half-effective
                half measure
half the people
            remain half pleased.
The half sated
            are half hungry.
The half free
            are half enslaved.

We are half afraid,
                    halfway on a rampage . . .
A bit of this,
                yet also half of that
party-line
            weak-willed "Robin Hood"*
who half goes
            to a half execution.
Opposition has lost
                its resolution.
By swashbuckling jabs
                    with a flimsy sword
you cannot be half
                a guard for the cardinal
and half
        a king's musketeer.
Can there be
            with honor
a half motherland
                and a half conscience?
Half freedom
            is perilous,
and saving the motherland halfway
                                will fail.

1989
TRANSLATED BY ALBERT C. TODD

*"Robin Hood": The Russian is Stepan Razin, the peasant rebel.

Contents

III.   SOVIET LIFE

IV.   BRIEF EXCERPTS FROM SELECTED PROSE:
The Poet's Role in Society

V.   BEYOND BORDERS

VI.   RUSSIAN GENIUSES

Contents

Editor-Translator's Foreword

"A POET in Russia is more than a poet." Yevtushenko was speaking of poetry's unique role in Russia, but the words apply equally to Yevtushenko himself — poet, prose writer, photographer, filmmaker, congressman, world traveler. In the civic tradition of Russian poetry, the poet is the voice of the people, the ombudsman, the champion of truth and justice, and the catalyst for social change. The dynamic of poet and tsar goes back at least as far as Alexander Pushkin and Nicholas I in the early 1800s, with the poet alternately in exile for his liberal views and in favor at court for his talent. Because poets express the strivings and needs of the people, they are revered in Russia as nowhere else. In preglasnost days, the message had to be elliptic, and poetry was read closely, between the lines.

Yevgeny Yevtushenko, born in Siberia in 1933, burst onto the scene when very young, his first poems published in 1949. He and his peers — Bella Akhmadulina (who became his first wife), Andrei Voznesensky, Robert Rozhdestvensky — became known as the *shestidesiatniki,* or poets of the sixties. They drew enormous, agitated crowds to their readings, and their popularity could be compared only to that of rock stars. Their bold verses, calling for freedom, thrilled audiences.

In fact, they shaped an entire generation, the generation of Gorbachev and Yeltsin, the people who began and are continuing perestroika in the Soviet Union. As Yevtushenko puts it in one of the essays in this book, their poetry was the cradle of glasnost.

Yevtushenko has remained in the center of the action in the Soviet Union as a writer and as a public figure for forty years. This volume, which takes its title from his poem on the dangers of doing things halfway, is a collection of his *publitsistika* (articles written on current issues), literary criticism, and travel pieces. The range and scope of his concerns gives an accurate picture of the social issues with which the Soviet Union has had to deal over the years.

Yevtushenko started his nonpoetic political protest activity with a telegram to Brezhnev condemning the Soviet invasion of Czechoslovakia in August 1968. One of the latest pieces in this volume is the antiracism manifesto Yevtushenko wrote for April, the independent writers' group whose meeting was broken up by anti-Semitic thugs from Pamyat in January 1990. In the intervening years Yevtushenko has been banned, threatened, censored, and punished — but not imprisoned. Some Westerners think that the only good Russian writers are those who have spent time behind bars. There are other ways to change the system besides going to prison. (And many bad writers were among the victims of the Soviet system — unfortunately, political martyrdom does not automatically confer literary talent.)

Yevtushenko helped to change the system by his public statements and actions on behalf of the oppressed and by his poetry and articles calling for reform. A common misperception is that Yevtushenko was so sensitive to political shifts that he often waited until it was safe to publish on a certain theme and then wrote "daring" verses. Actually, in most of those instances, it was just the reverse: it was Yevtushenko's pushing and demanding to get his verse into print that brought about the shift that made it "safe" to discuss the topic in print. Sometimes it took years for certain poems to see print, but once they did, they had their effect. His enormous audience was primed to expect and demand change. Yevtushenko expanded the limits, using his own head as a battering ram.

He has expanded the limits of his fellow countrymen's knowledge, too. Yevtushenko is a natural teacher. A seeker of Truth like all great writers, he is also a seeker of smaller truths and insights, all of which he shares with his readers. His insatiable curiosity about the human experience yielded discoveries that were unknown to the majority of his readers. In his extensive travels around the world, he became the eyes and ears of his countrymen. By writing about his experiences he gave Soviet readers an opportunity to compare their lives with those of the rest of the world. That information plus Yevtushenko's protests about the inequity of the situation led to a loosening of travel restrictions for all Soviet citizens and an impetus for change inside the USSR.

Yevtushenko's popularity with his readers is unflagging — even in the glasnost era, when long-banned works have become available, his books in huge printings sell out within hours of reaching the stores. His political activity in the years of perestroika has been channeled into a formal democratic role — he was elected a congressman, a People's Deputy, from the city of Kharkov with an overwhelming 74.9 percent of the vote (in a field of nine candidates). There was a national write-in vote to select the cochairmen to join Andrei Sakharov in leading the Memorial Society, dedicated to the memory of the victims of Stalinism. Yevtushenko was one of the three cochairmen selected, further evidence of the faith in his integrity and appreciation of his outspokenness among his countrymen.

This collection of articles is heartening proof that one man's voice, raised high and often, can alter the course of events. The exciting changes that the Soviet Union is undergoing today are the sum total of hundreds, thousands of voices. Yevtushenko's voice will live on long after this tumultuous period comes to an end.

The articles in this collection were written for a Soviet audience, and some of the references may not be familiar to Western readers. I have written introductions to place several of the pieces in the broad context of the major events of the perestroika years; footnotes give biographical data and other information that may interest the reader. I would like to thank Jean-Claude Bouis, whose generosity and enthusiastic support keep me going, and Mary Frances Lindstrom, whose efficiency keeps me sane.

Antonina W. Bouis
October 1990
New York

Prologue

Past and Present

Telegram to Brezhnev on Czech Invasion

When Soviet tanks rolled into Prague on August 21, 1968, to put an end to "socialism with a human face," Russian intellectuals were as shocked as the Czechs. Yevtushenko was in Koktebel, a Writers' Union resort on the Black Sea, when he heard the news and the appeals to him on Czech radio from Czech literary colleagues. Most of the writers at Koktebel expressed their outrage to one another. Yevtushenko, then thirty-five, sent a telegram to Brezhnev. His wife, Galya, packed a bag for him, certain that he would be arrested. Yevtushenko refers to his poem "Do the Russians Want War?," which became a popular antiwar ballad of the sixties.

General Secretary of the CC CPSU
Comrade Brezhnev, L. I.   *August 1968*

Dear Leonid Ilyich!

I cannot sleep. I do not know how to live my life after this. I understand only one thing, that it is my moral duty to express my opinion to you. I am profoundly convinced that our action in Czechoslovakia is a tragic mistake. It is a cruel blow to Czechoslovak-Soviet friendship and to the world Communist movement. This action detracts from our prestige in the eyes of the world and in our own.

For me, this is also a personal tragedy because I have many friends in Czechoslovakia and I do not know how I will be able to look them in the eye, how I will ever dare to face them again. I tell myself that what has happened is a great gift to all the reactionary forces in the world, that we cannot foresee the overall consequences of this act.

I love my country and my people. I am a modest successor to the great tradition of Russian literature, of such writers as Pushkin, Tolstoy, Dostoevsky, and Solzhenitsyn. This tradition has taught me that in some situations it is shameful to remain silent. I ask you to regard my views concerning the action in Czechoslovakia as those of a true son of this country, of the poet who once wrote the song "Do the Russians Want War?"

Speech at the First Congress of People's Deputies (June 1989)

In 1989 elections were held for the new Congress of People's Deputies. This was the first time that most of the 2,250 seats were contested by more than one candidate. Yevtushenko was asked to be on the ballot in a number of districts in Moscow and in other cities. He ran in the Ukrainian city of Kharkov, which is the third-largest university city in the USSR, and won with 74.9 percent of the vote in a field of nine candidates. His democratic program called for privatization of the economy and freedom of travel for all Soviet citizens. Elected to a five-year term, Yevtushenko travels regularly to see his constituents and lobbies for their interests in Congress.

The First Congress of People's Deputies was televised live, and the entire country was glued to the TV set all day, every day, for almost two weeks. Productivity went down 20 percent for the period. Naturally, not every congressman made a maiden speech. But several of Yevtushenko's colleagues petitioned the presidium to hear him, citing the fact that he was celebrating his fortieth anniversary in literature that month. His speech was one of the strongest made at the session, raising point after point, sore spot after sore spot in Soviet society.

IT IS NOT EASY sowing the seeds of perestroika in a soil cracked with national strife. What are toasts to the friendship of peoples worth, when blood flows beneath the banquet table?

The friendship of peoples must be started not even in school but in child care, on the street, the bus, in the store, where to our great shame many racial slurs can be heard.

Continuing the thoughts of Deputies Likhachev, Gorbunov, and Oleinik I proposed a new article in chapter 9 of the Constitution of the USSR:

"The sovereignty and national dignity of every republic of the USSR is guaranteed by all the other republics. Insulting any people, even the smallest in population, disrespect for its language, laws, culture, economy, customs, beliefs, and expression is considered a criminal offense and an insult to all Soviet peoples."

We cannot wash away the past if there is no soap.

The so-called strong hand is always ready to grow onto the flabby body of a weak economy. If there is no democracy in the economy, democracy will always be threatened. An undemocratic economy is caused by the cult of personality, which has never ended in our country — the cult of the personality of the state. The document read here in the name of our long-suffering peasantry is a cry of the land raped by endless contradictory regulations about how the land must live, what the land may or may not do. On this point I share the deep pain of my long-standing opponent Vasilii Belov, and on the other points we will argue later.

Continuing Adamovich's idea, I propose repealing all the sentences against the *kulaks*[1] by a special decree of the Supreme Soviet, thereby admitting at last the guilt of our society that criminally allowed the land to be deprived of so many of its real owners.

Supporting Starodubtsev, I propose throwing out from Article 19 of the Constitution of the USSR the insulting formulation about the need to erase the borders between city and village, which in fact erased so many villages from the face of the earth. I propose throwing out in its entirety Article 22 on transforming

---

1. Officially, the term *kulak* was used for rich peasants who gained their wealth by exploiting others. In fact, uncounted numbers of ordinary peasants were falsely charged and deported in order to meet the quota for "dekulakization," part of Stalin's forced and disastrous collectivization of agriculture, when private farming was replaced by kolkhozes (collective farms) and sovkhozes (state farms).

agricultural work into a form of industrial work, which demeans and makes primitive the great and poetic profession of harvester.

The cult of personality of the state has had a negative effect on industry, which has become not only a long-under-construction but an ever-under-construction edifice of the happy future.

Road workers add salt to the concrete to help the mixture "take." But if they put in too much salt, it eats away the iron armature. Our economy is like an oversalted corroded bridge, the repeated repair work on which has long surpassed the original cost. The branch ministries are like fattened repair offices, and Gosplan [the State Planning Agency] looks like a huge atelier for minor repairs for the clothes of the naked king. The cult of personality of the state has led to a state monopoly. The state, monopolizing all basic production — from paper clips to rockets — is like a clumsy dinosaur with rickety little legs bending under the body's weight, and a tiny brain in a head too far from the tail. The state monopoly of enterprises and land — this is not the so-cialism Lenin planned, but a semifeudal, antistate state capitalism. Antistate, because it is not profitable for the state itself. The index for determining the strength of a state is not the number of people with spoons but the life-style level of those who use the plows. To be as poor as we are with the phenomenal natural resources we have is the indisputable proof of the economic dead end of the cult of personality of the state and of state monopolism. We must give freedom of creativity, including economic, not only to the intelligentsia, but to all workers, peasants, and office workers.

Article 40 of the Constitution of the USSR, which begins with the words "Citizens of the USSR have the right to work," is not only primitive, but insulting. Even prisoners are also citizens and also have the right to work.

I proposed a new text for Article 40: "Citizens of the USSR have the right to *free labor*. Free labor includes the free choice of labor: collective, family, individual, state, kolkhoz, cooperative, stock, and lease. Free labor includes the right to buy the means of production and also the right to produce means of production. Farmers have the right to own the land as a means of production. The local soviets can sell land for a hundred years with the right of inheritance. Free labor is the right to sell the products of your labor at the producer's price wherever the producer decides to sell it. Free labor is the right of the producer to himself determine what salary to pay and how much to keep for development after paying state taxes. Free labor is the right to produce what is dictated by the needs of the market and the needs of the people and not what is forcibly dictated from above."

I propose removing the bragging formulation "The USSR has built a developed socialist society" from the Preamble of the Constitution. We must first build it and then brag about it. We should cut back and in several cases cease aid to poorly developed countries until our own is highly developed.

My constituents in Kharkov — the Leningrad of the Ukraine — where there is an intelligent working class and a truly working intelligentsia, gave me a firm mandate to enter the following article into chapter 7 of the Constitution: "Citizens of the USSR, independent of their party, state, or social position, have only equal rights with all the other workers in the sphere of consumer services and health care. The existence in open or hidden form of privileged special stores, pharmacies, and hospitals should be considered an anticonstitutional violation of the principles of socialist equality."

Comrades! Of course, deputies need privileges. Unfortunately, with today's situation with tickets[2] we need counters for deputies; we need urgent hotel space because of the urgency of our work. But to have luxurious deputies' lounges in airports and train stations when women, children, and old people are huddled on the floors outside is a monstrous shame. We, the Congress of People's Deputies of the USSR, are the highest organ of power. Let us with the permission of the chairman perform at least one tiny modest bit of democratic magic — let's vote to turn all deputies' lounges into waiting rooms for mothers and children and the el-

---

2. In today's Soviet Union, airplane and train tickets are in very short supply; flights are often delayed or canceled. Travelers are sometimes stuck in airports overnight or longer. People's Deputies are given priority for tickets and accommodations. The deputies' lounge, or *deputatskii zal*, is the equivalent of a VIP lounge. When Yevtushenko proposed abolishing the deputies' lounges, the response from the hall was rather feeble at first. But once Gorbachev, seated in the presidium behind the speaker, raised his hand to vote, the rest of the deputies followed suit.

derly. [The speaker raises his deputy voting card. The hall supports him. — Y.Y.] Thank you for your support!

At a meeting dedicated to his fiftieth birthday, Lenin prophetically warned: ". . . our party could, I believe, now fall into the position of a man who has gotten too proud of himself. This is a rather stupid, shameful, and laughable position." [V. I. Lenin, *Complete Collected Works*, vol. 30, pp. 326–327. — Y.Y.]

Wasn't there that haughtiness, comrades, that Party self-congratulation and self-glorification, when the portraits of leaders, and the slogans "Glory to the CPSU" and so on contrasted with the killing of millions of workers, with personal corruption, with the collapse of the economy, with the death of our boys in Afghanistan?

The historic achievement of the creative members of the Party and of Mikhail Sergeyevich Gorbachev personally is that they have courageously taken a course for new thinking. But new thinking is incompatible with the former inertia of the Party monopoly in preparing Soviet and state leaders. We have close to twenty million Party members in our country. But we have close to one hundred million adults who are not Party members! That's an inexhaustible supply of potential leaders, and we keep shuffling the same greasy *nomenklatura* deck. There isn't a single minister of the USSR who is not a Party member. You won't find a non–Party general director, either. I think there is only one non–Party republic minister in the whole country — Raymond Pauls — and only one non–Party editor in chief of an all-Union journal — Sergei Zalygin — and I think they should be put on the endangered species list just in case.

I do not understand the comments made here about the attacks on the Party allegedly organized by "dark forces" here at the Congress. There are only 292 non–Party members here, that is, less than 13 percent. What was said here is practically no more than an internal Party discussion! Neither Academician Likhachev nor Father Pitirim spoke out against the Party. Enough enemy-phobia! Let the thirty-eight Party committee secretaries who lost elections not blame it on attacks on the Party. That was simply the people's negative evaluation of their personal work.

We respect the Party for the best that it has done and is doing, and believe that it can do much more, but we do not need a new personal cult of personality or a cult of the Party.

Mikhail Sergeyevich, remember that now you are not only General Secretary of the Central Committee of the CPSU, but you are also president of the one hundred million party of non–Party members, and we the non–Party members ask you not to allow the old Party hold on jobs in our country. All of us, Party and non-Party, must be in a single, indivisible party — the party of the people.

I propose an additional article to chapter 7 of the Constitution of the USSR: "Citizens of the USSR, whether they are members of the Party or not, have the right to total equality in candidacy for any Soviet state post, including the very highest."

I propose changing the text of Article 6 to: "In accordance with the historic Bolshevik slogan, 'All power to the Soviets,' the main leading and directing force of Soviet society is the Soviet People's Deputies — the equal union of Party and non–Party people on the basis of the ideas of socialism. The highest organ of power is the Congress of Soviets."

I propose that by a special decree of the Supreme Soviet of the USSR we annul the sentences of all so-called dissident trials. We must return Soviet citizenship to everyone from whom it was taken unfairly. I propose taking away the licenses of all psychiatrists who violated the Hippocratic oath and filled mental hospitals with normal freethinking people.

Developing Drutse's proposal, and basing it on my profound respect for our army, I propose the following addition to Article 31 in my edition: "The Soviet Army has earned the noble reputation of savior of the world from fascism, and no one has the right to use it in punitive actions against Soviet or other peoples. The government figures who give such unconstitutional orders must be prosecuted."

I propose not only deleting Article 11 of the Ukase of April 8, which can lead to criminal prosecution for just criticism of people in power, but to review the entire extremely sloppy and dangerous decree.

There is, for instance, a spy-maniacal and ridiculous point on "foreign copying technology," as if all our stores were stuffed with our own domestic Xerox machines. Let us note that the idea of acceleration[3] has almost vanished, and that even Mikhail Sergeyevich no longer mentions it. Why? Because we have no means for acceleration, and the copying machine is one of them. So instead of Vasilii Belov's vigilant thesis that can be reduced to "Every Xerox under surveillance" I propose the thesis: "A personal Xerox for every Soviet citizen." Perhaps a Xerox would help him with his writing.

I propose opening a permanent all-Union newspaper, *The Deputy's Voice,* as the organ of the Congress of Soviets, with an unlimited subscription. The newspaper should have a non–Party editor, at least as a radical experiment.

We should announce a contest for a new anthem for the Soviet Union, because the words of the present one have aged hopelessly.

I propose the following amendments in the Election Law: "Elections must be universal, equal, direct, and secret. No *okrug* [regional] meetings. All elections with only one candidate, including election of the Chairman of the Supreme Soviet, will be considered void. All organizations, including the Party, have the right only to nominate candidates. The right of election belongs to the main organization — the people."

Comrades! Why did we win the Great Patriotic War? Because we all had the desire for a victory and a sense of a common enemy. Let us not look for enemies among ourselves, since we have common enemies — the threat of nuclear war, terrible natural catastrophes, ethnic conflicts, the economic crisis, ecological disasters, and bureaucratic swamps.

Perestroika is not only our spiritual revolution, it is our second Great Patriotic War. We do not have the right not to win it. But this victory must not cost human lives.

---

3. In 1985, at the beginning of Gorbachev's reforms, the slogan for change was *glasnost, perestroika, i uskorenie.* The two Russian words that entered English without translation mean, roughly, "openness, publicity" and "restructuring." The third appeal, the one that has an equivalent English word, "acceleration," did not become part of the reform package in the Soviet Union. It referred to a speed-up in productivity.

PART I

§ The Memorial Society

One of the greatest manifestations of glasnost, the policy of speaking openly, is the grass-roots movement to memorialize the victims of Stalinist repression. Hundreds of Memorial Societies sprang up all across the country, becoming the first unofficial organization of such size and scope. In the fall of 1988 several newspapers ran a write-in poll to elect the cochairmen of the national Memorial. Ales Adamovich, the Belorussian writer, Yuri Afanasyev, the radical historian, and Yevgeny Yevtushenko were the readers' choices for cochairmen, and Andrei Sakharov was elected honorary chairman of Memorial.

The society locates camp records, finds mass graves, documents the deaths of camp inmates, takes oral histories from both former prisoners and former guards, and is forming a library and museum dedicated to those years.

The moral authority of its chairmen protected and nurtured Memorial when it was in its infancy. On October 30, 1990, the society erected a monument to the victims of totalitarianism in front of Moscow's KGB headquarters. Yevtushenko is a tireless promoter of its goals and a fund-raiser in the Soviet Union and abroad for its activities.

℘ The Memorial
℘ Manifesto *(1988)*

THERE IS almost no family in our country in which someone was not killed or wounded in the war with fascism. There is almost no family in our country where someone was not killed, arrested, exiled, or wounded by every possible kind of humiliation in the war that was waged against our own people by those who spoke in the name of the people.

And if there are any families untouched by those two wars, is not our multiethnic people one family and should not our memory be our common family repository of sadness? Grieving for the victims of only one of these damned wars is as criminally unnatural as allowing only one half of the heart to feel compassion and cutting off the arteries of the other half.

The war against fascism lasted four years and we lost, according to official statistics, twenty million people, and even more according to other calculations.

The war of those who spoke in the name of the people against the people lasted decades, and no one has come up with the final number of how many millions were lost.

There is a theory that the repressions were a harsh necessity, without which we would have not survived the battle with fascism. But that theory is based either on historical ignorance or on historical cynicism. How can prewar destruction of the people be considered preparation for the defense of the people from destruction?

Here are the figures given by Lieutenant General Todorsky on the bloody purge of the Red Army's officers before the war: 3 of the 5 marshals were repressed; 3 of the 5 army commanders first rank; all 10 army commanders second rank; 50 of the 57 corps commanders; 154 of the 186 division commanders; all 16 army commissars first and second rank; 25 of the 28 corps commissars; 58 of the 64 division commissars; and 401 of the 456 colonels.

But there were also lieutenants and rank-and-file men who were first in Hitler's camps and then in Stalin's. Even when they escaped from the Nazi camps and fought against the fascists alongside Italian or French partisans, they were not saved from being counted as "traitors." Awkwardly, letter by letter we are learning the ABC's of historical memory.

We are beginning to honor the memory of leading revolutionaries, military leaders, scientists, and writers who were killed in prison cellars and behind barbed wire. Once-famous names, that were later pronounced only in a whisper, are resounding loudly now. But the national conscience and the national talent is not a privilege limited to celebrities. Our duty is to honor the memory of the murdered innocent grain harvesters, laborers, engineers, doctors, teachers, people of all professions, all nationalities and faiths, each of whom is a particle of the murdered national conscience, the national talent.

In all parts of the country, echoing each other, eternal flames burn, lit in memory of those who died in the war against fascism.

In all parts of the country, in accord with the will of the people, memorials must be raised to the victims of the repressions, like stone eternal flames. Half memory leads to half conscience.

Therefore, help Memorial.

Children on the banks of the Kolyma River to this day will bring you blueberries in human skulls they find and smile in innocent absence of memory.

How do we now decode B-13, B-41, or Ya-178[1] on the nameless, listing signs in the taiga? How are we to decipher the sign

1. These are labels on graves, referring to the camps in the Gulag system.

made in pencil on the plywood tag attached to an emaciated bare foot, when the tundra permafrost melts in the spring to yield one of its horrible secrets?

Belorussian peasants in the Kuropaty look with horror at the ravine piled with human skeletons, witnesses for the prosecution in the court of history.

Muscovites shudder as they learn of the existence, in the heart of the city in Kalitnikovsky Cemetery, of a terrible hidden ravine — the Moscow Babi Yar — where naked bodies with two bullet holes in the head, stuffed with a rag, were brought by vans at night.

Our moral law, "No one is forgotten and nothing is forgotten," should apply to both terrible wars, the Great Patriotic War and the war against our own people.

The memory we now have has no room for tears, blood, or hope. Not being armed with a knowledge of history can lead to being unarmed in the face of history.

You can't get away from history with monuments, giving them as bronze or stone bribes. The best memorial is memory. In the concept of Memorial we include the air of historical memory around the monuments. We see them not only as architectural complexes, but as a type of spiritual complex — a library of facts and a podium for public opinion.

The Memorial Society must become an organizer of the perestroika of memory, and this is work for the whole country, for all humans. Re-creating national memory without the help of its people is impossible.

Therefore, help Memorial!

The rusted barbed wire of former camps hiding in brambles is a snake that can deal a mortal wound. The toxin hidden in the barbs of the camp wire has poisoned those who see the path to the future not in democracy but in forced submission, not in pluralism but in assembly-line uniformity. That camp barbed wire was wrapped around so many talented sons and daughters of all the nationalities of our land — peasants, proletarians, intellectuals, Party and non–Party members, priests, and the devout. Who knows, if they were still alive then perhaps democracy and glasnost would have had their natural development earlier, and then there would not have been so many crimes and the war with fascism would have been won much faster, or perhaps the fascists would not even have taken power the way they did, referring to the "red terror" on a global scale, and the whole political ecology of the world might have been different. Our future was stolen from us for several decades. We must know how it happened, so that no one can ever steal our future again. The study of the past is the salvation of the future, its guarantee. The aim of Memorial is not the study of the past merely for archival precision but for precision in determining the prospects of the future, for making it impossible for our near or distant descendants to repeat the tragedies of our recent ancestors.

Therefore, help Memorial!

After the tragic years when conscience, justice, and truth were imprisoned, we must have a moral life sentence for "Stalinism," as an antinational phenomenon. It is not so much a question of Stalin and his circle, as of Stalinism as a practice, when the state is placed above man and class interests above human values. The results of Stalinism were paradoxically tragic — both state and man, both class interests and human values suffered. An analysis of the stifling of democracy in the past guarantees the defense of democracy in the future. Memorial in Moscow must be a national lecture and research center, where the morality of the present is developed on the tested facts of the past to create the foundation of the future. The research must not be directed only at finding negative facts and building up horror stories. We must publicize not only the crimes and treacheries, but the courage of the resistance, the exploits of charity, and the spiritual strength of nonparticipation. Many great books were written in those terrible years and many marvelous technological ideas were born then. But we must not use the talented and honest work of many in those years to justify the self-genocide that rampaged then.

The aims of the Memorial Society are not vengeful. We do not support the physical persecution of those who are implicated in one way or another in the bloody crimes of Stalinism. We feel that it is profoundly immoral to accuse without facts the still living or the dead. However, if there is incontrovertible evidence of guilt before the court of history, then let public punishment be the revelation of the truth of concrete crimes by concrete people, participants in the war against their own people. Hiding the truth about crimes creates the potential danger of their repetition.

The Memorial Society must become one of the centers of the most active support and participation in perestroika, glasnost, the new thinking, and democracy.

The Memorial Society must strengthen interrelations among the fraternal peoples of our country, because nothing brings you closer than common suffering.

The Memorial Society hopes that it will receive international support, for democratization and total de-Stalinization of our society is one of the main historical arguments for nuclear disarmament and mutual trust among nations.

Therefore, help Memorial!

Across a Precipice in Two Leaps? *(1988)*

THE IDEA of creating a memorial dedicated to the victims of the cult of personality did not appear just now, but after the historic breakthrough speech by Khrushchev at the Twentieth Party Congress.[1] This idea sounded in many of the speeches at conferences, meetings, and also in private apartments, trolley cars, lines. . . . This idea sounded at the Twenty-second Congress, too, but then it was jumbled, squashed, stifled — to put it bluntly, screwed. Among those who were frightened by the idea was the one who had proposed it, obliquely, Khrushchev himself. Why? Because he was, in the words of Churchill, a man trying to cross a precipice in two leaps. One foot, no matter how hard he tried to pull it out, was stuck in Stalinist times. He didn't have the courage to admit at the Twentieth Party Congress that he had been guilty of many mistakes and crimes himself. Of course, if he had admitted it, he could have been removed. But at least, with a clean conscience, he could have become a completely different leader of a completely different time. Having avoided a confession, he remained a partial man, that is, vulnerable morally. It was right to remove Khrushchev, but the wrong people removed him.

1. Khrushchev's "secret speech" to the Twentieth Party Congress on February 25, 1956, entitled "On the Cult of Personality and Its Consequences," denounced Stalin for the Great Terror.

Brezhnev was not a Stalinist. However, he made several Stalinist mistakes by inertia. Everything else — the awards made to himself, the loss of a sense of reality — lies on the shoulders of his entourage. But one of the lowest and most immoral acts of Brezhnev and his people is that the idea for a memorial was forgotten in the rush to set up the Churbanovs and Shchelokovs[2] in positions that were allegedly important to the nation. The idea of creating a memorial was resurrected with the ideas of perestroika. This idea came "from below," and its first enthusiasts were not united and at first looked like Don Quixotes. But they gradually united — not on the basis of unprincipled mafia ties, the way the enemies of perestroika have banded together, cravenly pushing Nina Andreyeva[3] before them and turning a human being into a trial balloon — will it fly or not? The uniting around the idea of a memorial happened like the confluence of small streams and rivulets into a mighty river that became a national symbol.

The first to turn to me with that idea were writers from the Urals. Then came workers, doctors, engineers, students. The idea sprang up all over the place, and so did the resistance to it. How could it not, if even at the Party Conference there were speeches made by some people that pushed back away from glasnost to the voiceless past, speeches that even the infamous Nina Andreyeva could sign?

2. Yuri Mikhailovich Churbanov (born 1936), general in the Ministry of Internal Affairs and Brezhnev's son-in-law. Nikolai Anisimovich Shchelokov (born 1910), Minister of Internal Affairs. These men, Brezhnev appointees, were accused of major embezzlement and corruption. The case, tried in 1988, threatened to expose and pull down the entire Party apparatus, implicating Yegor Ligachev and other Politburo hardliners.
3. Nina Andreyeva is a Leningrad schoolteacher who first expressed the antiperestroika sentiments of pro-Stalinists in a letter to *Sovetskaya Rossia*.

⸿ Defaming the Defamed

(1988)

I AM GLAD to be a witness of and participant in the Great Rehabilitation: the rehabilitation of revolutionary ideals, democracy, socialist glasnost, the rehabilitation of our faith in ourselves. This Great Rehabilitation is impossible without condemning the former "judges," their improper methods, which inculcated false theories both in politics and in science and which turned into antinational practice. This Great Rehabilitation is impossible without concrete rehabilitation of concrete people, concrete books, theories, which must be transformed into the national practice of democracy.

The Twentieth Party Congress started this Great Rehabilitation. Then the hands of those who feared the truth grabbed the hand of the clock of history. But they only slowed it down; they couldn't break it. History itself with the voice of the April Plenum announced the continuation of the Great Rehabilitation.

Supporting perestroika are all the best forces of our society, since only perestroika can guarantee spiritual and material development, and all of progressive humanity, since only perestroika can guarantee the safety of all peoples. Against perestroika are the reactionaries of the West and our domestic dogmatics, who are moving to ever more aggressive acts. I welcome the fair rebuttal *Pravda* gave to the antiperestroika manifesto in *Sovetskaya Rossia*.

There was only one name signed to the manifesto, but it could have included the many other enemies of perestroika who are gradually losing the mask of political mimicry.

There are two litmus tests to determine a person's attitude toward perestroika: "Tell me what you think of those who put them away, and tell me what you think of those who were put away, and I'll tell you what you think about perestroika." (Naturally, I am excluding criminal murderers, fascist collaborators, and other scum from the category "those who were put away.") Some people fail the first litmus test by not having enough information about the crimes of those who did the putting away, even though it's time people stopped excusing themselves for their naïveté. Most often it is not the naïveté of not knowing but the unwillingness to know. The second litmus test catches those who are hostile to the rehabilitated. What could be more ignoble than defaming the defamed, slinging mud on the reputations of those who died in their own blood! These inhumane attempts are usually explained away with words like, well, we're for rehabilitation but not for idealization.

Just imagine that a man returns to our house after many years of suffering behind barbed wire, unjustly accused, called a spy, murderer, and saboteur. The first natural reaction, if we are human, is joy, happiness that he is alive, that we can embrace him, feel his heart still beating. Perhaps this man, when he was free, had his faults. Perhaps, once, in the heat of argument he unfairly criticized a writer and sometimes made errors both in theory and in practice. . . . But it would still be immoral of us to react to his return initially by unleashing a torrent of rebukes and accusations over mistakes he once made instead of first and foremost rejoicing in his exoneration and his return!

Petty attempts to defame the Great Rehabilitation are doomed to failure. But only if we fight back in time, responding to every attempt with scrupulously, painfully gathered truth. We cannot allow the defamed to be defamed again.

We Cannot Correct the Past

TRAGICALLY, we cannot return to the past in order
to warn people of what awaits in the near future, which has just
become the past.

We cannot with hindsight protect the Revolution from dark
destructive forces that arose from the agitated swampy bottom and
began to devour the Revolution.

We cannot warn Bukharin or Kirov or the many others not to
support their potential murderer, who slowly but surely clam-
bered to the heights of power, standing on the helpfully offered
shoulders of his potential victims.

We cannot warn the thoughtless gang members of the poverty
committees, intoxicated by invented class hatred, that the cost of
the X's on the doors of innocent "kulak" houses would be starvation, the loss of a common language with the earth, and then
the humiliating purchases of grain, hypocritically packed in anti-
capitalist slogans, from the "damned capitalists."

We cannot share a crust of bread with Mandelstam, who died
in the camps, or defend Shostakovich, Akhmatova, and Pasternak,
who died apparently at liberty but actually behind invisible barbed
wire.

We cannot resurrect the millions of our countrymen killed by
the Nazis in the war, its destruction unleashed by Stalin, who

criminally trusted Hitler, nor resurrect the millions destroyed by domestic killers in the war against our own people, which turned into an unprecedented suigenocide.

We cannot wish anything that could make the blasphemed and destroyed houses of God grow back together out of the pieces.

We cannot do anything to wash away the filthy, bloody spot on history of the anti-Semitic sabbath of destruction of the so-called cosmopolites,[1] and then the Doctors' Plot, or the shame of resettling the Chechens, Crimean Tatars, the echelons of people from the Baltics . . .

We cannot lower the gun sights of our soldiers, minds clouded by the crazed order to shoot at our brothers and sisters in Novocherkassk.[2]

We cannot turn back our tanks crossing the borders of Czechoslovakia at the stupid will of our craven bureaucrats, and we cannot return the boys killed in the sands of Afghanistan to their mothers.

We cannot wipe away the shame of the so-called dissidents being thrown into prisons and psychiatric wards, or of the Gorky exile of Sakharov, or of Solzhenitsyn being forced into a plane that may never bring him back.

But if we cannot save anyone or anything in the past, we can still save the present from a repetition of the tragic mistakes and crimes that brought our country to the brink of spiritual and economic catastrophe. And that repetition remains a possibility as long as clubs and tear gas can be used today when the innocently murdered are mentioned, as long as some organs of the press and some writers can attack glasnost.

Perestroika is our hope and our last chance. We love our country not with blind servile love, but with the love of patriots with "their eyes open," as one of Pushkin's teachers, Chaadayev, taught us.

1. *Cosmopolite* is a code word for *Jew* in Soviet anti-Semitic circles. Cosmopolites were attacked in 1949 as a threat to the Soviet nation. A purge of Jewish professionals began in 1953, with the so-called Doctors' Plot, when Jewish Kremlin doctors were accused of attempting to poison Stalin. Jews were forced to leave their jobs in hospitals and pharmacies and the pressure quickly extended to almost every other profession.
2. A peaceful strike in 1962 in Novocherkassk over wages and living conditions ended in bloodshed, when the army fired on the strikers. This incident was hushed up until the glasnost era.

Let our young people, born after Stalin's death, accept the historic guilt for Stalinism, even though they are not personally guilty. A smug and indifferent sense of not being guilty of anything is a sin against the homeland. Citizenship begins with a sense of historical guilt, a sense of responsibility for everything that happened in our country and in the whole world. Saving the present with the memory of the past, we save our future and that of our children's children. Thus, history is saved by historical memory. That, I feel, is the main goal of the Memorial Society and the goal of our society in general.

Personal Happiness Based on the Blood of Others *(1988)*

SOME ACCUSE ME (and other properestroika writers as well) of throwing out the baby with the bathwater. That in speaking of the bitter episodes of our history we cross out our great victories. That's not true. Our literature is only beginning to reveal our history to us. And that is another of the great victories of our society. Even Stalin once said that being able to admit one's mistakes is a revolutionary's most important quality. He said it, but he didn't follow his own advice. However, after the war, he once touched on it, almost mentioned the repressions. . . . But he retreated at the last second. He never did repent.[1]

We are right to be proud of today's glasnost. It is proof of the viability of our society. The spiritual revolution taking place now is equal in significance to the October Revolution of 1917 and the taking of Berlin at the end of World War II. But we must not gag the opponents of glasnost. That is the pluralism of opinion without which we cannot get away from our dead end.

We are learning that even the famous battle cry "For the Homeland! For Stalin!" was imposed from above — even the veterans themselves say so. They also say that prices were lowered under Stalin. Yes, they were. But at the same time so was the

---

1. Stalin touched on the repressions at a 1945 banquet in honor of Victory Day.

value of human life and human conscience, and that is horrible.

Now we are wise enough to understand that deceit in the spiritual sphere inevitably is reflected in the economic sphere. They are related, alas. I was born in Zima Junction. I recently read unpleasant things about my hometown. My first reaction was dislike of the article's author. He was talking about people I held dear. But then I thought, "But it's the truth." And since it is, it is necessary. Glasnost is a lot like medicine. You have to hurt a person in order to save him.

I can picture how people in my hometown are writing letters disagreeing with him. I can understand that too. There's an opponent of glasnost sitting inside me, too. I was also trained to put up with almost any filth at all as long as no one breathed a word of it. The operating principle was you can wipe the floor with me, just don't call me a rag.

In 1954 *Komsomolskaya Pravda* printed a letter from an Old Bolshevik who did not like that I described the dead drunkenness and poverty as well as the lighter sides of life in my poem "Zima Junction." I was accused of "spitting on my homeland." No more, no less. Similar responses filled the local paper. It's been thirty-four years. And now, the same arguments are used in response to my recent poetry. Yet more proof of how deeply the rot has penetrated in us.

But even worse are silence and indifference. I have a bone to pick with our young people in this regard. Part of our youth does not believe the adults — and we deserve that. The insufficient participation of young people in today's revolution is also our fault. But how long can we ask for forgiveness? Enough time has passed for them to see what's what. It's as simple as can be: we can't change anything without their help. And if young people still turn away from us, it's beginning to be their fault. They are wrong in regard to us and to our descendants. This phenomenon deserves a name — historical dependency.

Why not just dependency, but historical dependency? Some young people leave in the middle of the movie *Repentance*.[2] As if

2. *Repentance*, an anti-Stalinist film by the courageous and talented Georgian filmmaker Tenghiz Abuladze, was a tremendous hit in the USSR in 1987–88.

to say, what does it have to do with us? But real culture requires a people to accept all its country's history, all its guilt. Even that for which it is not personally responsible. Young people from Germany come to England to rebuild Westminster cathedral, bombed by the *Luftwaffe* during the war. It is not their fault, it was their fathers who did the bombing, but guilt for their people urges them to pay off their historical debts. The best segments of American society created a public outcry at home so that their troops had to get out of Vietnam. I am not making direct analogies here, but nevertheless . . .

You must understand: the past does not exist alone! We suffer over the past in the present. And as long as we suffer, we are human beings. Bad teachers teach us in school that people are born to be happy, as birds are born to fly. And so we bring up candidates for the post of fortune's child. They are not prepared for suffering. And even worse, they are not prepared for compassion.

Many young people are embarrassed to show their feelings. They are afraid of being accused of sentimentality. But when did that word become insulting? It means fullness of emotion. But no, some young people pretend to be supermen. It's silly, of course, but it corrodes the heart. We hear more and more frequently about the inexplicable pathological cruelty of adolescents. Believe me, I have nothing against happiness. Let there be happiness. But not at the expense of others. Not based on other people's blood, on crushed hopes, on mutilated lives.

PART 11

Glasnost and Perestroika

Cradle of Glasnost

(1987)

GLASNOST was not created in a test tube. Glasnost is the child our country was pregnant with even in the most terrible times, and the boots of the Cheka [secret police] could not kick that child out of its womb, the way they did the child of pregnant Leningrad poet Olga Berggolts in 1937. The blows on the womb carrying unborn glasnost could not deform it before birth. The overdue child was weak and seemed in danger of not surviving. The day of Stalin's death became its birthday. But Stalin lived on after his death, and died slowly, sometimes feigning death, and still has not died completely. The tyrant's poisoned breath entered the infant's lungs, corroding them. The infant had weak muscles, fragile bones, but one thing was strong — its voice. The infant howled so loudly that it was heard not only throughout the country, but beyond its borders. The infant glasnost did not cry simply, it rhymed. The cry was poetry.

The early poetry of my generation is the cradle of glasnost. In 1953 a twenty-year-old poet from the Siberian Zima Junction began to understand two tragedies at the same time: the tragedy of World War II and the tragedy of the war Stalin and his henchmen were waging against their own people. Of course, this understanding could not be deep for reasons of both the poet's immaturity and his lack of information. The understanding was only partial at first because the poet had been brought up as a child in the spirit of love for the "best friend of Soviet children." This poet, as an adolescent, had dedicated his own naive childish poems to Stalin and wept when he died. Where did his anti-Stalinism come from then? Did it come only after Stalin's death? No, no matter how paradoxical it may sound, the anti-Stalinism had existed earlier, but parallel with Stalinism in the young heart. Even children in those days could not avoid seeing the arrests, the toadying up to the leader, and the terrible fear. The instinct of terror imbued children, forcing them not to think about the crimes happening all around. But the instinct of truth was stronger than the instinct of fear. Stalin's death released the instinct of truth.

When I began writing my poem "Zima Junction," among the first truth-seeking poetry after so many years of official lies, there was no Solzhenitsyn, no Sakharov, no novels by Pasternak, Grossman, or Dudintsev,[1] there were no dissidents, no abstract artists, no film *Repentance*. Akhmadulina and Voznesensky[2] had not started publishing their poetry, the word *jazz* was banned, and there was no private travel abroad for Soviet citizens. In 1953 it seemed I was all the dissidents rolled up into one. In 1957 I made a youthful declaration:

> *Borders bother me.*
> *I'm embarrassed*
> *not knowing Buenos Aires,*
> *New York.*

After the long years of Stalinism, when all the borders were closed, this was the first rebellious cry against isolation from the world. In 1960 I wrote "Babi Yar" against anti-Semitism, in 1962,

1. Boris Pasternak's novel, *Doctor Zhivago*, was completed in 1957 and published abroad. It was not published in the USSR until 1989. Vassily Grossman's *Forever Flowing* appeared in the West in 1970. Vladimir Dudintsev's *Not By Bread Alone* was published in 1956.
2. Bella Akhmadulina, born in 1937, and Andrei Voznesensky, born in 1933, along with Yevtushenko became the brightest stars of the "Young Poets," whose works shaped a generation of Russian readers. Their influence and celebrity in the 1960s has no parallel in other countries. It can be compared only to that of rock stars in the West.

"The Heirs of Stalin," with a call to throw off the oppressive shadow of the tyrant pretending to be dead.

> *As long as Stalin's heirs are still alive on earth,*
> *I will think*
> *   that Stalin is still in the Mausoleum.*[3]

But it does not follow that all my early poetry was thoroughly political. That would not be true. My first poems, which gained significant reader response, were love poems. But even those poems, to some degree, independent of my wishes, became political, since in them I defended man's great right to the personal property of his individual feelings and thoughts and rose up against the criminal collectivization of human souls. Looking back at my early poems today, I see much that is weak and naive. Some of them resemble an anthology of my lost illusions. But still there are poems that I could call an anthology of realized hopes.

When I wrote "Babi Yar" there was no monument near Kiev to the victims of fascism. Now that poem has been turned into a monument. "Heirs of Stalin" is turning into a monument for the victims of Stalinism. But the best monument to the early poems of our generation is the liberation from the tyranny of censorship, from the tyranny of the observing eye of Orwell's Big Brother. And this liberation is what we call glasnost.

---

3. Originally, Stalin's embalmed corpse was placed alongside Lenin's in the Mausoleum in Red Square. The body was removed in 1963, after the revelations under Khrushchev of Stalin's crimes.

Censorship Is
the Best Reader (1990)

LATELY I've been uncomfortable. Something's missing. I'm ashamed to admit that I miss censorship.

In order to explain this paradoxical and almost pathological nostalgia, I'll tell you a true story that verges on parable.

Once upon a time in the Stalin years there lived a young sailor, Vadim Tumanov, boxing champion of the Far East. He loved poetry, even though he didn't write any himself, and declaimed Esenin's poetry on the deck of his little vessel. Esenin was called the "epileptic poet" then, rarely reprinted, and not taught in the schools. On top of all his other sins, Esenin had committed suicide (although now there is talk that he had been murdered), and in those days that was practically an antipatriotic act, for pessimism was considered a bourgeois vestige. Delighting in Esenin, Tumanov also made mocking references to Mayakovsky, whom Comrade Stalin himself had called "the best, most talented poet of the Soviet era." This lack of correspondence with the literary tastes of Comrade Stalin during Comrade Stalin's lifetime was rather dangerous. The political officer of the freighter, frightened by the young sailor's readings of Esenin to an ideologically unstable crew, denounced Tumanov, who was sent off to the camps for anti-Soviet agitation.

However, life behind barbed wire was unbearable for the sailor-boxer's freedom-loving soul, and Tumanov escaped with a few criminal prisoners. Along the way they robbed a bank and killed a policeman. They were captured, beaten mercilessly, thrown behind barbed wire once again, and given longer sentences. After the first attempt, Tumanov escaped several more times, but he was always caught in the end. Once the guard dogs took a chunk of his back out along with a piece of his quilted jacket.

One of the cruelest guards in Kolyma was Colonel M——. After yet another capture, he forced the fugitives to crawl in front of him and eat dirt. When one man refused, M—— shot him. Tumanov's turn came. "Eat dirt, scum, or I'll shoot you too!" M—— shouted, waving his gun. Tumanov refused and M—— didn't shoot — he may have liked his stubbornness or something. . . . From a romantic poetry lover Tumanov gradually turned into a tough convict. He had a knack for finding gold. Back then convicts who exceeded the quotas were given reduced time — one year for every five in the sentence. In ten years or so, Tumanov got out and with the personal permission of the Chairman of the Council of Ministers USSR, Alexsei Kosygin, opened a gold-mining cooperative. Their gold cost five times less than state gold and the salaries paid to the miners were ten times higher than the state salary. Tumanov became the first legal Soviet millionaire. They tried to jail him several times, but his financial books were always in order, and he won several cases in a row.

In 1977 Tumanov was my incomparable guide to the former camps on the northern Kolyma River, the subject of so many camp songs. When we got back to Moscow, Tumanov and I tried to get into the National — one of the hardest restaurants for a Soviet to enter — for dinner. The massive redwood doors with bronze handles were guarded by doormen in livery with gold galloons. The doormen looked like statues depicting vigilance. However, Tumanov and I knew that all pretensions of watchfulness vanished when money was shown by the client banging on the door. Our legal Soviet millionaire waved a purple twenty-five-ruble note through the glass and the doorman reacted, even though he tried to maintain an insouciant gait. When the door opened a crack Tumanov instantly slipped the bill through and it disappeared in the doorman's hand as if by magic. The doorman was bulky and red-faced, with a nose that looked like a fire extinguisher, and he displayed no particular interest in us other than that of a lackey — will the gentlemen be placing any more money in his gray hairy hand? He opened the door to let us through and suddenly something happened to his face — it shifted in several directions simultaneously with mixed feelings, fear and joy, with joy taking the upper hand.

"Tumanov? Vadim Ivanovich?" he gasped, his eyes teary with recognition.

"Colonel M——? Colonel M——?" muttered Tumanov, smiling in disbelief, as if meeting one of his dearest friends whom he had given up for lost.

Even though Colonel M—— (retired) did not return the twenty-five-ruble note out of joy, the former jailer and the former prisoner embraced almost like brothers. A classic story, reminiscent of the relationship between the fugitive Jean Valjean and police inspector Javert in Victor Hugo's *Les Misérables*.

And this is exactly the relationship that developed for many Soviet writers, including me, with the censors.

When we tried to help our words escape beyond the barbed wire of Party dogma, the ideological guard dogs trained by their masters attacked us, tearing out chunks of our living flesh with their fangs. The masters wanted us to crawl in front of them and eat dirt. However, when we refused, sometimes the masters and the dogs began to respect us — if, of course, they hadn't killed us already.

Writers and censors — weren't both inside the same enormous concentration camp?

Today, in this strange unaccustomed absence of censorship, is it possible to find readers as diligent, thoughtful, sensitive, and subtle as the censor? Weren't we writers glorified in the readers' and in our own eyes by the fact that the censors considered metaphors, epithets, and rhymes so threatening to the state? With quick eye, the censors looked for political hints within filigree verse designs as if they were puzzle drawings for children, where the hunter and his rifle are concealed by the branches of the bush. With acute ear, the censors listened to the ticking of explosive mechanisms within iambs and trochees and with surgical elegance they removed dynamite from sonnets!

The Russian printed word has almost never known similar censor-free times, neither before nor after the Revolution. Then how did Russian literature survive? How did they manage, even in the most difficult times, to get novels and poems past the censors, works that should not have fit through any door? The same way that fish sometimes miraculously get through a sluice with the water. Russian censorship was like an accordion — when its pleats were folded tight, the lines of verse fluttered like butterflies trapped in a bellows. But as soon as the pressure eased for an instant, the butterflies, which had seemed dead, flew up into the air. The tsarist censorship in the late nineteenth and early twentieth centuries had gotten tired, with weak eyes, and began liberalizing, but it still existed, like an aged watchdog trying to prove its loyalty despite its lack of teeth. The first Russian period of total noncensorship was a brief slice of time between the February revolution of 1917 and 1918. But the tsarist censorship, aged, gouty, and wheezy, gave way to the new censorship — young and tough.

It was historically apt that the first victim of Bolshevik censorship was Gorky, who had supported the Bolsheviks before the Revolution both morally and economically. Part of the print run of his volume of political essays, *Premature Thoughts,* in which he spoke out against the violence and cruelties of the Revolution, was destroyed. The new regime made it very clear that it had learned from the tsarist regime and would not allow anything to be said against it. Censorship in the 1920s extended only to political content and did not touch upon the form of art. The avant-garde was willing to compromise on content because the regime gave it freedom of form. That compromise was its death sentence. In the 1930s the plasma of grayness and monotony spread all over the gigantic expanses of the country, gradually sucking up not only the content but the form along with many avant-gardists, who were tortured to death in the camps or cast into poverty and oblivion. The form of official art became like the content — pompous and wedding-cake-like. Any printed matter — from postcards to posters announcing soccer games and concerts — had to be passed by the censors. Editors knew what was possible and what wasn't and didn't bother to bring things that were obviously hopeless to the censors. The most hopeless case both before and after the Revolution was "Philosophical Letters," written by Pushkin's spiritual teacher, Petr Chaadayev, in 1831 and first permitted by the tsarist censors in 1914. The book had to wait for Soviet censorship's permission from 1917 until 1987. I was a witness to how the censors tried to remove Pushkin's satirical verses about the tsarist censors from a play at the Taganka Theater in the 1960s. Quotes were vetted ruthlessly, even from Marx and Engels and Lenin if they were in a context that could be seen as criticizing the system and not just a specific situation.

The censorship of the Stalin era was crude, wielding axes and other unsubtle instruments, but the post-Stalin censors were much more refined, using microscopes, loupes, ideological scanners, scalpels, and tweezers. In the heightened reading culture of the censors the most guilty were the poets of my generation. At first we tricked them easily by the titles, which allegedly put the action in a capitalist setting: "Monologue of a Beatnik," "Monologue of a Blue Fox in an Alaskan Breeding Farm," "Monologue of an American Poet," "Monologue of a Broadway Actress." We went deep into history and our historical characters from the seventeenth or some other century cried out in contemporary pain. But our censors gradually caught on. Their favorite word was "allusion," pronounced with the sensual triumphant feeling of a jailer who had found a metal file baked into an apple pie.

For the first printed version of my narrative poem "Bratsk Hydroelectric Station" in 1963 the censors demanded 593 changes in four thousand lines. Otherwise the poem wouldn't have been published for twenty-five years or so. I don't know whether I was right or not, but my guilt is expiated at least partially by the fact that for many years a few chapters from this poem of mine were the only evidence on the horrors of the Stalinist camps reprinted in the USSR for the mass reader.

The Jesuitical character of the censors was exquisite. In 1964 the editor of the journal *Znamya*, Kozhevnikov, not a liberal by any means, showed me galleys with my poetry, marked up by red pencil. I asked him, "Did Glavlit do it?"[1] He shook his head and pointed with his own pencil to a level clearly higher than Glavlit. "If you want to save your poems, go see Ilyichev,"[2] he said. "Complain about me."

I realized that all the pencil marks belonged to the Party Secretary of Ideology himself, and not to mere censors. I asked to be received and put the galleys down on Ilyichev's desk, expressing my outrage at the bureaucratic behavior of the editor in chief of *Znamya*, just as he had told me to. Ilyichev picked up the galleys, as if seeing them for the first time, as if they weren't covered with his markings in red pencil, and he sat down to read them closely, exclaiming from time to time over lines he particularly liked. When he finished reading the verse cycle, he sighed deeply, wrinkled his bald brow and looked at me with his beady eyes over his spectacles, which were creeping down his short, shiny nose.

"Things are bad for your little sailor, oh, so bad," he said shaking his head, almost sobbing, and drilling his eyes into mine.

"What sailor?"

"Your sailor, this one." Ilyichev jabbed his finger at my poem "Citizens, Listen to Me." "There's your little sailor, Yevgeny Alexandrovich, he's sitting all alone on the deck, no one needs him, and he's singing and strumming his guitar. . . . And no one's listening, Yevgeny Alexandrovich, not a soul. And yet I was a little sailor once, too, look —" And the Secretary of Ideology of the Central Committee of the Communist Party showed me his sturdy fist, covered with reddish hairs, on which there was a faded tattoo. Ilyichev jumped up and paced around me with the quick steps of a chubby but solid man.

"Your sailor is on a ship, Yevgeny Alexandrovich. And the ship isn't an ordinary one, it's called the *Friedrich Engels*. And look what's going on on that ship of yours: everyone's drinking

1. The central censor's office.
2. Leonid Fedorovich Ilyichev, ideology secretary under Khrushchev.

vodka, or playing cards, or dancing — and not an iota of attention for your sailor. It's all too symbolic, Yevgeny Alexandrovich, it's turning into a symbol. The ship is our country. The crowd on deck, the flowing vodka — that's our Russian people. And the little miserable sailor, that's you, Yevgeny Alexandrovich. And you're not miserable at all — why make these things up? And who's supposed to have made you so miserable — surely not the Soviet state?"

Ilyichev stopped his badgered running around me, sat down, and pushed a cup of cooled-off tea toward me along with a plate of cookies.

"Don't be shy, Yevgeny Alexandrovich, try our Party cookies. Of course, you know the artist Kuindzhi. I have one of his canvases in my modest collection, by the way. You can't compare my collection with yours. I've heard about it, I have. But did you know that he was also a celebrated bird doctor? You know how it happens with songbirds, when they get sad in captivity and try to break out of the cage and damage a wing. . . . It's hard to sing in captivity, Yevgeny Alexandrovich, oh, so hard. . . . After all, I'm in a cage in this office, you know. . . . But, no more about me. . . . So, Kuindzhi saved the wings or set the bones for many birds and he fed them herbs when their throats were sore. And when he died, they say that the owners of the songbirds all came to the funeral with the caged birds, opened the cages, and the birds sat on the coffin and sang their song of thanks to him."

Ilyichev leaned over the table, smiled crookedly, and whispered in a way that made me recoil, "And when I die, Yevgeny Alexandrovich, will any songbirds memorialize me with their songs? So who's the wretched sailor, Yevgeny Alexandrovich, you or me? Eh?"

Ilyichev leaned back in his chair, shut his eyes, and groaned. But when he opened his eyes again they were energetic, collected, and businesslike.

The red-haired hand with its tattoo handed over my galleys. His voice was ordinary, indifferent, when he said, "We'll deal with Kozhevnikov, Yevgeny Alexandrovich. He's been in his editorial chair too long, he has. But you help me get this poem published. Come on, think of another name for the ship instead of the *Friedrich Engels*." Ilyichev smiled with all the charm he could muster. "But not the *Karl Marx*."

That's the kind of subtle reader we Russian poets used to have! But God forbid they should ever return.

℘ Sakharov (1989)

SOMETIME in the mid-seventies Sakharov invited me to his apartment and asked me to sign a collective letter calling for the repeal of the death penalty. I too was for the repeal, but back then I did not particularly believe in the effectiveness of collective letters. Their authors, so-called signers, were then individually called on the carpet. Some of them recanted, claiming that they had been led astray, and repented. The bureaucracy did not simply punish, it also bought people and created schisms. The era of executions had passed — this was the period of quiet choking in back alleys. People were blacklisted simply for humanistic initiatives, not only for speaking out against the government. Part of the liberal intelligentsia, squirming under the weight of the "cult of impersonality," followed the Soviet modification of Galileo's last cry, "It still revolves nevertheless . . ." which added the forced ". . . but of course, only on orders from the Party."

I offered to write my own individual letter demanding the repeal of the death penalty. Sakharov understood my reasoning and said that that would be all right, too. I added that nevertheless I did not believe that these letters would achieve anything positive. He thought and said, sadly but firmly, "Yes, you're right, of course. . . . In the present situation it's merely a gesture. . . . But today a humane gesture is important . . . even if it's futile."

He did not change my mind, but it was impossible to get him to change his. He was silent, apparently mentally going through the list of the few remaining famous intellectuals who might sign the collective letter, and then asked, "You're close friends with Lyubimov. Do you think he would sign?" The Taganka Theater was then under constant threat of having Yuri Lyubimov, its chief director, fired. I replied, "Lyubimov's signature under this letter won't make a decisive difference, but if he signs it we might lose the Taganka Theater."

Sakharov looked at me with his kind, shy eyes, which were at the same time strong and hit right at your conscience. He asked, just as sadly but firmly, "Doesn't it seem to you that if our intelligentsia doesn't sign letters like this, we will lose — and forever — the Taganka Theater, and Lyubimov himself, and much more?"

That's how he lived — sadly and firmly. What had changed the young successful atomic scientist, winner of three gold Hero of Socialist Labor stars, and who according to law should have had a monument erected to him in his lifetime? What had turned him, a man so removed from politics by nature, into one of the era's central political figures?

The pangs of conscience, traditional to the Russian intelligentsia. The hydrogen bomb that he developed eventually led to an explosion of his conscience, which in turn undermined the foundations of the world's largest militaristic bloc (threatening all of humanity) — the bureaucracy.

But Sakharov treated even the bureaucracy with his usual courtesy and politeness, sending the Brezhnev leadership his amateurish but prophetic manifesto on peaceful coexistence, in which he proclaimed the theory of convergence between socialist and capitalist countries as the only means of salvation. The bureaucracy not only turned away from Sakharov, but like a multiheaded monster began clicking numerous bared, spitting, and biting jaws.

Sakharov found himself in Pasternak's position, not a politician but in the epicenter of politics, because in a conscienceless administrative system, an unkilled conscience is a political phenomenon. But Sakharov went further than Pasternak and heroically sacrificed his science, consciously becoming a political fighter. As a political fighter, Sakharov was unique — history has not known such a gentle, shy fighter, such a polite and awkward hero. Sakharov was a unique politician, because there was nothing of professional political cynicism about him. His unarmed wise naïveté, bordering on the childlike, raised the shamefully fallen prestige of politics per se. Sakharov was a unique patriot who protested against our troops in Prague and then in Afghanistan, thereby proving that if patriotism toward your country is in contradiction to patriotism toward humanity, it ceases to be patriotism.

Sakharov lived according to the ancient British principle: only a true gentleman takes up hopeless causes. Yet nevertheless, the causes he took up turned out not to be hopeless. Yes, it was thanks to Gorbachev's telephone call to Gorky that Sakharov returned from exile. But perestroika and glasnost became possible not only thanks to Gorbachev, but also thanks to Sakharov and the entire human rights movement.

The official statement by our government that human values take primacy over class interests — isn't that Sakharov's thesis, which just recently was still called "antipatriotic"? Isn't betting on the development of joint enterprises with foreign partners the first clumsy but promising step of Sakharov's convergence, spat upon not so long ago? Didn't Sakharov help bring down the Berlin Wall by calling for the destruction of all barriers? It turned out that political amateurism with a pure conscience is much more effective than professional politicking with a dirty conscience. When just yesterday, the live Sakharov, deputy badge on his lapel, walked along the Kremlin cobblestones, slick with spilled blood, his figure seemed tiny and defenseless before the gigantic shadows of Ivan the Terrible and Stalin. But after Sakharov's death, his shadow, imprinted on the Kremlin walls forever, will keep growing bigger as the shadows of the tyrants will diminish.

Sakharov did not appear out of the blue. He was born out of all the best that the great Russian intelligentsia left us. From Tolstoy he took and put into practice the thesis of nonviolent resistance. From Dostoevsky, the thesis that all the best ideals of mankind are not worth the tears of an innocent child. From Chekhov, that there are no little people or little sufferings. Sakharov won. Sadly, but firmly.

℘ *Pass to a Trial* *(1989)*

The trial in 1966 of Yuli Daniel, who wrote under the name Nikolai Arzhak, and Andrei Sinyavsky, who wrote under the pseudonym Abram Tertz, on criminal charges for writing and disseminating anti-Soviet literature was a great blow to the freedom of literature. The two men were sentenced to five years of hard labor. Daniel stayed in the Soviet Union and died in 1989. Sinyavsky emigrated to Paris, where he publishes émigré literature. He returned to the Soviet Union for the first time to attend Daniel's funeral.

IN HIS LAST INTERVIEW with *Moscow News,* that of September 11, 1988, Yuli Daniel said, "Strangely enough, what I remembered was that the courtroom was filled with many well-wishers; I felt a warm wave of sympathy. I remember Yevtushenko's aghast face, and other faces; they all expressed compassion."

Before the trial I had not known its protagonists personally — I had only read Andrei Sinyavsky's introduction to a one-volume Pasternak, and I had come across Daniel's translations from time to time. I knew the pseudonyms Nikolai Arzhak and Abram Tertz from samizdat,[1] but to tell the truth, I didn't care much for their works and I had even considered the possibility that it was just

---

1. *Samizdat* literally means "self-publish." Before glasnost, banned literature was "published" on typewriters and carbon paper and circulated secretly. Possession of samizdat literature was a criminal offense.

mystification created abroad and not anything sent out of the USSR. The exposure of the pseudonyms and the arrest of Sinyavsky and Daniel had stunned the intelligentsia.

I was received by Secretary of the Central Committee of the Communist Party P. N. Demichev and asked him not to have a criminal trial. Demichev told me that he was against a trial, too. He said that Brezhnev had been informed of the arrest post factum and that his decision was to ask Fedin, then chairman of the Writers' Union, to determine whether the question should be handled by a criminal trial or by a comradely investigation within the Writers' Union. Fedin waved his hands in disgust and said that it was beneath the Writers' Union's dignity to deal with such criminal activity. Besides the collective letter against trying Sinyavsky and Daniel, there were other such letters, one of which had my signature. Nevertheless, despite the protest, the trial was held. *They gave out tickets to the trial!* Actually, passes. With great difficulty, I managed to get a pass at the Party committee; you could get them only for one session. I was a bit late, since it was difficult getting through the crowd and the police outside the courthouse. When I got into the small room, which held about one hundred people, the session had started. No sooner had I sat down when Judge L. Smirnov, who had noticed me come in, accused Sinyavsky of acting "against" the respected poet Yevtushenko in the article he had written for *Novy mir* and for which the type had been broken just before the trial.

This was one of the most disgusting moments of my life. I felt myself being pulled into a filthy provocation. When I was denounced politically in newspapers and accused of "unwashable bruises of betrayal," our courageous courts kept quiet about it for some reason, and suddenly they were "defending" me, accusing two of my colleagues of treason! It must have been at that moment that Daniel saw my "aghast face," as he called it. I was helped by Sinyavsky (yes, it was the accused who saved me, sitting in the audience). Sinyavsky said that it had not been an article against Yevtushenko, that he liked many of my poems, and that he criticized only certain of my works in the article. He did not look at the judge, but at me, over people's heads, and in his eyes I read something like, "They want to make enemies of us, but we must not give in." And that's how it was.

(Many times many people passed on warm words about me from both Sinyavsky and Daniel, who did not forget my signature on the letter in their defense nor the other aid I gave them to the best of my abilities. In that lies the moral distinction of Sinyavsky and Daniel from some of the others who left for the West, whom I had also defended more than once in difficult moments of their lives, but who then "repaid" me following the old and sad law: "No good deed goes unpunished." God is their judge.)[2]

After that noisy trial of writers a new term came into use: *podpisant,* or "signer," meaning a person who signs his name in support of a dissident. Signers ended up blacklisted on TV, their galleys were either taken apart or held up, their trips abroad were canceled, and some were even fired. I became one such "signer" — and I also had to put up with a lot of unpleasantness; however, unlike many of my colleagues, I was protected by my national and international fame. Despite its attempts to stop my trip to the USA in 1966, the bureaucracy failed. Today's deputy chairman of the Znanie Society,[3] Comrade Semichastny, now tries in his self-serving memoirs to depict himself practically as an arts patron. (For instance, he alleges that he tried to soften Khrushchev's anger against Pasternak. That's a lie. I was present at a Komsomol [Communist Youth League] meeting where Semichastny attacked Pasternak with inspired sadistic frenzy.) When he became head of the KGB, Semichastny tried to use the Sinyavsky and Daniel case to "tighten the screws" even more. At a meeting with the *Izvestia* editors, he mentioned that they'd have to start arresting people again. In response to the question of how many, he said, "However many we need." Before my departure for America, Semichastny attacked me at a meeting and said that

2. Yevtushenko rarely receives public credit for his generosity to other writers, both supporting and protecting writers in trouble and promoting budding authors. There have been incidents of people expressing their gratitude to Yevtushenko for his help privately in Moscow and then publicly denouncing him for his supposed lack of support once they reach the West, attributing their release only to the pressure of Western public opinion.
3. The Znanie (Knowledge) Society organizes lecture tours throughout the Soviet Union, especially to provincial areas.

our policies were too ambiguous — with one hand we arrest Sinyavsky and Daniel, with the other we sign papers allowing Yevtushenko to travel abroad. That was a dangerous symptom. However, I already had my visa.

During my trip to the USA in November 1966 I was invited by Senator Robert F. Kennedy to his New York headquarters. I spent several hours with him. In the middle of the conversation, Kennedy took me to the bathroom, turned on the shower, and informed me confidentially that according to information he had, the pseudonyms of Sinyavsky and Daniel had been revealed to the KGB by American intelligence services. I was naive back then and didn't understand at first: why, for what purpose? Robert Kennedy laughed bitterly and said that it was a very profitable propaganda move. The topic of US bombing in Vietnam took a backseat to the stories of persecution of writers in the USSR. I asked Robert Kennedy for permission to pass this information along to the Soviet government, since I considered this action harmful to the interests of our country. Kennedy agreed on the condition that his name not be mentioned. I went to see someone in our mission, whom I'll call B.D., a noble diplomat. He did behave in the most noble way in this story. I told him about the information. Not a single muscle moved in his face. B.D. did not even try to find out how I had gotten it. He was satisfied with my gentlemanly formulation "a major American political figure." B.D. asked me to compose a telegram which he would send on to Moscow in code. Understanding the danger of such a telegram to me, I asked him who would read it. "Just the ciphers man and me," B.D. assured me. I was afraid, of course. The people who arranged the trial of Sinyavsky and Daniel were certainly pursuing their personal aims, since they could have gotten into the higher echelons only by "tightening screws," accusing their rivals of being soft. But, I left the telegram in our mission.

The next morning at seven the phone rang in our hotel room. A man's voice said that they were waiting for me down in the lobby. The mission had sent a car for me on an urgent matter. My wife and I agreed that if she had not heard from me by one that afternoon, she was to call a press conference. There were tears in her eyes, but she was brave. I wasn't very happy, but I had been prepared for it. Below I was met by two men, on the young side, with unremarkable, athletic faces. When I asked, "What happened?" one replied, "You'll soon find out."

It was dumb that during our insignificant conversation the second man turned on the car radio, with a hand gesture hinting at eavesdropping. That fake-serious move made me laugh and improved my mood. We went into the mission building, but when the elevator doors opened, the opera buffa level went up. One of them blocked the floor buttons so that I couldn't see which one his partner pushed. When we came out, I saw a door without a number or a name. The room was almost empty — a desk, two chairs, a table lamp, and nothing more. Everything that happened afterward seemed to be from a bad American spy movie, of which these two had seen too many. I was offered the chair in front of the desk. One of them stood behind me. The other, following Hollywood clichés, took off his jacket, tossed it on the chair back, and sat on the desk, crossing his legs picturesquely.

He undid the top button on his shirt, loosened his tie, and asked, staring into my eyes with what he thought was a penetrating look, "Who was the political figure you wrote about in your telegram?"

I realized that they had read it. I thought undeservedly badly of B.D. just then. I stalled. "What telegram?"

"The telegram in which you try to slander the intelligence organs," roared the one behind my back.

"I'm not slandering anyone," I said, realizing there was no point in pretending anymore. "I passed along information given to me by an American politician. If it's true, then the ones who arrested Sinyavsky and Daniel have damaged the prestige of our country and took the bait . . . "

"That's slander!" the other one, on the desk, roared too.

"If it's not true, I'm not responsible for it. They'll figure it out in Moscow," I replied.

Then they began a rapid-fire list of all the politicians I had met during my trip, including Senator Javits, UN Ambassador Goldberg, and Bobby Kennedy. Trying to stay calm, I said that there are rules of human decency and I was not about to violate them. This simple statement irritated them particularly.

Suddenly I heard something that made my skin crawl. "New York is a city of gangsters. If something happened to you, *Pravda* would print an obituary with sentimental notes about the poet who perished in the stone jungles of capitalism. . . ."

But my fear passed suddenly, when I realized that they were blackmailing me brazenly, unforgivably. I turned abruptly and grabbed the rear investigator by the tie.

A squall of majestic and powerful Russian words, learned on Siberian train platforms and in flea markets, in the alleys and bars of Maryina Roshcha, poured out of me, a squall so mighty that my investigators shut up, exchanged a look I did not understand, and left.

That's when I really got scared — when I was left all alone in an empty room. The emptiness, the uncertainty, the loneliness were worse than threats. I don't know how long I was in there alone, maybe only five minutes, maybe a half hour. At last I went over to the closed door, tugged, and found it opened quite easily. I was in an empty hallway not far from the elevator. I pushed the button and in a second leapt into it, almost knocking down a waitress in an apron who was carrying a tray covered with a white starched napkin.

"Are you going to B.D.'s?" I asked hopefully.

"I am," she said. "Can I have your autograph?"

"I'm going to see him, too," I said quickly and just as quickly signed the napkin.

B.D. was on a couch in a Manilovian robe with Hussarlike piping, reading a book on Eastern philosophy. Nothing moved in B.D.'s face when he saw me or when he heard what had happened to me. He did not ask any foolish questions, only asked for a detailed description of my "investigators." It was not easy, since their main distinction was their lack of distinction.

"You have a good American friend, Albert Todd, the professor who set up your tour. Why don't you go see him now and tell him what you told me."

I was stunned. There was an unwritten rule — don't tell foreigners what went on inside the Soviet embassies. And here I was being asked to do it. . . .

"I'll let you have my car to go to Todd's. You can trust the driver fully," B.D. said. "Would you like me to give you this marvelous new edition of Bo Zui I?"

A half hour later I was at Todd's house, from where I immediately called my wife and then told him about the "Hollywood interrogation" and the blackmail.

Todd blanched as he listened to me and rushed off to make a phone call, shutting the door behind him. Todd did not ask who had told me about Sinyavsky and Daniel, either — he was a gentleman like B.D. Two hours later a car drove up to Todd's house and two men got out, also without any distinguishing features, but of an American type. They took up positions near the doorway. Todd went downstairs, spoke with the driver of the Soviet car, shook his hand, and saw him drive off. For a while those two untalkative men accompanied me on all my trips in the gangster city of New York. Then Todd and I left on tour of the American provinces — without their accompaniment. We came back about a month later. The Soviet Mission to the UN gave a huge reception in my honor. B.D. was at the door. He was in a good mood, as usual.

"Your two overly persistent fans were sent to the homeland," he half-whispered to me between handshakes with the Peruvian and Malaysian ambassadors, and then asked, "Have you read Kobo Abe's new novel? So charming!"

Semichastny was soon removed from office as were others close to him, who are now trying to present themselves in reminiscences and interviews as the engines of progress, no less. But unfortunately, the dissident trials soon took on the momentum of snowballs turning into avalanches. Even before the Sinyavsky-Daniel case I had written a letter in defense of Brodsky, and afterward, in defense of N. Gorbanevskaya, A. Marchenko, I. Ratushinskaya, L. Timofeyev, F. Svetov, and others, not to mention letters in defense of those who were not subjected to criminal prosecution but just as damaging civil prosecution. One of the most cynical inventions in the fight against freethinking was sticking people into mental hospitals.

The dissident trials undermined the prestige of our country not only abroad but primarily in our own eyes. They destroyed the feeling of dignity — human and civic.

Perestroika is the reestablishment of civic dignity. That's why, along with clear victories of democratization, any attempt to diminish our dignity, so painfully restored, seems particularly unbearable: the use of clubs and tear gas in Belorussia, the Draconian legislation on special passes for journalists, provocative cruelty in Georgia. In order to guarantee legal dignity in our laws once and for all it is important to recall the disgusting humiliation of that dignity — in the dissident trials.

Letter to the Writers' Union, 1967

Alexander Solzhenitsyn had become a literary outcast by the mid-1960s. He wrote an open letter for the Fourth Congress of the Writers' Union on May 16, 1967, protesting his treatment. Many writers signed a petition and wrote letters in his support. It did not help. Solzhenitsyn was expelled from the Writers' Union in 1969, and arrested on charges of treason and deported from the Soviet Union in February 1974.

His monumental work on the camp system, The Gulag Archipelago, *began publication in the USSR in 1990. His citizenship was restored in August 1990. The intransigent Solzhenitsyn has not ruled out a return to his homeland, once his historical cycle,* The Red Wheel, *is published there, too.*

To the Presidium of the Congress of the Writers' Union USSR from member of the Writers' Union Yevtushenko, Y.A.

May 23, 1967

Even though I am not a delegate to the Congress, I am addressing its presidium with the following statement:

I have received a letter from the writer A. Solzhenitsyn, which has elicited great concern with its tragic tone. I know that several other writers and the presidium have received this letter. It seems to me that the presidium's moral duty is to deal with this letter with full seriousness, particularly where it refers, first of all, to the state of censorship in our country and secondly, to the personal fate of one of the most talented Soviet prose writers, whose name is widely known to our people and the people of other countries.

I am deeply convinced that the activity of the censors goes beyond what is permitted in the Constitution and hinders the normal development of our literature. After a half century during which our Soviet literature proved by blood and tears its loyalty to the common cause and its unity with the thoughts and dreams of the people, the existence of censorship in its present form is an ugly, clumsy vestige, one that threatens to turn into a tumor and must be excised from the healthy body of our society. From every platform, in every newspaper we speak of the fact that the guarantee of moving forward is trust. Censorship is the symbol of mistrust, and its existence is abnormal, especially in our socialist society, whose moral laws must be comradeship and trust. Responsibility must be placed on the shoulders of editors, who, as we know, do not appear out of thin air, but are confirmed by Party organs. The censors must deal only with military secrets. Should we fear anti-Soviet materials? I've been working in literature for eighteen years, and many works have been criticized in that time, but has even one work printed in the Soviet press been anti-Soviet? Is that thanks only to the censors? First of all, it is because the spirit of Soviet literature is healthy and does not need artificial filtering. The vestige of censorship must be cut off.

Perhaps Solzhenitsyn's letter does exaggerate things somewhat, but we must understand the man's position, and we must help him, not rebuke him.

Of his unpublished works I have read only *Cancer Ward* and I am convinced that with some work this novel, which has truly marvelous pages, can and should be published. The scandalous fact remains that the KGB confiscated a writer's manuscript and distributed it in a closed fashion.

The scandalous fact remains that Solzhenitsyn's book of stories has not been published. I consider it my duty to warn the Congress that if we do not take immediate action, something tragic may happen to Solzhenitsyn. The history of our literature unfortunately has sorrowful lessons for us.

Letter to Gorbachev, 1986

The Writers' Union has dachas, or summer houses, in the village of Peredelkino, outside Moscow. These are allocated to members for use as studios during their lifetimes. When Pasternak died, his family stayed on in the dacha rather than turn it over to the next writer on the waiting list. For years the writers' community was torn over the issue of making the dachas of Pasternak and of Kornei Chukovsky, the great children's writer, into museums. There was enormous resistance, both from political diehards and from literary widows who felt that their homes should become memorials, too. After a hard-fought campaign, the supporters of the museum idea won and the Pasternak museum opened in February 1990.

General Secretary of the CC CPSU
Comrade Gorbachev, M. S.   *1986*

Dear Mikhail Sergeyevich!

We ask the Central Committee of the CPSU and you personally to help in the creation of a museum in the house of the outstanding Soviet poet Boris Pasternak in the writers' colony in Peredelkino. Pasternak's relatives have moved out; the house is fully renovated. Fortunately, the poet's entire library, furnishings, and personal effects have been preserved. We feel that it would be a mistake to lose this opportunity to create a museum where everything is original. The approaching date of Pasternak's hundredth birthday, which will be celebrated by UNESCO on a world scale, is not far away — in 1990. Pasternak is not only a domestic phenomenon, he belongs to world culture, and we all bear responsibility before our descendants to preserve his memory.

False Alarm

I HADN'T SEEN the pathetic slogan of sad memory, "No to Homeless Cosmopolites!," since the days of the Doctors' Plot when anti-Semitic feelings were being fanned in every possible way. But it was that slogan that was hysterically waved on the stage of the Wings of the Soviets Sports Palace on January 23, when as part of a Voices and Colors of Russia Festival there was a meeting of the editorial boards and writers of the journals *Moskva, Molodaya Gvardiya,* and *Roman Gazeta* with their readers. Actually, Pamyat[1] participated, too, since the slogan The Pamyat Movement Will Win and the red banner with Saint George instead of the hammer and sickle were also being waved in the audience. Saint George the Dragon Slayer on a banner in the hands of Russian soldiers defending Russia from the enemy was a symbol of Russian courage. But let's not forget that the same Saint George in the hands of Black Hundreds[2] was the symbol of the pogroms. It's not a question of Saint George per se but what the

---

1. The three journals listed are known for their right-wing political views. Pamyat is a semiofficial organization ostensibly dedicated to the preservation of Russian culture and cultural monuments, but which has an extremist faction of anti-Semitic bullies, who break up liberal meetings and threaten Jewish writers, lawyers, and political figures. Pamyat's emblem is Saint George the Dragon Slayer, the old banner of prerevolutionary Moscow.
2. The Black Hundreds were anti-Semitic reactionaries active before the Revolution, with a membership similar sociologically to the Ku Klux Klan's.

dragon is supposed to represent — a real enemy or one invented to have an excuse to brandish spears right and left.

So, who were the dragons listed in the speeches that night? A whole terrarium of strange creatures with hissing, toxic tongues — Trotsky, Sverdlov, Bukharin, Kaganovich, Zaslavskaya, Aganbegyan, Korotich, B. Vasiliev, Nuikin, Shmelyov, Strelyany.[3] The journals *Znamya* and *Ogonyok* and the newspaper *Moscow News* were accused of kowtowing before the West.

I realize that neither the chairman nor the presidium can be held fully responsible for the behavior of the audience or for every speech. But if the chairman and the presidium do not react to insulting speeches and hooliganish catcalls, then they share the responsibility. For instance, the deputy editor in chief of *Molodaya Gvardiya*, Vyacheslav Gorbachev, in his speech read statistics meant to incite nationalist feelings: how many academicians are Jewish, how many writers, how many college graduates, et cetera. I was reminded of the story about the Soviet conductor and the American conductor. The Soviet conductor, in order to prove that there was no anti-Semitism in the Soviet Union, said, "Look, for instance, in the orchestra I've brought to the USA, I have seven Jews." And the American responded, "You know, I've never thought to count the Jews in mine."

At the meeting there were cries from the audience: ". . . Korotich is in the USA right now. He was invited by Bush. . . . They have the same leaders." A cry: "Why doesn't he stay there!" "They are trying to confuse people, to blacken Stalin. . . . Of course, Stalin did make a few errors, but . . ." (stormy applause drowning out the meek "but" and turning into an ovation).

This outcry had nothing to do with literature: inciting hatred is a political phenomenon.

I had the strange feeling that I had seen this emotional high brought on by one's own shouts somewhere before. I remembered the groups of teenagers with sheeplike eyes strolling in Pushkin Square a few years ago to celebrate Hitler's birthday. Have these

---

3. This list of "dragons" in need of slaying includes four Jewish Bolsheviks (Trotsky, Sverdlov, Bukharin, and Kaganovich), the editor of the liberal and very popular magazine *Ogonyok* (Korotich), and a number of economists and writers associated with economic reform and perestroika.

young people grown into a new more legal herdlike existence with chauvinist slogans? Chauvinism is the cheapest way of feeling superiority that is not based on knowledge, or talent, or work, or spiritual kindness, but merely on nationality.

The slogans hauled out of mothproofed trunks could easily turn into the military arsenal of the reactionaries. Perestroika is an attempt at spiritual and economic liberation. But sometimes the base passions are also released, leading to mutual enmity instead of mutual understanding.

I am against arguing by force, cudgels, and whistles and by forbidding or breaking up meetings. But there are times when one cannot be silent and must resort to moral arguments. We must not allow democracy to be used against democracy, glasnost to be used to stifle glasnost. Much in history will not be clear to us until all the archives are declassified. But one crime has been declassified forever — inciting hatred by using unproven accusations. This was what led to the millions of corpses that blocked our path to democracy for so many years.

Soviet and American filmmakers have discussed stopping the creation of the "image of the enemy" on screen. Unfortunately, the people in our country who like to make an enemy out of their own countrymen have not been similarly enlightened.

At the meeting I heard: "Listen, the people on the square are sounding the alarm." History has shown that there is nothing more "anti" the people than the attempts of a single group to speak in the name of the people and denying everyone else that right. Calling for the restoration of the Cathedral of Christ the Savior without maintaining Christian tolerance is a destruction of the cathedral of hope for universal brotherhood.

We must restore all the desecrated Russian shrines. But we must not forget that our national shrines include kindness and hospitality and universal responsiveness. Russian patriotism is Pushkin and Tolstoy, not the fabricators of the Protocols of the Elders of Zion.

It's not the people sounding an alarm — that is the sound of a false alarm meant to deceive the people sent by the monopolizers of Russian patriotism.

Declaration against Racism *(1990)*

This manifesto condemning racism was written by Yevtushenko for April, the liberal group of writers that has formed a properestroika alternative to the Writers' Union. Their first meeting on January 18, 1990, at the Writers' Union was broken up by Pamyat rowdies. The Pamyat leader was sentenced to two years imprisonments for inciting violence and racial hatred.

THAT WORD *racism*, to which we were taught aversion from childhood, was always perceived as something far from us, foreign, capitalist. The older people among us remember the little black boy in the movie *Circus*, who was saved from the American racist and tenderly passed from hand to hand. . . .

Our Constitution makes it illegal to incite hatred among nationalities. We saw one of the bestial faces of racism during World War II, which was won by all the nationalities in our country. But then we saw a different face of racism, our own. State genocide toward entire nationalities — Kalmyks, Checheno-Inguts, Crimean Tatars. . . . The murder of the great Jewish actor Mikhoels, the attack on the so-called cosmopolites in 1949, the Doctors' Plot of 1953, the monstrous anti-Semitic lampoons in the newspapers. After Stalin's death it seemed, at first, that this could never be repeated. We were sincerely outraged by the Ku Klux Klan, the Saint Bartholomew's Nights in Ireland, the endless bloodshed in the Near East.

However, racism, like AIDS, recognizes no borders. The germs of racism grew marvelously in the nutrient medium of the stagnation period — in personnel policy, where question 5 on the application forms took on such tragic significance.[1] Lately, shuddering with indignation and shame, we see outbreaks of a spreading racism epidemic, on your own street, or in the next town, or in a distant republic.

On January 18 it happened in Moscow, at the Writers' Union Club. A meeting was planned of April, a group of writers supporting perestroika. But about two hours before the meeting a group of individuals with no relationship to literature (about fifty people, most of them with Saint George on their chest) took seats in the hall. Armed with a megaphone, they created an anti-perestroika, chauvinist witches' sabbath, provoked a fistfight, insulting the writers, some of whom were People's Deputies, with Black Hundreds–type exclamations, physical assaults, waving anti-Semitic flags. They threatened anti-Jewish pogroms. These new domestic Nazis shouted "Lousy Kikes!" "Go to your Israel!" at everyone there. Their pathological racist hatred makes them consider Jewish anyone who is not anti-Semitic. How else can you interpret the slogan, "A. N. Yakovlev, go to Tel Aviv!" Several brawny men viciously beat up the famous Russian writer Anatoly Kurchatkin, who tried to calm them down, breaking his glasses and giving him a black eye, and they struck one of our oldest prose writers, Elizar Maltsev. In their rage, these storm-troopers of Russian Nazism even attacked women writers, some of them quite elderly.

The vandals were removed from the auditorium only with the help of militia reinforcements, who were quite late, and a number of the ringleaders mysteriously escaped being charged. One thing is clear — this was not a spontaneous outbreak, but a prepared action. I get the impression that the extremists from Pamyat and organizations around them are hoping that the disorders they create will lead to an imperial militarized dictatorship.

One of the most dangerous forms of organized crime today is racism. Racism is an opportunistic forgery of the struggle for na-

---

1. "Stagnation period" is the current code word for the Brezhnev years, 1964–82, which followed the thaw under Khrushchev. Question 5 appears on every Soviet passport and on every application and form — it asks for nationality. Since religious affiliation is not asked, the nationality question determines whether a person is Jewish or not.

tional interests. Actually, racism is an instrument for manipulating people for the careerist aims of a narrow reactionary group. We connect the brawl in our writers' house with the anti-Semitic attitude of the last plenum of the Writers' Union of the RSFSR [Russian Republic], which was synchronized with a gathering of this sort, organized by Pamyat on Red Square. These and other actions in Moscow and Leningrad are strengthened by constant ideological preparation in numerous articles with a blatant racist taste published in *Molodaya Gvardiya, Nash Sovremennik, Literaturnaya Rossia, Moskovsky Literator,* and others. We are bitterly shocked by the position of some famous writers who are on the boards of these publications. Sometimes they not only passively allow their names to be used but openly support racist tendencies. We would like to remind these writers that a shift to reactionary positions usually ends in creative barrenness. Embracing racism has not given birth to a single great writer, but it has discredited many.

With wrath and scorn we condemn all forms of nationalism and chauvinism, including anti-Semitism. In the last statement by April on the nationalities issue, we already said that there would be no united front of Russian chauvinism. Now, in this heated atmosphere, we say: there is a united, unwavering front against chauvinism, against any form of violence no matter what national flag it hides behind. We call on all citizens of our country to join in this united front, the working class, which has not lost its sense of proletarian solidarity, and the intelligentsia, which has not forgotten its humanistic destiny.

The victims of slaughter in Baku, Sumgait, and Fergana, Azerbaijani refugees from Armenia, Armenian refugees from Azerbaijan, and the residents of Nagorny Karabakh,[2] where shots ring out day and night, and the peaceful Volga Germans who have to pay for the crimes of fascism, and the Crimean Tatars, who return to the land of the ancestors only to find tent cities, all cry out to our consciences.

Imperial thinking should be alien to us, because the law of history is clear: all empires eventually fall apart. We are not for

2. Nagorny Karabakh is the territory in dispute between Azerbaijan and Armenia.

the breakdown of interethnic and human relations, we are for a free union of free sovereign peoples. We must defend the right of the Baltic peoples for a sovereign path of development and the right of Russians and people of any other nationality living in the Baltics not to lose confidence in tomorrow. It is unbearable to see homeless Meskhetian Turks, or the tragic conflicts in Tbilisi, Southern Ossetia, and Abkhazia. We are against forcibly insisting that only one point of view is correct, because that is a kind of ideological racism. We are against any religion considering itself the representative of God and calling for war against other religions, for that is religious racism.

There's been enough fire and blood! Enough mistrust, mutual demands, and rebukes that turn into mutual enmity. Enough national egoism, enough nationalistic "localism." Let's look into one another's eyes. Don't we have common misfortunes? Are wisdom and conscience determined only by a blood test?

With bitterness and pain we see racism around us — not imported, but our own, domestic brand. Have we come to a new gigantic self-genocide — civil war? No one knows better than we that civil war is first and foremost fratricide.

We believe in the spiritual potential of each individual nationality in our country and in all of its people together. We are for democratic pluralism, but not for indulging fascism. There is no other name for propaganda of hatred for other people. We demand that our government finally start using its power against the pogromers who are trying to use democracy only to destroy it.

For What Does the Chernobyl Bell Toll?

(1987)

JOHN DONNE'S LINE used by Hemingway for the title of his famous novel *For Whom the Bell Tolls* comes to mind more and more with each tragedy of the twentieth century, as if they are connected, like links in an endless chain. I'm not a specialist, but of all the monuments dedicated to the dead of World War II, I like the one in Khatyn with its severe, miserly sorrow, where bells on the crematorium smokestacks ring in the wind that carefully touches them. The bells of Chernobyl ring far away, but their echo reached beyond the seas and elicited in most hearts not political gloating but painful thoughts on the interdependence of all human lives under the sign of nuclear threat. The bells of Chernobyl ring not only for those who died in the catastrophe, not only those who might die tomorrow or the day after from its direct and oblique aftereffects, but for those who might never be born into this world because there will be no world.

"The accident in Chernobyl has shown yet again the abyss we face if there is nuclear war. . . . We understand that this is another toll of the bell, another dire warning."[1] Those words were exact and became another warning toll themselves.

---

1. These words are Gorbachev's, but Yevtushenko chose not to identify him as the speaker.

The facts are tumbling out, piling up on the pages of our press, but there are few conclusions. What is the main thought that comes to mind? The thought that a crime leading to the death of people can be accidental, involuntary, part of the daily grind, part of the most sincere attempt to help the so-called production process, speeding it up. It gives me the creeps to listen to the calm, weary commentary of a man who works at the plant: "What really hurts in this story is that we'd had the warnings before. Resolutions were passed . . . papers written, but nothing was done, nothing at all. And we ended up with a serious business, and we were empty-handed, and we had to make things up to handle it as we went along, inventing . . ."

O! accidental mother of so many crimes — fecklessness! "Resolutions were passed, papers written . . ." We have always blamed, especially of late, the bureaucrats who put "resolutions" and "papers" above people. But let's think about why those resolutions aren't acted upon and the "papers" remain just paper. Because any bureaucrat who puts paper above people doesn't care about the paper either. A bureaucrat like that cares only about himself. Yet he doesn't consider himself an egoist because in his own eyes he is the embodiment of the state and all his ambitions, power, and egoism are masked as state interest and will. This is where accidental crimes start.

Aren't people who fish in poisoned, radioactive rivers, against prohibitions, an example of fecklessness that cannot be eradicated from criminally thoughtless heads? And I also thought: are there really that many subtle villains in history, criminal masterminds from the movies? Instead, underdeveloped consciousness, stupidity, and stubbornness turn into villainy toward our contemporaries and descendants. It's still the same Chekhovian irrational villain unscrewing bolts from the tracks of the train of the future.

The outstanding hematologist A. I. Vorobyov, who worked with the American Dr. Robert Gale, said, "I think that this accident will put an end to humanity's medieval thinking. The conclusion must be unambivalent: not only nuclear war but war between nuclear powers becomes impossible. Humanity must abandon the medieval psychology of imposing its will with the aid of a fist. And there is nothing else left for us, because if we bomb only the atomic energy plants with ordinary warheads without nuclear charges, and only in the Soviet Union, Europe will be gone, and so will North Africa. . . ."

Here's my hypothesis: if our self-genocide had not destroyed so many thinkers and harvesters, there might not have been the Chernobyl apocalypse, or the accident with the *Nakhimov*, or the explosions in Arzamas, or in Sverdlovsk, or the train fire near Bologoi, or the destruction of the Aral Sea.[2] All this destruction was caused by the destruction of professionalism.

The criminal amateurishness of overblown authorities, who united into a mafialike conspiracy, leads to people moving up the ladder until they reach their level of incompetency. Incompetency in a responsible position has the potential for villainy. One of the signs of creative professionalism, with the exception of the professionalism of crooks, murderers, and kidnappers, has always been a conscience. Academician Sakharov, one of the creators of the atom bomb, one day grew horrified of the danger lurking in his creation, and it was his pangs of conscience that made him a great citizen of our country and of the world. The city of Gorky, where he was exiled, became the capital of free thought. We will never be able to scrape the air of Chernobyl from our lungs, but, in the expression of Ivan Drach,[3] the contemporary Pontius Pilates have already washed their hands of the radiation. I would not like to believe Chaadayev's sad prophecy that our nation exists solely to teach humanity a terrible lesson. Let us not allow one another to give in to the destructive radiation of civic pessimism; let us be preventive fire fighters against all new Chernobyls. But our life with its deficits and daily shopping suffering has turned into a kind of daily life-style Chernobyl. And if the well-meaning villains in the uniform of special forces use army shovels and chemical bombs,[4] this will lead to a moral Chernobyl. Let us be vigilant

2. The reference is to various accidents that were almost certainly caused by carelessness. The cargo ship *Nakhimov* collided with another vessel near Novosibirsk in 1987; a train carrying chemicals exploded at the Arzamas station in 1988; the Aral Sea, thanks to crackpot "scientific" plans to irrigate cotton fields in Uzbekistan by diverting rivers, is dying.
3. Ivan Drach, Ukrainian writer, People's Deputy of USSR.
4. The reference is to the massacre by the Soviet Army of peaceful demonstrators in Tbilisi, the capital of Georgia, on April 9, 1989.

and not let people, who under the guise of saving our historical path from an accident caused by loose screws, tighten those screws so hard that they kill freedom and people. No! to all Chernobyls — atomic, life-style, and moral! No! to a slavish worship of the atom! Yes! to respect for every atom of the human body and soul!

Politics Is Everyone's Privilege *(1987)*

IN PASTERNAK'S NOVEL, *Doctor Zhivago*, there is this conversation between two Russian intellectuals. One says, "To a certain degree I am with you. But Lev Nikolayevich Tolstoy says that the more a man gives himself up to beauty, the farther he gets from good. . . ."

The second asks with mocking skepticism, "Do you think it's just the opposite? Beauty will save the world, mystery, and so on, Rozanov and Dostoevsky?"

The first stands firm. "Wait, I'll tell you what I think. I think that if the animal dormant in man could be stopped by threats — it doesn't matter of what — lock-up or otherworldly revenge, the highest emblem of mankind would be the circus animal trainer with a whip and not a preacher who sacrifices himself. But that's the point, that for centuries what raised man above the animals was not the stick but the undeniability of unarmed truth, the attraction of its example. . . ."

Thus spoke two Russian intellectuals before the revolution of 1917, but that argument continues today all over the world. Let us pose two questions. First: is it true that the dormant animal of war lives in the dark caves of the human subconscious and demands the flesh of those close to us as its inexorable bloody food and that politics is merely the justification of that vile but natural appetite? In other words, are wars a physiological need of our psychology? And second: can the unarmed truth of protest not only stop nuclear weapons but destroy them?

Let us agree that we are against war. But let's look inside ourselves, let's do a little self-surgery on our psychology with a sober and ruthless scalpel.

Is there one of us who has never fought against a family member? Has at least one of us not wounded or murdered his parents with naive childish cruelty, with monstrously shameful deeds, and then when grown up, has not killed his children with lack of attention, indifference, nervous meanness, or humiliating condescending didacticism? Hasn't each one of us killed the ones we love along the tragic immortal formula of Oscar Wilde, "Each man kills the thing he loves," and killed them not necessarily with "physical betrayal" but spiritual cheating, when the heat of passion changed to habit, which kills love, and the brief unity of souls and bodies turned into that strange alienation between men and women who are no more than neighbors in bed?

We condemn bombing of countries when other people's houses are turned into ruins, but many of us are guilty of ruining our own houses, our own families, and behind many beautiful facades of apparently happy families are nonstop local wars. If you take all the tragedies of families blown up by divorce in the whole world, it will add up to misfortune as great as Chernobyl. How can we hope for peace in the gigantic multifamily family of man, if there is no peace in so many private families? Of course, this may appear microscopic, incomparable to the scope of nuclear war that threatens us, but global morality has to be related to personal morality.

We are torn asunder by many other undeclared wars. The illiterate, incompetent mediocrities who end up in power are occupiers who invaded the spots that should belong to more talented people. The manipulation of public opinion through the mass media is chemical warfare, poison gas for the brain. Bureaucracy is daily aggression. Exploitation, both spiritual and physical, is armed invasion. Chauvinism, racism — even in their veiled manifestations — are potentially fires that burn everything to the ground. Hunger, epidemics are the forcible annexation of living souls to the grim territory of death. The specter of nuclear war is a gigantic monster grown from the embryo of all the other wars, local and global.

The most dangerous thing is that humanity is infected from childhood with the virus of accepting war. But does that mean that war is inevitable? Yes, war is a chronic, genetically encoded sickness of humanity. But it is a bad physician who tolerates even the oldest inherited disease, because in betraying his patient, he betrays his Hippocratic oath. It is a bad politician who does not want to try or is tired of trying new methods to save his exhausted patient — our common planet Earth.

On the other hand, medicine or politics that shows off and pretends to know all is a very dangerous phenomenon — a semiscience, which in medicine can lead to individual fatality and in politics to fatality for the world. Dostoevsky wrote about semiscience in *The Devils* this way: "Semiscience is a despot the likes of which has never been seen. A despot who has his priests and slaves, a despot before whom everyone vows with love and superstition, heretofore unthinkable."

For the semiscience of today's politics to become a science, a new discipline has to be added to its teaching. Tolerance. We must be cured by truth of the ambitious attempts to look good in our own eyes and others'. Politics is not the elitist privilege of professional politicians, but the privilege of people in all professions. The times when narrow nationalism could have been progressive are over, for any kind of nationalism armed with the atom bomb is internationally dangerous. Moreover, aggressive nationalism with the atom bomb stops being nationalism, because it is suicide for its own nation, too.

The historically determined division of mankind into three worlds is unnatural — they are merely three different approaches to the future — but we have only one world. Perhaps one of the models will predominate, convincing the rest of the world of its superiority, but not by being forced on people, because it is hopeless in the long run to buy love with state bribes or demand that love with missiles up against someone's throat. Perhaps the future will consist of all three attempts, filtering out their flaws and leaving their best features.

But perhaps there is a fourth, completely different path, to which we have not yet matured morally, which we do not even suspect exists. The question of the future is not the privilege of the so-called superpowers. We must not accept atomic elitism, especially because it is deceptive. Every single person, no matter his nationality, is a superpower.

That is why I welcome the idea of the simultaneous disbanding of the military organizations — both NATO and the Warsaw Pact — as a great opportunity to free the colossal joint resources that could be used to save so many people from hunger and disease. That is why I welcome the idea of Professor Stephen Cohen to create a Soviet-American Peace Corps to help the developing countries.[1]

This may seem idealistic, but idealism that rejects the false ideals that separate people and that confirms the ideals developed through suffering and that unites people is just what we need. A shortage of idealism is the tragedy of the twentieth century after Auschwitz, Hiroshima, the Stalin camps, the McCarthy witch hunts, the Vietnam War, the assassinations of the Kennedys, Martin Luther King, the Pol Pot terror in Cambodia, and so much else.

The shortage of ideals turns into a shortage of openness and confessionalism. We waste so much time in stupid pastimes that only create the appearance of human communication. Try answering the formal question "How are you?" seriously, and tell how things aren't going well in your family, how you have trouble sleeping, how you've lost faith in yourself, and the questioner will recoil from you as if from a madman. Perhaps he doesn't sleep nights either and he has trouble at home, but he is afraid of confessing, afraid of seeming weak.

The fear of confessing for oneself turns into a fear of national confessing. While secret services are achieving heights of perfection in mutual eavesdropping, nations are losing the salvation of listening to one another's heartbeats. Many political negotiations break off because they are built on mutual accusations instead of

1. Stephen F. Cohen, the noted Sovietologist who teaches at Princeton, mentioned this idea in his keynote speech in May 1987 at a conference in Moscow sponsored by the Physicians for Peace.

mutual confessions. The fear of losing face leads to one's losing it. The world will be saved only if politics will be built on mutual courage to admit mistakes and not on the comfortable cowardice of considering your partner the symbol of world evil.

We must forget mutual gloating. Humanity is a single body and it would be criminally stupid for broken legs to dance a jig when learning of a stomach ulcer and gallbladder stones hopping with glee hearing about pneumonia. In that sense everyone on Earth, including politicians, must be a physician and not gloat over others' illnesses.

The main goal now is to put a stop to nuclear war by taking the risk of trust. The risk of trust is the only risk that is not dangerous, as long as it is mutual. But what will the world be like, if we do save it from war? Will it be a world without ideals, based on commercial-biological deals? Will it not have great poetry, or great love, and will we be turned into computers, secretly hostile to one another, but coldly calculating that fighting is irrational? Are we going to replace the ideal of brotherhood with the necessary, but profoundly pragmatic, détente?

Detente must now be only a step to the peak, where there is no mutual fear, where people talk to each other as naturally as they breathe. One of the causes of the shortage of idealism is a shortage of a new philosophy that would combine the invaluable experience of former philosophies with the enormous experience of two world wars and prophetically add the potential horrifying experience of a third war, hanging over us. I think that humanity is pregnant with this new philosophy, and it is already kicking, ready to come out.

Ecclesiastes says there is a time to sow and a time to reap, a time to embrace and a time to refrain from embracing, a time to love, a time to heal. . . .

This is the season to heal.

We had a man surrounded by legend, an outstanding specialist in suppurative surgery and a man of deep religiosity. His name was Voino-Yasenetsky.[2] One of the legends, or perhaps it's a true

2. Valentin Feliksovich Voino-Yasenetsky (1877–1961), professor and surgeon, was also an ordained bishop in the Russian Orthodox Church. He spent time in Stalin's camps.

story, is about the time Stalin called him in and asked sarcastically, "How can you believe in the existence of the soul? You've opened up so many bodies. Have you ever seen anyone's soul inside there?"

"Do you believe in the existence of the conscience?" Voino-Yasenetsky asked him in turn.

Stalin thought and after a pause replied, "I do."

"When I open them up, I've never seen a conscience, either," Voino-Yasenetsky replied calmly.

Dostoevsky said that beauty will save the world. I think he included the conscience in the concept of beauty.

¶ Every Person Is a Superpower (1978–1989)

THOREAU SAID: "I'd like to remind my fellow citizens that first of all they must be human and only then — under the appropriate conditions — Americans." These words apply equally to people of all nations, including us Russians. But some of us make war, even against our own convictions. Tolstoy said, "If everyone fought only according to his convictions, there would be no war."

But was that great writer absolutely right? Really, it's hard to meet people who would dare to declare openly that their conviction was the necessity of war. Personally, it's never happened to me. If you look around in a good mood it might seem that we are surrounded by nothing but proponents of peace. In Hamburg I spoke with a former Hitlerite general — now a sweet old pensioner, whose son was studying Russian literature at college. He told me that he hadn't retired because much worse people would have replaced him. An old theory! Besides which, the general said, he was also human and afraid. His wife, who was present at our conversation, added touchingly, "Our phone was constantly bugged." The general said that he tried to do everything he could to soften the cruelty of war. He recalled that near the Russian city of Orel he had personally given orders to hand out rolls of wallpaper to the Russian prisoners of war so that they could wrap their frozen feet in it.

Of course, there are people participating in an unjust war who do it not out of conviction but out of fear, because insubordination is punished. But some people participate in unjust wars because they have been persuaded in their justness. Once I picked up a book at a Moscow used-book store by an unknown author, S. Kuzmin, called *War in the Opinions of Leading Men,* published in Saint Petersburg seventy years ago. Very revealing are the opinions of some "leading" men, who made war their profession. "War is the moral medicine Nature uses when she runs out of other means to return people to their true path" (Bismarck). "War supports all the great and noble sentiments in man" (Moltke). "I advise not labor but war. War and courage have done more good deeds than love of one's neighbor" (Nietzsche). War always had not only its direct executors but its justifiers. Propaganda was always the oil that kept the war machine going. Pessimism, which insists that war is part of man's nature, had an influence on people from ancient times. "War is the natural state of peoples" (Plato). But this book of aphorisms about war proves that the peace movement has existed as long as humanity. "Murder committed by ordinary men is punished. But what of wars, slaughterhouses, when whole nations are exterminated?" (Seneca). The Christian rhetorician Lactancius, in the third century, warned, "Bearing arms is not permitted to Christians, for their weapon is only the truth." Hugo exclaimed, "A society that allows war, a humanity that allows poverty seems to me a society, a humanity of the lower kind, and I want a higher society, humanity." The great Frenchman was right in speaking of war and poverty in the same breath, since war is the moral poverty of humanity. In Sebastopol, Tolstoy said to people, like a reproachful teacher, "War is not a courtesy, it is the most vile thing in life: you must understand that and not play at war." A furious Gladstone angrily threw this into the teeth of war's apologists: "Militarism is the damnation of civilization." Hobbes hated war, but he did not believe in the possibility of destroying war: "The condition of man . . . is a condition of war of everyone against everyone." Spencer, on the

contrary, saw the opportunity to destroy war in the moral perfection of people: "Absolute morality is the regulation of conflict
in such a way that pain shall not be inflicted."

The seventy years since this book was published have made
war much more horrible. But it is the same seventy years —
which include two world wars, the Cuban missile crisis, the Ko-
rean and Vietnam wars, the tension in the Middle East, the dangerous incidents on the Sino-Soviet border, the Afghan war — it
is these years, as no others, that have strengthened the idea of the
total destruction of war. It sometimes seems that the atom bomb,
if it only had reason and conscience, should commit suicide. The
Helsinki and Vienna accords show an unprecedented unanimity
among the most disparate countries with the most different political systems when it comes to the question of destroying war. If
man created war, he can destroy it. It's not hard to destroy the
bombs, but it is hard to destroy that which gives rise to war.
Distrust is the mother of war. In recent times aggression and annexation had an openly barbaric character, with no attempt at
political disguise. Now politics rules the world, and war is simply
its weapon. To all the other racisms we have added a new one:
political racism.

Political Racism

The source of political racism must be sought in religious racism.
The crucifixion of Christ by the sellers and Pharisees was one of
the first manifestations of religious racism, though of course not
the very first. When the lions tore apart the Christians in the
Coliseum, it was an attempt of the collapsing empire to tear apart
a new idea that was establishing itself.

Fascism was a combination of racism in its primary meaning
with political racism. And what do we observe today? Racism in
its primary meaning remains long-lived — whites despise blacks
only because they are black, blacks not trusting whites only because they are white. Religious racism is also alive, and even
though the commandment Thou shalt not kill applies equally to
Catholics and Protestants, Protestants are still killing Catholics
and Catholics are still killing Protestants. But the most horrible

of all is political racism, when the unwillingness to allow a person to have his own political point of view on his society turns into hatred, sometimes greater than hatred for skin color or faith.

The common fight against fascism united millions of honest people of the most different religious and political views from the capitalist and socialist worlds. Despite all its horrors, and perhaps thanks to them, World War II gave mankind an example of the possibility of uniting in the future, too. However, as it so often happens in history, struggle against a common enemy unites people and victory separates them. The microbes of political racism, lying low during the war, crawled to the surface once more.

As a very young poet in 1949–50, I frequented the cocktail hall on Gorky Street and I remember an American — in bright yellow shoes, with an impossible tie that looked like a peacock tail. I think he was from the embassy. And where else could he have come from? We didn't have foreign tourists in those days. The American always sat alone at his table, puffing on his pipe, and observing with a mocking smile how no one dared sit at his table, even though there were lines for seats. At that time we were no longer tossing our allies up into the air. It seemed that there was no air at all then. It's strange to remember that now, when young Americans with fringed jeans and guitars have become an integral part of the Moscow landscape; when quite recently I drank vodka in the gold mining town of Aldan with the representative of an American firm teaching Siberian workers how to use Caterpillars; when thousands of Muscovites listen to American jazz at the Sports Palace or to Britten at the Conservatory and thousands of New Yorkers come to the Felt Forum at Madison Square Garden to listen to a Russian poet. You have to be blind not to see that we are living in a new era. Isn't it a new era, when all of humanity watches the TV as slowly the hands meet in space of men from different countries and different political systems — hands that managed to reach each other through the iron curtain of political racism?

I remember the words of an American boatswain I met in the Philippines: "When we push the buttons, we don't see the faces." Culture is a nation's face, and we must see each other's faces and know them so that it becomes morally impossible to push that button. But for that we must be able to see, we must remove the shards of the iron curtain from our eyes.

We Must Belong to the Party of Children

Humanity is confused by political terms, mixing them up with moral ones.

If a communist and a noncommunist were standing on a bridge and saw a child drowning in the river, the better man would be the one who jumped into the river. And if both of them did it, then their spiritual unity at that moment would be higher than their political differences. We are all children of humanity, and yet humanity is our child. This child must be saved, because it is in danger. Everyone, independent of party membership, must first belong to the party of the child who must be saved. In Alaska I met Padre Spolettini, a priest in a tiny wooden church in an Eskimo village. My ideas of a Jesuit were mixed up with mysterious conspiracies, with poison-filled rings, with hooded robes and daggers. The padre gave all his money to the village library, trying to give the Eskimo children a minimal education. The padre energetically battled for the Eskimos' rights and against the slaughter of animals in Alaska, was at home in an igloo, and the Eskimos called him father without any religious servility, but simply in a human way. He did not resemble the metaphorical Jesuit in the least. Then I thought: how important is it what a man calls himself? You can call yourself a Christian yet be a Pharisee Inquisitor. You could call yourself an atheist but be more Christian in your treatment of others than a hypocrite proudly proclaiming that he is a Christian. Is terminology so important? Isn't what a person really is the important thing? Can't we develop principles, despite various religious and political convictions, in the name of the basic values of human life — peace, health, well-being, culture, freedom? John Kennedy, of course, was the representative of a certain class, its pupil and its defender. But on June 10, 1963, he said, "So, let us not be blind to our differences — but let us also direct attention to our common interests and to the means by which those differences can be resolved. And if we cannot end now our differences, at least we can help make the world safe for diversity.

For, in the final analysis, our most basic common link is that we all inhabit this small planet. We all breathe the same air. We all cherish our children's future. And we are all mortal."

They say that there can be various kinds of disarmaments — good and bad. But with the state of weapons today even an imperfect disarmament is of course far better than war.

Children Behind Glass

A few years ago I was returning from Australia. My seatmate on the plane was an Australian farmer around seventy years of age — a sturdy, red-cheeked man, filled with health and optimistic curiosity. He had saved some money and wanted to take a look at the world toward the end of his life.

Until that time the farmer had never left Australia and his knowledge of his homeland was limited to his own sheep pastures. For instance, he told me that he had never seen an aborigine. Everything delighted him — the way the stewardess, hips swaying, rolled a cart with tiny bottles down the aisle, and that somewhere below, showing emerald green through the clouds, were islands he had never seen, and that he had a new Polaroid camera bouncing on his chest with which he planned to capture the anticipated beauties of the world. The farmer was on his way to Paris, I was headed for Moscow, but an airline strike forced us to spend a few days in Delhi. We were put up at the same hotel and we chipped in for a taxi to Old Delhi. In anticipation of exotic sights, the farmer got his Polaroid ready. But not far from the entrance to Old Delhi the cab driver demanded that we shut the windows despite the incredible heat. We understood the reason for his insistence once we got into the city. The driver was forced to slow down to a minimum, because the car was surrounded by exhausted, half-naked people, who reached out to us begging, "Money! Money!" Their demands were not shouted and there was almost no hope in their voices, and that's what made it so horrible. We saw skeletal ghosts with immobile eyes, turned onto their own hunger, pressing against the windows, and there were not dozens, not hundreds, but thousands of such people. They were the people who are born on the street, sleep on the street, and die on the street, without ever learning what having a roof over your head means. It was particularly unbearable seeing children, so skinny that they seemed transparent. Their black eyes stuck to the car windows and their thin hands scraped fingernails on the glass. If we turned our pockets inside out and gave away every last coin we had, we wouldn't have been able to help them all.

The Australian farmer forgot all about his Polaroid and gasped hoarsely, "Back . . . Back . . . I can't stand to see this." That night he had heart trouble for the first time in his life, and they called in a doctor. The farmer muttered feverishly, clutching my hand, "I had no idea it was like this. I'm an honest man, I never stole anything, I've worked all my life, but I felt like a criminal. . . . Yes, we're all criminals, if there are children living like that today." I felt like a criminal too. I'd met so many children like that in Togo, Liberia, Ghana, Mexico, Uruguay, Ecuador, and the Philippines! A child of the war, I know very well what hunger is and I understand those who are hungry. With every child who starves to death, a future Mozart, Shakespeare, or Eisenstein may be dying. Once upon a time the Russian philosopher Fedorov dreamed of resurrecting the dead, considering it a common cause that would unite all of mankind. Today's goal is much more modest — to keep the living from dying of hunger. It has been calculated that every fourth person on the globe goes to bed hungry. But today's hunger might seem like paradise if we don't stop the arms race and start preparing for the war on future famine. In 1900 the world population was 1.5 billion. In 1960, it was 3.5 billion. By the year 2000 there will be 7.5 billion people. And in 2060, 20 to 30 billion. Yet the earth can feed no more than 12 billion people and then only with optimal organization of agriculture and expenditure of natural resources. What will save the earth and man? Mechanized reason? But before entrusting thinking machines with this important question, man must first create an ethics for the thinking machine. Man can look to no one but himself for help. If he is drowning in a sea of problems today, he has to pull himself out by the hair. But sometimes humanity resembles a strange drowning victim, who pulls himself out with one hand and pushes himself under with the other.

Political racism is particularly disgusting next to the hands of starving children scratching at raised car windows. The cost of every nuclear warhead is enough to save tens of thousands of innocent children from starvation. "The best ideals of humanity are not worth a single tear of an innocently tormented child," said Dostoevsky. The little hands of starving children are invisibly scratching at the windows of each and every one of us, calling to our consciences.

There Is No Superpower but Man

I don't like the expression *superpower,* just as I don't like the expression *superman.* Gorky said, "Man — that has a proud sound," and superman has a vile one. Does it imply that just man is a not-quite creature which can approach perfection only by overcoming the human in itself? Being not a superman, but a man in his original essence is the real approach toward perfection. Getting up physically from all fours is biological evolution, getting up morally from all fours is moral evolution, which unfortunately does not always correspond with the biological. The idea of superman, sung by Nietzsche, tragically was materialized in caricature in the Nazis, who burned immortal books and posed for photographs with bravado against a background of corpses. Marching with sleeves rolled up across a flaming Europe, they did not even notice that they were marching on all fours. The author of *Zarathustra* were he alive would have been horrified by such a monstrous embodiment of his dream of overcoming human weakness. How often were the commandment Thou shalt not kill, conscience, kindness, and honesty listed as human weaknesses, and cruelty, blind obedience, and denunciation raised to the ranks of strengths. Overcoming these so-called weaknesses forced man to overcome his human nature. People suffering from an inferiority complex are tempted by the possibility of individual or collective chauvinistic self-elevation: it gives the sense of false, albeit pleasant, superiority. If you are a superman, that is, higher than a mere man, then you can oppress the rest, step over their bodies, and not burden yourself with such old-fashioned human weaknesses like pangs of conscience.

We can more or less trace the etymology of *superman,* but where did the disgusting term *superpower* come from? For it places the two countries, the two nations, above all other countries and above all other nations. I know our people, I know the American people fairly well, and I can definitely state that the line "from superman to superpower" is morally unacceptable for both nations. Aggressive permissiveness can be the behavior only of individual moral monsters, but it must never become the expression of any nation as a whole. Did either of our peoples, when they fought with guns in their hands against the materialized theory of "superman," intend to then transform that theory on a state level by declaring themselves "superpowers"? And yet the term *superpower* has an author. The author is the atom bomb. The great discovery of breaking the atom, which could (and still might) have become the source of well-being for nations based on mutual trust, has become in the atmosphere of distrust the source of fear for the future. The tragic paradox is that both great countries, working on creating the atom bomb for a common victory over fascism, ended up with their own bombs on opposite sides of the iron curtain. The atom bomb dropped on Hiroshima killed 71,000 people. That bomb is still killing innocent people with radiation sickness. And beyond these victims, the bomb killed many more morally — it deprived many nations of mutual trust. If it were in my power, I would send every citizen of the earth to the Hiroshima museum. Peace must be taught by the memory of the horrors of war. And if that memory weakens, it would not hurt to remember the words of Thomas Paine, one of the first to fight for American democracy: "When the experience of the past does not help, we must turn once more for knowledge to primary sources and reason as if we were the first thinking people." The visitors' book at the Hiroshima museum has many notations from Americans. The most frequent remark is "Never Again!" But reality is such that, according to the statistics of the Stockholm International Institute on Issues of Peace, back in 1973 the world stockpiles of nuclear weapons of all categories was 50,000 megatons, that is, approximately 2.5 million times more powerful than the bomb dropped on Hiroshima. I recently read that there are enough nuclear weapons to kill every person on Earth 150 times over. Even if that figure is exaggerated, there is little to be happy about.

What will happen to us all, if history is ruled by the laws of drama that, according to Chekhov, demand that the rifle shown in Act I must go off by the third act? The nuclear "superpowerness" of the USSR and the USA may be only temporary. Atomic tests are heard in other countries. Some people may be annoyed by someone else's "superpower" status — they too want to be superpowers at any price. Damn the striving for superiority over other people that has replaced the striving for personal moral perfection. But there is no military power that can help a man become a superman or a power a superpower. There is no superpower higher than man. The superpower is man himself. The annihilation of war cannot be the work of the superpowers alone. The annihilation of war must be the work of the only superpower — man himself. And if people can recognize their spiritual power then Edison's prophecy may come true: "The day will come when science will give birth to a machine like a power that is so horrible, so unendingly terrible, that even man — a militant creature bringing suffering and death on others with the risk of bringing that suffering upon himself — will shudder with horror and reject war forever."

℘ A Personal Opinion

(1986)

THE CONCEPT of "people," of "humanity" consists for us primarily of individuals. Not only of celebrities, for celebrities are not always the best representatives of their people and of humanity.

A personal opinion is sometimes costly. But without a personal fair opinion there is no personality, no individual, and without individuals there can be no people. A personal opinion grows into a national one when there is no personal greed to it, merely concern for the people. A personal opinion trapped inside becomes self-destructive. But a personal opinion expressed fearlessly in the name of others creates a personality. This kind of personal opinion ceases being purely personal and becomes the voice of everyone else. Naturally, this is only when that personal opinion is not used to suppress all other opinions. The fresh wind of glasnost is the freedom of creativity, but not in a narrow literary sense; it is freedom of creativity for the whole nation, including literature. Today's fresh wind consists of personal opinion, the breath of many people whose name is "the people." But we must not accept any form of depersonalization so that the paper clips of bureaucracy don't crimp that fresh wind of personal opinions. The windowless walls of new buildings used to be painted (and still are) with gigantic ugly figures with hearty pseudo-optimism on their faces and faked, heavy-looking sheaves and hammers in their hands. At best, people disregard this propaganda, but at worst it works in reverse, giving rise to mocking skepticism and even cynicism. It is time to replace cosmetic ornamentation of reality with a businesslike resolution of real problems. This is the main direction of our life today. Some orators, still using the old methods of adding a little incense of flattery into the businesslike spirit, are being taught a lesson. Persistent requests "to the top" on issues that could be solved on other levels with just the slightest bit of elementary independence are being received with a just and firm suggestion "not to put everything on the shoulders of the government" and the people told to solve it themselves. The slogans of our new times are a constructively critical approach, a condemnation of enforced pomp, and the development of democratic glasnost. Glasnost is impossible without the precious right to have an unpunished personal opinion.

If a personal opinion is mistaken, then it can and must be corrected by the opinion of the collective, but without harsh administrative instruction, without pressure — by reasoning. But without the right to a personal opinion the national collective opinion cannot exist. The opinion of the people is not a circular issue from above but the sum of all personal opinions. [The writer] Andrei Platonov expressed it perfectly: "Without me, the people is incomplete."

There was a time when the supremacy of just one opinion prevailed and the role of the rest was reduced to that of cogs in the machine. To that single opinion, often incompetent, we entrusted not only domestic and foreign policy, but also biology, linguistics, cybernetics, music, and literature. Other personal opinions, even those of leading specialists in their fields, were ignored and often punished as ideas allegedly against the "opinion of the people." Using only one opinion to realize ideas and discounting the many other important opinions led to many mistakes for which we are still paying today in our backwardness in various fields of science and production. I doubt that all these tragic mistakes were the result of evil intent. But the subjective, willful "Do it this way!" does not have the moral right to become an order unless it has first been a "How should it be done?" that was asked of millions of other opinions.

During the dangerous period of World War II, Stalin's famous appeal to the people began with the rather unexpected and human "Brothers and sisters," which touched many people who still bore the unhealed wounds of undeserved losses and insults. The opinion "The enemy will be vanquished; victory will be ours" was not a personal one then — it was the people's. The joining of state and people was the secret of that great victory. But after the victory the opinion of those "brothers and sisters" became nonexistent. If peasants had been asked for their opinion, they would have said that seeds for harvest should not be collected just to meet the plan, that domestic cattle should not be taken away, that this would lead to more problems in agriculture. But no one asked for their personal opinion. If our readers and our music lovers had been asked their personal opinion, they would have said that neither Anna Akhmatova, who had written "The hour of courage has struck on our clocks, and courage will not fail us" during the war, nor Dmitrii Shostakovich, whose Leningrad Symphony became a world symbol of our homeland's defiance, could be accused of being antirational. But no one asked their personal opinion.

Many things are being done now, albeit far from everything that could be done, to improve quickly our agriculture and the life of our farmers, and both Akhmatova and Shostakovich are acknowledged Soviet classics, but can we forget the bitter lessons of history that showed how destructive the gap can be between the opinion "above" and the opinion of the people?

The development of economic thought is impossible without the development of thought per se. Bold transforming decisions cannot be made if there is negativism toward radical change, if there is cowardice, which creates an impenetrable swampy jungle for valuable initiatives. The people must help the government with their work and their frank glasnost in expressing their personal opinions, not for the sake of hearing their own voices but for the sake of our common goals, which cannot be divided into opinions from "above" and from "below." Doomsayers warn us that glasnost might turn into anarchy. Truth from a friend is medicine, and from unfriendly hands can be poison. Now that our government is matured and strong we must not fear self-criticism from personal opinion, for this frankness is a sign of our maturity and strength. Glossing over problems is a sign of weakness. The fear of losing face leads to losing face. General silence is a hidden form of anarchy. There is nothing more harmful than a situation in which everyone votes obediently, out of inertia, instead of voting out of conscience and caring. This form of voting turns into conscious or unconscious sabotage of the very resolutions passed. Glasnost should not be a goal in itself. Glasnost must not turn into the babble of people with nothing to say. We are not for a glasnost of chatty nonsense, but for the glasnost of ideas that can be turned into the energy of action. But against the background of calls for civic courage and truthfulness, there is the constant resistance of doomsayers who want to balance and average out the view of many historical events and of today's life. Interfering with the expression of a personal opinion by writers, directors, artists, scholars, and workers, these hopelessly obsolete dinosaurs are still trying to put their personal opinion above all others. If a technical commission votes against the construction of a new airplane and yet that plane is still made and flies to the greater glory of the homeland, then that commission must be judged by the people. It is time to declare incompetent those people who blocked the way of valuable inventions, stopped the publication of literary works, the production of plays and films, and the exhibition of paintings which later gained world renown.

The lathe operator who unexpectedly takes the floor at a meeting and speaks the truth in the face of the squirming bosses; the milkmaid who forgets the piece of paper in front of her and squeezes out every word from her long-suffering peasant heart; the scientists who battle pseudoscience and those who try to hinder progressive creative thought; the writer who uses a congress on Russian linguistics as a tribune to express his great concern over the fate of northern rivers — we are all equally responsible before history and our personal opinions flow together like rivers into a single opinion of the people.

The great power of our personal opinion is the lever of collective democracy. Collective democracy is impossible without individual democracy.

℘ Execution by Conscience (1988)

Vladimir Alexeyevich Soloukhin, born 1924, is a "village writer," whose prose is set in the northern countryside. At the height of the persecution of Pasternak, the Writers' Union orchestrated attacks on the poet. There was a meeting of the Union in 1958, after Pasternak received the Nobel Prize for Literature, to denounce him. Under glasnost, there has been much discussion of the roles played in that ugly scenario, and many writers, including Veniamin Alexandrovich Kaverin (born 1902), have repented publicly.

THE WRITER Soloukhin tried to justify his betrayal of Pasternak at a meeting in 1958 and betrayal in general as practically an inevitable behavioral norm under certain circumstances. In this case we are dealing with a rare genre in the press — repudiation of repentance for an evil deed.

Here are a few excerpts from Soloukhin's speech, quoted thirty years later in the journal *Gorizont*.

> [Pasternak] is an internal émigré, so why not let him become a real émigré? In connection with this, I thought of this analogy. When our party criticized the revisionist policy of Yugoslavia, there was talk — what if it moves away completely and goes to the other camp? And wise Mao Zedong in a verbal appearance said that it could never happen because the Americans need it to be in our camp. . . . And so Pasternak, when he becomes a real émigré — he will not be needed there. And we don't need

him, and he will soon be forgotten. . . . And that will be the real execution for his act of treason.

In the course of thirty years Soloukhin had the opportunity to save his soul — with nothing more than repentance. Those who spit at the condemned are damned. But we must not seek revenge against those who have lost the way — we must give them the opportunity to cleanse themselves with repentance. Every sinner has that chance. But damnation will fall from the faces of those who branded other human faces with their spittle only if they find the courage to blame themselves for the "holy simplicity" of adding kindling to the bonfires of the inquisition. The repentant shall be forgiven! But the black stamp of unforgiveness will lie on the foreheads of those who add to their sin with the pride of unrepentance and the attempt at justification of their sin, the shameful blaming of others.

In thirty years, Vladimir Alexeyevich, the sin of your betrayal seemed to be hidden well and deep under the gravestone, away from the glare of publicity, but glasnost washed away its foundations, like springwater, and your guilt stuck out, like the hand of a murdered child out of a melting snowbank. You wanted to cover up that hand with the golden sand of your praise for Pasternak on television — hoping the past would be forgotten. But your two-facedness shocked a reader, perhaps a fan of your *Vladimir Country Roads* or *Letters from the Russian Museum,* and she asked bitterly: who are you really — a fighter for Russian culture or one of its murderers? And you, instead of repenting at least now, for which much would have been forgiven, replied so angrily, as if to a mortal enemy, or as though that reader was your conscience, which scared you to death and which you began to hate? And then you began to pull Kaverin, who even repented for not having been at that meeting, into the black funnel of sin. How could you put yourself, an unrepentant evildoer, and the bitterly and unsparingly repentant "nonparticipant," our most senior writer, famous for his conscientiousness?

Many of our writers, myself included, had their arms twisted, and yet we did not agree. Don't try to blame everyone else in order to protect yourself. My refusal and the refusal of others whom they tried to get involved in this case, was not merely cowardly silence, as you are now trying to prove with your all-justifying thesis: they proposed, I spoke. They "proposed" to me and other writers, and we did not speak. That was taking a position right there. It's terrible to read and find a writer, not a former camp commandant, not a Beria investigator, but a writer, and one not without talent, using the creepy self-justification of professional executioners: "The times were like that," "It was simply in the spirit of the times — they proposed, I spoke," "You must remember that there was yet another concept — party discipline," "No, my dear, good friends, if we're going to cleanse and repent, let's do it together," "Let's mention the times, because the times, as we know, change. . . ."

Wasn't spitting at the condemned vile and base in all times — the times of Pontius Pilate and of Stalin? Isn't betrayal of people villainous in the times of Ivan the Terrible and of Khrushchev? Isn't the moral executionism of the stagnation period no more vile than trying to justify it now during perestroika? What disgusting examples of potential betrayals for our descendants, for if they learn experience's lessons, they will be able to betray their best poets, their best people without a twinge of conscience and then justify themselves with a shrug: "the times were like that." That's a recipe for destroying all our hopes for perestroika, a recipe for the moral corruption of souls.

Soloukhin's self-revelations are horrifying: "I'll amaze you, but I'll tell you that I never felt an acute desire to repent and 'cleanse' myself, not because when I spoke out then I was so smart and good, but because I do not feel any particular sin." I don't believe Russian literature has heard such cynicism, when one person tries to smear his grave sin all over other people, from any other writer.

Since earliest times talent in Russian literature has been measured by the most important yardstick — pangs of conscience. Pushkin was tormented by not having shared the better fate of the Decembrists. Dostoevsky, having seen the hell of the dead house, tormented himself for having been punished with freedom that was not shared by so many other prisoners. Tolstoy suffered over his aristocratic origins and inherited wealth, which were like a curse. They suffered for sins that they did not commit nor even think about. And if they were guilty of something, they paid with their sins not in words, but in their own blood. "For a drop of blood, in common with the people, forgive, O Homeland, forgive me!" wrote Nekrasov.[1] They were not ashamed of repenting. They cleansed themselves with repentance. The great moral postulate "everyone is guilty of everything" is not intended to make justification easy. Soloukhin turned it around, blaming everyone in the sin of Pasternak's civil execution, so that he and his thirteen comrades in arms are allegedly "no worse than the rest." No, those who damned him from the pulpit are worse than those who sat silently in the pews. Those who pronounced fiery speeches about the enemies of the people at the trials of 1937 are incomparably worse than the silent crowds who stood with pathetic parcels to pass to prisoners on Sailor's Rest Street.

Soloukhin joyfully manipulates biblical imagery to defend his anti-Christian theories with feigned Christianity, although for some reason he relates the crucifixion of Christ only with Caifa and Pilate, with great Freudian obviousness delicately omitting mention of the greatest traitor, Judas.

But there were not only those who spat lining the road to Golgotha. There were also the compassionate, not courageous enough to try to save the condemned, but brave enough at least to weep tears of sympathy, dangerous enough, before the executioners. After all, spitting is more shameful than crying, even if it is helpless.

There is a difference between lips sullied by spitting at the condemned and lips whispering a prayer to ease his mortal agony. Of course, those who spat and drove nails through the condemned's hands are not the only ones who are guilty. Those who felt compassion but did not rise to save them are not totally forgiven by history or their own consciences. But execution by your own conscience is a sure sign that your conscience exists.

---

1. Nikolai Alexeyevich Nekrasov (1821–1878) was a leading civic poet, concerned with exposing society's flaws and the hardships of the peasants. One of his major poems is "Who Is Happy in Russia?" He was also editor of Russia's preeminent literary journal, *Sovremennik.*

⸂ *Fear of Glasnost* *(1987)*

IN THE EARLY SIXTIES young people used to read poetry from the pedestal of the Mayakovsky monument in Mayakovsky Square. One day Black Marias appeared, and the athletic young men who jumped out of them began taking away the poetry lovers for disturbing the peace. I saw them beat up a young man because they thought the Mayakovsky poems he was reading were his own "anti-Soviet" poems. No one reads poetry at the Mayakovsky statue now. The fear of glasnost has killed that wonderful tradition. The fear of glasnost recently killed the attempt at a Holiday of Laughter on the old Arbat — there were so many cordons of police that no one felt like laughing. The fear of glasnost is why we practically have no worker or student discussion clubs, only pathetic ersatz organizations. The fear of glasnost is not in the brain but in the bone marrow — years like 1937 leave their trace. The fear of glasnost is the fear of independent thought. How can people start the new thinking if they've never had their own old thinking? The fear of glasnost is the self-defense of the faceless. The fear of glasnost is patriotism of the banner-carrying kind — destructive protectionism. The fear of glasnost undermines national pride. How can you be proud of a society that shuts your mouth? The fear of glasnost undermines the country's safety, for holes can appear in the sky if the army cannot be criticized. The fear of glasnost is the potential for repeating the mistakes of history. The fear of glasnost blurs people's morality. The fear of glasnost is the factory of nihilism. The fear of glasnost is an obstacle to peace, because without mutual sincerity people cannot have mutual understanding. The fear of glasnost is often dictated by considerations that are purely personal, but they turn into sociopolitical ones. Glasnost, won after years of exhausting struggle, cost our people too much to give it up now to the fear of glasnost.

What Do Russians Want? *(1986)*

THIS QUESTION is posed, with furrowed brow, by the president of America, an office worker in Copenhagen, an Australian trucker, and maybe even a Japanese geisha. The question itself is wrong, because in the Western press all Soviet people are considered Russian. So let's use the word "Russian" conditionally, understanding the question as "what do the Soviet people want."

In propaganda films of the Stalin era our people were shown to be idiotic, happy living statues with hammers and sickles in their hands. In Western propaganda films they were shown as KGB agents, boxers with SS eyes, dulled, drunken state robots.

For me the word "Russian" is not an abstraction, it represents concrete people. This includes geniuses and mediocrities, generous people and stingy ones, bureaucrats and fighters against bureaucracy. Fans of Shostakovich and fans of Michael Jackson. They are people who hang pictures of Stalin from their rearview mirrors and those who were in Stalin's camps. The mosaic can be continued ad infinitum.

So how can I answer the rhetorical question "What do Russians want?"

Let's try to determine what they want by focusing not on the geniuses and villains but on the ordinary, so-called "average man." The average Soviet man has undergone a spiritual revolution — he has realized that he lives badly and that there are countries where people live better. The average Soviet man has lost a lot in idealism, but he won by developing revulsion for enforced ideals. The average man does not believe and will not believe words that are not supported by actions. The average man has become skeptical, after so many unfulfilled promises, but skepticism is less dangerous than uninformed optimism. The average man wants to live according to his own initiative rather than by centralized instructions. The average man doesn't give a damn what milk his children drink — state, kolkhoz, or private — what he cares about is that the milk be available, always available, and that it be inexpensive. The average man's attitude to alternatives in economics is the same: he doesn't give a damn what direction it follows as long as it brings milk for his children. The average man wants to dress well, and he knows very well that the state can never be a good tailor or cobbler. The average man is tired of standing in line, yet just recently he didn't even notice that he was spending half his life in lines. The average man wants a society without privileges and special stores for the bosses, or Beriozka stores, because all that demeans human dignity. The average man has suddenly discovered that he is often helpless before authorities, and he wants guarantees of personal safety. The average man has gradually realized that the *propiska* [residency permit] and domestic passports are shameful rudiments of serfdom. The average man has come to understand that the system of checking loyalty before trips abroad is insulting. The average man has understood how dangerous the concentration of power is in one man and he does not want the horrors of the Terror to be repeated. The average man has figured out that the lightning bolts of terror not only strike the big trees but they burn the grass around them. The average man does not want the window to Europe hewed by Peter the Great to be hammered shut from either side. Geniuses can exist in the most totalitarian conditions. The level of genius is not the spiritual level of a nation. The spiritual level of a nation is determined at the level of the average man. The changes that are happening in our so-called average man are astonishing. The average man is still sleepy but waking up. If he manages to overcome the inertia of the habit of having someone else think for him, if he manages to be cured of dependence and submission, as of a long-standing illness, he will cease being "average." The level of the average man fell catastrophically after we lost so many millions in the civil war, and World War II, and in the war of totalitarianism against its own people. If we manage to raise both the material and the spiritual level of the "average" man, this will be the greatest accomplishment of perestroika.

Letter to Gorbachev, 1987

Under glasnost many revisions of Soviet history have been reexamined; heroes of the Revolution who had become nonpersons under Stalin are being rehabilitated. Nikolai Bukharin (1888–1938), a Bolshevik leader who was executed for treason by Stalin, was an advocate of a market economy and other measures that are now seen as inevitable and necessary aspects of perestroika. He was first "rediscovered" by a group of activists in Naberezhnye Chelny, an industrial city that is home to the KamAZ, or Kama Automobile Plant. They set up the Bukharin Club, started social reforms in the city, and invited guest speakers to address local workers and intellectuals. By 1987, the feeling that Bukharin should be officially rehabilitated was growing, and the club asked Yevtushenko to present their petition to Gorbachev.

General Secretary of the CC CPSU
Comrade Gorbachev, M. S.   *June 1987*

from Secretary of the Board of the Writers' Union USSR
and laureate of the State Prize USSR, poet Yevtushenko, Ye. A.

Dear Mikhail Sergeyevich!

I am forwarding a letter to you with a petition for the rehabilitation of Party leaders unjustly accused in their time and executed, and among them first of all, Nikolai Ivanovich Bukharin, whom Lenin called the "legal favorite of the Party." This letter is signed by representatives of the progressive part of our working class in KamAZ. The best representatives of our intelligentsia could have signed this letter too. Everyone who not only gives lip service to perestroika and glasnost but inculcates them in our lives certainly shares the opinion of the writers of this letter. Bukharin's rehabilitation has long been overdue and the seventieth-anniversary year of our state is the best time to do it. We inheritors of the revolution do not have the right not to remember with kind words all those who created it.

Sincerely and respectfully yours,

Yevgeny Yevtushenko

PART III

Soviet Life

Party of Non–Party Members *(1988)*

THERE'S THIS PARTY. It has no Politburo, no oblast committees, no regional committees. It is unorganized, and therein lies its weakness, but it is not overorganized, and therein lies its strength. The party of non–Party members is strong because it has no *nomenklatura*. By party of non–Party members I do not mean any social plankton, but only those who together with the best Party members form an unformed but truly existing Popular Front of Perestroika.

This Popular Front is not simply a front of resistance to bureaucracy, but a front advancing against it. It is a front fighting the grim ghosts of the past, to keep them from being resurrected in the present. It is a front fighting for a life in our country where we will never have to be ashamed of even a single line. The party of non–Party members has more people than the Communist Party and is a gigantic historical force that is not yet fully self-aware.

The shufflers of personnel files are frightened by the echo of "uncontrollable" in the word "non-Party." But history shows that many of its tragedies and crimes were the fault of "controllable" people, while the "uncontrollable ones" were often, in the final analysis, the heroes of history. A person easily controlled by the bureaucracy is essentially an antipatriot, for bureaucracy is actually war against your own people. A person controlled by his own conscience is not without a party even if he is not a member, because he belongs to the party of the people.

Neither partyness nor non-partyness is a moral qualification. The Party is also filled with social plankton. As children we were taught that "the Party is the avant-garde of the working class." But this formula by no means should be construed as an automatic enrollment of every Party member into the avant-garde or of every non–Party member into the rear garde. Beria was also a Party member, but he belongs to the avant-garde of bastards. A Party card is not evidence of progressive thinking or a clear conscience. A Party card by itself cannot be a pass to the front ranks of our society, for otherwise those front ranks could easily turn into the back ones.

Let's return to the expression "avant-garde of the working class." At this stage of modern society this expression has broadened, since our intelligentsia is not an elite separate from the working class, but represents a spiritual working class. A real intellectual may not have bloody calluses on his hands, but he has them on his heart. Weren't the non–Party members Tsiolkovsky, Vavilov, Chayanov, and Andrei Platonov[1] the avant-garde of the spiritual working class? How can you exclude from the avant-garde of the working class those non–Party academicians who fearlessly entered the contaminated zones of Chernobyl? How can you exclude from the avant-garde of the working class non–Party teachers, doctors, nurses, or, for instance, the gray-haired, crystal-pure non–Party accountant through whose hands pass billions of rubles while he earns kopecks? Isn't that army of working people who are for some reason disparagingly called *sluzhiteli* [literally, "servers," the Russian word for white-collar workers] part of the

---

1. Konstantin Eduardovich Tsiolkovsky (1857–1935), a mystic and scientist known as the father of Russian rocketry. He was concerned with making interplanetary travel a reality because he believed that everyone would be resurrected physically after the Second Coming and there would not be enough space on earth for every human who had ever lived.

Nikolai Ivanovich Vavilov (1887–1943), a geneticist who stood up to the Stalinist machine's oppression and distortion of Soviet science; was killed in the Great Terror.

Alexander Vasilyevich Chayanov (1888–1939?), an economist, proponent of the co-operative movement; died after his arrest in the Terror.

Andrei Platonovich Platonov (1899–1951), a writer and critic, was also persecuted under Stalin. *See* "The Proletariat Does Not Need Psychosis: Andrei Platonov," pp. 310–329.

working class? Doesn't retaining a clean conscience even without a Party card put you in the avant-garde? Aren't our best writers, artists, and actors, whose easy life-styles create envious gossip, part of the avant-garde of the working class? (Just to clarify things, I'll tell you that the average earnings of members of the Writers' Union is 162 rubles a month.)[2] And isn't our long-suffering, exhausted, and mutilated peasantry, whose best sons have miraculously managed to preserve the talent to whisper in the same language with our exhausted Mother Earth, also the avant-garde of the working class? Why were strangers from factories and plants, many of whom had never held a piece of living earth in their hands, instructed to teach the farmers how to plow and sow, thereby relegating the peasantry to a lower class beneath the workers?

The disrespect for the peasants was cleverly disguised by placing mute tokens like Maria Demchenko and Mamlakat Nakhangova into presidiums. Also mute was the marvelous native genius, the miner Alexei Stakhanov, who was barbarously torn away from his jackhammer and pushed "up" as a public mannequin to create the appearance of the dictatorship of the proletariat.[3] The dictatorship of the proletariat was actually replaced by the dictatorship of the bureaucracy. The phrase "The Party is the avant-garde of the working class" became hypocritical in the mouths of Stalin and his entourage, for in destroying Party and non–Party members they gagged the Party and the people. Inside the Party itself, the party of mediocrity triumphed. The director Mikhail Kalatozov told me that Stalin particularly liked an American film about an old pirate who locked himself up in his cabin and played chess by himself. He molded the figures out of bread to represent the other pirates. When he won a piece and swept it from the board, he

2. In 1990 the average wage in the USSR was a little over 200 rubles a month. At the official exchange rate of $1.66 to the ruble, that makes $332. Any comparison of salaries, however, is misleading, because so many budget items (rent, milk and bread, children's clothing) are state subsidized and unnaturally low-priced while other items, in very short supply, are disproportionately expensive.
3. Yevtushenko is referring to the mockery of placing unqualified "representatives of the peasantry" into official positions where they merely rubber-stamped presidium decisions. Alexei Stakhanov, the miner who surpassed all production norms, gave his name to the term "Stakhanovite," for a Soviet industrial worker awarded recognition and special privileges for exceeding quotas.

also murdered the actual man. By the end of the film, the pirate was alone and laughing wildly, drinking rum out of the bottle, as he piloted the ship toward an iceberg in the fog. Stalin, despite the Politburo members who pleaded weariness, forced them to watch the film again. "An edifying movie," he said with a chuckle.

Stalin destroyed the best revolutionary cadres and then destroyed many of those who had destroyed them, and he kept the Party apparat in fear, even as he bribed them with various privileges: special stores, food parcels, dachas, cars and drivers, and even "blue packages" (a special monthly salary that was tax free). Stalin and his circle, corrupt themselves, corrupted the Party. Stalin's personal asceticism, modesty, and lack of greed are a lie. The level of morality and talent of Party members fell catastrophically. The difference in promotion to responsible posts was sharply felt between Party and non–Party members. More and more careerists joined the Party. Many talented people did not want to join, because along with a quick rise it implied a greater dependence and enslavement.

After the Twentieth Party Congress new fresh forces joined the Party hoping that they would be able to promote democratization faster from within. It was not easy for them. Some were broken and grew cynical and sold out. The more steadfast ones, sometimes gritting their teeth in shame, did not abandon their hopes for a revolutionary perestroika and bore the flame inside their hearts. It is these people who heroically turned the ship of state out of the swamp of stagnation into the open seas of glasnost. But many became mired in the swamp muck and we cannot expect any love for the future waves of glasnost from them — they might be swept off the deck. Of course, these kinds of craven wait-and-seers exist among the non–Party people, too.

The dividing line today is not between Party and non–Party members, but between those who fight for perestroika and those who sabotage it. It is the hands of the saboteurs that are trying to choke the cooperatives with taxes and all sorts of other limitations. It is their hands that invisibly bless anti-Semitic explosions. What are they so afraid of and why are they scaring others? Because under glasnost a terrible state secret might be revealed — their total uselessness and inability to rule.

Many join the Party in order to help perestroika, to fight inside the Party against those who defile it. But the leaden ballast of careerists will continue to exist in the Party as long as the priority of promotion in work and public life continues, related not to ability or merit but to the red party card. The Party becomes weaker when its membership does not have to compete fairly with non–Party members. The state is impoverishing itself, robbing its own cadres, by not entrusting more posts to more talented non–Party members. Are our workers building two different socialisms: one for the Party and the other for non–Party members?

Some of the non–Party people are devout. During the historical celebration of the thousand years of Christianity in Russia, leaders of the Russian Orthodox Church met with the leader of our Party and expressed their support for perestroika. The Constitution has sacred words on freedom of religion. But if freedom of religion is constitutional, then any persecution of the devout is illegal. Expulsion from the Komsomol or the Party not for belief but merely for attending church, having a church wedding or baptism is hopelessly out of date — a vestige of the twenties. Is it impossible to believe in God and at the same time in socialism? The freedom of atheism should coexist with the freedom of religion. Overthrowing vulgar theories, history has shown that devoutness can coexist with patriotism and civic courage. The Russian Orthodox Church, which blessed our troops, collected money for defense, including wedding bands of the faithful. The synagogue in Irkutsk has a wall with an eternal flame and a marble board listing those devout Jews who died in the war against fascism. Muslims from Central Asia, Catholics and Protestants from the Baltics fought shoulder to shoulder, like brothers. Now all the churches in our land are active in the struggle for peace, for nuclear disarmament. Why is it, then, that when it is learned that a Soviet citizen is religious, it becomes hard for him to move ahead at work? Soviet Congresses of People's Deputies that do not have representatives of the devout cannot represent our people. Ilya Nikolayevich Ulyanov, Lenin's father, was deeply devout. A few years ago, visiting

Ulyanovsk, I was outraged to see that someone's tactless hand had painted out the carved Orthodox cross on his headstone. It showed through anyway. The criminal punishment for insulting believers must be raised. The greatest danger to our society lies not in those who believe in God but in those who believe in nothing.

Our country is undergoing the Great Rehabilitation not only of names but of ideals as well. We have made great strides in glasnost. Now we must convert glasnost into material values. The heroic struggle of our press against the tyranny of shortages will be meaningless as long as the people who control medicines, food, and goods don't have to stand in line with the rest of the people. The shortages will not disappear as long as there is a shortage of trust for non–Party people. Without trust for non–Party members, national self-rule is impossible, since the majority of the people are non–Party members.

All the best people of our country — Party and non-Party — should be equal within the party that unites us all, the Party of Perestroika. There is such a party.

$\mathcal{S}$ Wooden Moscow

(1981–1989)

A Rally Like a Dream

THE PAVED LOT in front of the stadium is filled with twenty thousand people, chanting: "United we stand!" In the crowd there are no bureaucrats, smoothly shaven with Sony electric shavers or Gillette blades, neither of which are available to the general public, no kings of the black market with fat hairy fingers covered with rings, no pop stars in mink coats. This crowd consists of Muscovites who probably earn 150 to 200 rubles a month. A student in a knit ski cap is waving a banner that says, "Go democracy!" A young nurse with a freckled face holds a flag made of a white sheet with a blue cross. A small, shabby old man of a profession hard to guess grasps in his tattooed hand a thin stick to which he has attached a homemade sign: "Yeltsin is invigorating somehow," which is completely at odds with his hangdog look. From the tribune, orators demand freedom and rule of the people. Photo correspondents from all over the world hang from every lamppost like starlings. An American journalist comes over to me and says with a smile, "The last election campaign in America looked like conformism from over here. I never thought Moscow could be like this. . . . " To tell the truth, neither did I. Of course, not far from the rally, beyond the railroad tracks, there are khaki-colored vans, and in them are sturdy fellows dressed in the gray jackets of the special troops, ready to go. And I'm sure that there are people in the crowd who represent the collective eye of Big Brother. But the militia is not breaking up the crowd, not pulling the speakers down from the tribune, because no such order has been given yet, and they are even listening with unfeigned childlike interest to the particularly rebellious speeches. A red-haired policeman who looks like a farm boy, hearing a call for a multiparty system, wrinkles his brow and shares his concern: "Does that mean that if we have three parties, then there will be three regional committees, and we have to feed all of them?"

That rally seems incredible, almost like a dream to me because I remember a different Moscow, of the Stalin era, when people were afraid of the sound of the elevator at night, because they could be arrested at any moment not only for a speech calling for freedom (there hadn't been speeches like that in a long time), but simply because the multiheaded monster of the police machine had to have new human victims to stay alive. Just last year several horrible secrets of Moscow were discovered. Next to the Bird Market is a previously undistinguished cemetery — Kalitnikovsky, with a marvelous ancient Church of All Sorrows. And suddenly it turned out that beneath the "official" cemetery there is another secret one, covered with dirt and squashed by new coffins. When Stalin died, Beria gave orders to have it covered up immediately, to hide all traces of the crimes. Even many longtime residents of Moscow had no idea that under the fresh graves there was an old common grave for tens of thousands of people, shot with and without trials in the wild Saint Bartholomew's nights of the 1930s. A few old women who had been children then miraculously survived, and they told everything they remembered. With the intense curiosity of children they went to see what was going on there at night when people drove up in closed vans. Hiding in the bushes, the children saw a horrible picture: a van would drive up right to the edge of a long deep ravine, the back doors opened, and Soviet Sonderkomand in long aprons, rubber boots, and gloves would use special poles to push out naked corpses, one after the other, shot in the back of the head and the wounds stuffed with rags. Many of the corpses were not very fresh; they had distended bellies, which burst with a horrifying bang as they landed.

The tragic irony was that the Mikoyan meat-packing plant was located right across the way, and an enormous electric sign depicting Stalin shone above it, while the plant's dogs approached the edge of the ravine and howled in the moonlight.

Moscow remembers all this and does not want to see a repetition.

I don't like the Moscow of bureaucratic offices, I don't like the Moscow of stores. I love the Moscow of workers, who not only play dominoes on Saturdays and Sundays but now also attend political rallies, reviving the almost forgotten revolutionary traditions of the proletariat.

I love the Moscow of students, whose eyes gleam today not only with poetry but with social hopes.

I love the Moscow of scientists who demonstrated in support of the candidacy of Academicians Sakharov and Sagdeyev,[1] against the science bureaucrats.

I love the Moscow of theaters, music, paintings, museums, churches, cemeteries, and kindergartens.

I love the Moscow of homes where you can always be fed and always get a loan if you need it.

I love the Moscow of beautiful women who catch the eyes of the whole world.

I love the Moscow of babushkas.

Moscow is the grandmother of the future, carrying it in a baby carriage.

Moscow Secrets

In order to understand a city, you have to fall in love there at least once, get sick at least once, be robbed at least once, find something accidentally at least once, bury someone at least once, and walk through the city with a child in your arms at least once.

1. Roald Zinnurovich Sagdeyev (born 1932) was head of the Soviet space program. In recent elections to the Congress of People's Deputies, he ceded his place on the Academy of Sciences list to Andrei Sakharov. Sagdeyev was elected, too. He married Susan Eisenhower in 1990.

All these things happened to me in Moscow, and therefore the city is mine — it is filled with shades of my happiness and misfortunes, ghosts of people who have died for many but are eternal residents of Moscow for me. When tourists visit the Kremlin, the Bolshoi Theater, and museums to the quick patter of guides, I am glad that I have another guide — my memory, which leads me down byways where tour buses never go. Some cracked wooden house, miraculously retaining its unique face filled with aged beauty and doomed to being razed because it spoils the view from the nearest high rise, is my own little Bolshoi Theater, where the romantic operas of life are played to the popular American song "Rio Rita," which came through the open window from a gasping record player with a rackety needle.

When I recently passed the construction site of the Olympic Stadium in the neighborhood of the former Meshchanskaya streets, famed for their hooligans in my childhood, I thought with sadness about how many of my memories were buried in the foundation of that stadium and how the thousands of fans roaring in the stands would never know the secrets of our childhoods, pressed down by the marvelous sports palace, including the site of my first kiss.

I came to Moscow from Siberia in 1944, when I was twelve. My mother — a popular singer — was at the front, my father, divorced, was somewhere in Siberia, and I lived alone in a communal apartment inside an old wooden house, surrounded by bird cherry trees and poplars. Like many children of that period, I was left to my own devices. My nanny was the street. The street taught me to fight, steal, and be afraid of nothing. There was one fear the street did not take away from me — fear of losing my bread cards. I carried them in a canvas bag tied around my neck on a shoelace. Then one day after a fight, the bag was gone. An old woman, standing in line, gave me her late husband's cards and said, "You can eat for the dead man. . . . "

With the other boys I sold cigarettes, buying them in packs and selling them singly. But on Victory Day all the cigarette vendors in the city were giving them away, the ice cream women were giving away ice cream in Red Square. It looked like all of Moscow was in Red Square. All the women, spinning in waltzes to accordion music, were wearing oilcloth boots — I don't remember anyone in shoes. American and English officers were tossed into the air, and we kids scrambled for foreign coins that came out of their pockets. One American gave me some gum; I thought it was candy and swallowed it. Wounded soldiers sat with their arms around each other and drank on the steps of the Mausoleum. French couples kissed under the blue Kremlin firs.

Every city is made up of hundreds of thousands of secrets, invisible to the tourist eye. "Then why bother going to strange cities, if you're never going to get to the bottom of their secrets anyway?" a lazybones might ask. To understand the secrets of other cities, you have to make your own secrets there. There's no point in going to a country if you don't have a deep interest in its history, culture, and life today, but only a desire to show people slides when you get back of yourself in front of the Eiffel Tower, the Empire State Building, or the Kremlin. It's time to get rid of the anachronistic and harmful sense of being a "foreigner" wherever you are, and if stupid bureaucrats in some country try to remind you of that, do not forget that besides the bureaucrat every country has many wonderful people who live, love, suffer, and feel joy, people who are perhaps incredibly close to you in their hopes and perhaps in their secrets. The key to that which seems foreign is art and literature. You can't understand even contemporary Leningrad without Dostoevsky or modern Moscow without Tolstoy and today's Russian poetry. Literature and art are the invisible threads that give all the people separated by borders the sense of themselves as a single family of man. But literature alone is not enough, because it is sometimes fatally behind the constantly changing world. Having an opinion of a country or a city where you have not been is at best frivolous and sometimes even amoral. No books, and certainly no newspapers, can replace your own eyes. Proximity to the greatest pages cannot give you the understanding that can sometimes come from hand touching hand.

Moscow has changed extraordinarily since my youth. If those women who did not have dress shoes and waltzed in heavy soldiers' boots on Victory Day could be brought by a time machine right to today's Red Square, thirty-five years later, they would be confused and think that they were in a different country that had made a copy of Red Square and where everyone had learned Russian — which has also changed significantly since then. People of the war period would find it hard to believe that the girls in white dresses and boys in jeans dancing to rock music by the ancient walls of the Kremlin after the graduation dance were their descendants.

I took my small son to watch the fireworks from Vorobyovye Hills to celebrate Victory Day and I was surprised to hear German being spoken nearby. Not far from me was a German man — perhaps a journalist, perhaps someone from the embassy or in trade, I don't even know if he was from the FRG or the GDR — with his blond son on his shoulders, who shouted in glee each time the fireworks spread a peacock tail in the sky. Could we have ever thought, we boys of the war years, who played war (and no one ever wanted to be the Germans), could we have imagined that someday a little German boy would be enjoying the salutes in Moscow celebrating our victory?

Gina Lollobrigida and Red Square

One morning my phone rang. A melodic female voice said in Italian that it was Gina Lollobrigida. I hung up, thinking some silly girl from the foreign languages institute was making a joke. It was too incredible to think that it could be the celebrated movie star of the sixties, who had impressed my youthful imagination not so much with her acting as with the seductive beauty of her eyes, which looked like wet dark cherries, and the embarrassing and alluring and world-famous globes bursting out of her blouse. But the call was repeated. The woman, who insisted she was Gina Lollobrigida, said that she was a photographer now, had come to photograph Moscow, and wanted my help and advice in picking locations.

Our meeting took place in the rehearsal hall of the Bolshoi ballet, where the young ballerinas smelled of sweat like whipped horses. The image of the screen Gina, always either seductive or seduced, had materialized into a not young, but still charming, fully businesslike woman, hiding her famous eyes under sunglasses and her famous breasts under cameras, which hung in bunches from her neck. Gina was accompanied by an escort of photographers, hauling her extra lenses, film, and flash; at the same time, they photographed her taking photographs. That kind of an escort contradicts my understanding of photography as an art and I asked Gina to get rid of them. She agreed and said, "First let's go to Red Square. But that's for everyone. . . . After that show me your Moscow."

And I thought for the first time, what is my Moscow? There is a tourist Italy and the Italy of Italians. There is a tourist Moscow and the Moscow of Muscovites. And inside that Muscovite Moscow there is my personal one. Gina Lollobrigida stood on the paving stones of Red Square, and dropping to one elegant, black-velvet knee, took pictures of the changing of the guard in front of Lenin's Tomb and then of Saint Basil's. But did she know that according to legend the builders of the cathedral had had their eyes put out so that they could never build another better? No wonder the tsar was dubbed Ivan the Terrible.

In the fall of 1941 I watched soldiers climbing up ladders to the stars on top of the Kremlin towers to cover them up with sacking. One of the carvers of those stars was an elderly Latvian we called Karlusha. He lived in our building on Fourth Mesh-chanskaya with a lot of cats. We used to catch them and with childish cruelty tie their tails to his doorknob. Karlusha was arrested before the war, and he vanished forever, and it's too late to ask his forgiveness.

The Mausoleum too was covered with painted plywood in an attempt to camouflage it from air attack. The coffin with Lenin's body was evacuated, but that was kept secret. I learned about it during the evacuation when all the echelons were stopped to let through one very short train. The rumor was that it was filled with gold. The boys and I went over to the guards and said, "Misters, are you carrying gold? Can we see just a little piece?" An officer sighed deeply and said, "It's more precious than gold. . . . It's Lenin."

On October 16, 1941, many thought that they would be leaving Moscow. I remember a boy sadly letting his goldfish out of the aquarium and into a brook beneath the shade of the antiaircraft guns above him. People were scurrying in all directions with packs and suitcases, and a fat woman was pushing a baby carriage in which lay a rolled Persian rug, a crystal chandelier, and a bronze bust of Napoleon with his hand in his jacket. A strange old man with a chessboard in his hand wandered around, trying to stop people and get them to play a quick blitzgame with him. "Just think . . . just think . . . All my colleagues — José Raul Capablanca, Lasker, Euwe — are all evacuated to Siberia, and no one even imagines that I am Alekhin. . . . Remember this, that on October 16, 1941, there was no one to play chess with Alekhin!" A close look at the old man showed that he was wearing hospital pajamas and slippers under his raincoat.

I thought of all that while Gina Lollobrigida climbed up on Lobnoye Mesto, the old execution spot, without any historical fear of the ghosts of tsarist executioners, and photographed Red Square from this special vantage point.

I also saw my return to Moscow from Siberian evacuation, and soldiers taking off the sacking from the stars, and fascist banners falling by the Mausoleum, and women waltzing with soldiers and officers, who smelled of victory-spoils kirsch. A few legless veterans were lifted up by the crowds in their wicker baskets and they swayed over Red Square like gruesome living memorials to the war.

"Well, I'm finished with Red Square," she said, loading her Nikon with new film. "Now you promised to show me your Moscow."

"Yes, yes," I muttered, shaking off the flood of memories.

How could I explain to Gina that Red Square was also my Moscow, because it was filled with ghosts invisible to tourists?

We got in my car and drove to the area of the old Meshchanskaya streets, where I spent my childhood, playing soccer in the empty lots instead of going to school, where my grandmother once led me tied to a rope, like a calf.

There were two Moscows right after the war — stone and wood. I grew up in wooden Moscow — in a small, two-story house hidden in trees. It was heated by firewood. There was no bath or shower, and like the majority of Muscovites in those days we solemnly went to the steam baths on Saturday, performing the ancient ritual of lashing each other's sides and backs with birchleaf brooms. There are many more apartments with baths in Moscow now, but paradoxically, the lines for the bathhouses have gotten longer, and there is a shortage of birch brooms. Now people go the *banya* not simply to wash, but to have a good time, to talk to people in clouds of steam, where everyone is naked and no one is superior because of the clothes he wears.

In the early years after the war we all dressed about the same, and only a tiny minority lived in separate apartments with a bath and other conveniences. Private refrigerators appeared around 1950, if I'm not mistaken, and before that people hung their groceries outside the window in a string bag to keep them cool. My mother, a former singer who lost her voice singing at the front, my grandmother, my little sister, and I lived in two rooms of a communal apartment. The satirical works of that period describe the nastiness of the communal kitchens, where neighbors spat in each other's pots of borscht and residents beat up the one who always left the light on in the toilet. However, there was nothing of that sort in our apartment. On the contrary, our common kitchen was like a small parliament, where everything was discussed — family and politics — and the big room of that parliament was the inner courtyard, where long meetings were held on the shady benches and all the residents were equal — plumber, professor, writer. That was the way Moscow was then.

When I arrived at Fourth Meshchanskaya with Gina Lollobrigida, our house was still standing, but it was empty, and bulldozers were standing next to it, ready to tear it down. It was in the way of the construction for the Olympic Games. Two of my former neighbors were standing by the house, sipping vodka from the bottle, and watching its destruction. I had a drink and so did Gina, unrecognized by them. We went to look at the other wooden streets, but to my sad surprise there were film crews hurrying to capture the last remaining pieces of vanishing old Moscow. I wandered through the cemetery of memories of my childhood with Gina Lollobrigida, a strange guest from another world. Accustomed to avoiding recognition, Gina seemed uncomfortable not being recognized at all, and even took off her dark glasses. But no one knew her anyway.

She may have been the last photographer to get pictures of the old Moscow village yards with dahlias and daisies, windows with wooden shutters and fretwork, and on the sills the traditional red geranium (the triumphant symbol of the so-called bourgeoisie, which had been often attacked by Komsomol poets and which nevertheless survived), the green spikes of aloe, which, according to Moscow superstition, prevents all diseases, and also tubby jugs of dark homemade liqueur, with drunken cherries bobbing in them. The windows of old Moscow were unthinkable without this entourage, or without net curtains, behind which were the curious faces of Moscow babushkas — the caryatids of the capital.

No matter how much Gina shot, she naturally saw things in her viewfinder completely differently than I saw them, and it could be no other way. No camera exists that can take pictures of memories.

After the photo session Gina asked me to take her to a place "where young people have fun." I chose the Lyra Café on Pushkin Square [now the McDonald's], where female students, secretaries, and factory workers come in couples at six o'clock and modestly order iced coffee, leaving two chairs free at their tables. By seven, those chairs are filled by their improvised escorts — Muscovites or men in town on business — and bottles of champagne and jars of salted nuts are on the tables, and the electric guitars are wailing wildly, and everything is swirling in a seemingly unstoppable dance carousel until the fateful hour of eleven [closing time in all state-run restaurants]. We managed to squeeze in at a table belonging to two sailors and their girlfriends. They were hospitable and made room for us, and soon Gina was dancing to the rock music with a sailor. Gina was astonished that no one recognized her here, either. She decided to help the recognition along and asked me to translate for her. She asked our tablemates if they knew any Italian actors. After some thought, one Red Fleet boy named Alberto Sordi.

Gina went into open attack.

"How about Gina Lollobrigida?" she asked.

"I think she played Cleopatra, right?" said one of the girls. "Or I'm confusing her with Elizabeth Taylor. . . . But they're both dead, I think."

I have to give Gina her due — she had a sense of humor, and

she laughed and then said to me, "I'm glad I died. I'd rather take pictures than be in them."

Wine in Tablets

I spent my childhood in lines, as did almost all the children of our generation, writing down our numbers on our hands with indelible pencil.[2] Now, despite the higher prices for cars, there are lines for them. Back then you could easily buy a car, released for private sale for the first time, but there weren't many buyers. The huge ZIM limousine cost 40,000, the Pobeda 16,000, and the Moskvich a mere 8,000 (in today's rubles 4,000, 1,600, and 800 rubles [$6,640, $1,750, and $1,150]). Even in times of food crisis the stores always had champagne, canned crab, and codfish in oil. Now they are hard to get, because everyone knows they are delicacies. Back then our tastes were simpler and no one knew what delicacies were.

When I was fourteen, I learned of the existence of cocktails from Hemingway's books. My school friends and I decided to celebrate New Year's à la Hemingway and mixed everything we could get our hands on in a pail: beer, cider, cheap fruit wine, and vodka, adding icicles with rust from the roof into our devilish mix. There's no need to say that we barely survived our experiment in introducing civilization to our stomachs.

In 1949, after the publication of my first poems, I invited my friend, the son of the janitor, and two girls from a clothing factory to the Aurora Restaurant. When I saw "dry wine" on the menu and ordered it I was very disappointed to see that it didn't come in tablet form. Wanting to show off her restaurant expertise, one of the girls asked the waiter for "A bottle of satsivi!" The waiter, a gray-haired man with a thin, intelligent face, who looked more like a violinist than a waiter, replied politely, without letting on that satsivi was a Georgian dish, "I'm sorry, we've run out of the bottled satsivi. Would you like it as an hors d'oeuvre instead?"

The first wealthy children began to appear in Moscow. It was a narrow caste of sons of academicians and famous composers.

2. During the years of World War II, women and children had to line up for bread. They would show up the night before, get their number in line written in indelible pencil on the palm of their hands, and then return at dawn to take their correct place.

They wore only foreign clothes: long jackets that looked like half-length coats with enormous padded shoulders, parrot-bright ties, and cherry-colored shoes on white rubber soles. Their long hair was slicked back with brilliantine. They drove around in their fathers' cars and relaxed in the company of models. This clan was later dubbed the *stilyagi* [from the word for "style"]. Their manner of dressing and dancing was a sort of protest against standardization, but it was protest in caricature. Their hangout was the cocktail hall on Gorky Street. In 1954 after a murder in the *stilyaga* clan, the cocktail hall was declared "a breeding ground of a bourgeois way of life" and shut down. Volunteer police sought out the remaining *stilyagi* and battled against long hair and narrow pants with scissors; they also made sure the dances were within the bounds of ideological restraint. The *stilyagi* disappeared. But the minuet and the Cracowiak did not catch on in the dance halls. The young people stubbornly danced to rock and roll.

The final break in taste took place in 1957 during the Youth Festival, when thousands of foreigners flooded the streets of Moscow, mixing with the young Muscovites. Once upon a time the satirical magazine *Krokodil* depicted Coca-Cola and Pepsi as "bourgeois poison," and today you buy Pepsi at the Bolshoi. Almost all of Moscow's youth wears jeans, if not made in the USA, then in a socialist country, which leaves something to be desired, incidentally. Jeansomania, however, seems to be dying out — corduroy seems to be taking its place. Bars are opening up where drinks advertised as cocktails are made, though rather ineptly for the time being. Jazz groups, once semiunderground, are playing in big halls with concerts of Western songs and their own. Moscow is much less patriarchal and cut off than it used to be. When Boney M appeared, they had to call out mounted police to control the crowds.

But far from everyone likes the import of modernization. Many find the new boulevards roomy, but not cozy, and they express nostalgia for the crooked, old, and charming streets with wooden houses and red geraniums. There are more conveniences, but less coziness. It's a paradox: people who strove desperately to have a separate apartment now sometimes sigh for the communal flats, because people lived there without a sense of alienation.

Muscovites are creating courtyards again, planting trees in empty lots, planting flowers on balconies and entryways, because Moscow is not Moscow without green yards. The rattle of dominoes on a wooden table under the "mushroom" umbrellas is the usual music of Moscow's courtyards. Ineradicable is the Moscow custom of pickling cucumbers and tomatoes, making sauerkraut, marinating mushrooms, and putting up jams for the winter. People buy Pepsi-Cola for its exotic taste, but prefer the traditional Russian *kvas,* for which they line up on hot days with their pitchers and jars at the cistern. Moscow by nature is somehow eternally patriarchal, and modernization does not catch on in everything and thank God for that. Why should Moscow turn into an average European city? Old Moscow lives inside modern buildings with gas stoves and bathtubs, for you can still hear the drawn-out choruses of songs coming from the windows of high rises just as they used to come from the windows of wooden houses.

It is no accident that despite the love of Muscovites for modern music, Moscow gave birth to two outstanding minstrels: the singer-poets Okudzhava and Vysotsky. Bulat Okudzhava, who sang the praises of the old Moscow streets, is a subtle lyric master, the father of Russian bards. He began writing his songs in the late 1950s. Despite the fact that his songs were not played on the radio or television or recorded, they spread like wildfire and were heard in every Moscow house, in student and worker dormitories, even in Shostakovich's apartment.

Vladimir Vysotsky, an actor at the Taganka Theater who played Hamlet and Brecht's Galileo, came later. His songs were the complete opposite of Okudzhava's: they were not as melodic but much harsher, much more exposed. Vysotsky's voice was hoarse and growling. The words of his songs are written in Moscow's rude slang and sometimes resemble satire set to guitar. Vysotsky died young and his funeral turned into an all-city procession: about three hundred thousand people followed his coffin.

I am happy that people in Moscow love poetry as in no other city. I think that in Moscow it would be possible to fill a stadium with one hundred thousand people for a poetry reading. It hasn't happened yet, but I'm sure it will.

Isaac Melamed, the Victorious

The legendary director Vsevolod Meyerhold had an assistant, Isaac Melamed, who miraculously survived the historic cataclysms. I never met Meyerhold, but I did get to know Melamed. It happened in the fifties, at the National Café, where Melamed came every night with his friend and drinking companion — the brilliant writer Yuri Olesha. Both Melamed and Olesha were not rich, to put it mildly, and the kindly waiters allowed them to bring their own vodka without the café's surcharge. Melamed was a confirmed bachelor, as thin as a rail, with sunken cheeks covered with freckles, and with red curly hair, a fiery halo around his head. He always wore the same soiled jacket, dusted with dandruff, pants with frayed cuffs, and he sometimes wore his shirt inside out to make it look fresher. He also always wore a bow tie. Melamed had huge, surprised eyes with a touch of sadness, and he could spend hours at the table talking about Dante, Goethe, and Shakespeare. But when he left the café, he descended from the heavens of art to the sinful world and proudly asked for a loan for the trolley.

One time something extraordinary happened. A long banquet table was set opposite theirs, full of well-fed foreigners who looked like businessmen, and who were drinking vodka to wash down black caviar and smoked salmon. Suddenly one of the foreigners — freshly shaven, rosy, sleek, with diamond cuff links and stickpin — choked on his caviar sandwich, spat it out, knocked over his chair, and shouted loudly: "Melamed! *Mein lieber* Melamed!" He rushed over to our red-haired oracle and crushed him to his chest, covered with a napkin, speckled with caviar eggs. Melamed said nothing as the foreigner embraced and shook him, laughing and practically crying at the same time. We exchanged looks, since none of us could have imagined that Melamed — our modest Melamed! — could even remotely know a capitalist. And suddenly Melamed's staved cheeks also trembled and recognition flashed in his eyes. "Paul!" he shouted and now they were both shaking each other, knocking over the small decanter of store-bought vodka that had been poured into it under the table. The foreigner, a president of some West German company, began waving packs of Marks and rubles around, demanding champagne, which appeared immediately. Explaining nothing, they started singing Tyrolean songs and then arm in arm headed off into the unknown.

The story of their friendship was later told to me. In 1941 Melamed volunteered for the war and put "German" down as a language he knew, even though he had only studied it at school. German was in high demand then. Despite his purely symbolic weight — a little over 50 kilograms, just enough to be a man — and his skeletonlike frame and starving-Indian look he was sent into the paratroopers. Melamed was sent down with a parachute in the Belorussian forest to learn the language. All the paratroopers were killed in landing — except for Melamed. He may have been saved by his light weight. He got stuck on a pine tree and hung from his straps. He cut them and sank to the ground. He remembered his assignment and tried to do it. After our artillery attacked, Melamed found a German lieutenant in the woods, with a leg wound. He dragged him along on his own back. For those of us who knew Melamed's physical abilities, this was unimaginable. He had no orientation: he had had almost no preparation and his compass broke when he landed. Melamed's knowledge of German was weak, but he had plenty of time to learn: he wandered around, dragging Paul on his back, for almost a month. Melamed operated on Paul, digging the bullet out of his leg with a knife, and made him a crutch out of young pine trees, and the German limped alongside Melamed in the direction of the prison camp, which seemed better than the war he was sick of. They became friends along the way, and Paul taught Melamed Tyrolean songs. When they crossed the front line, the SMERSH[3] agents arrested Melamed, too, seeing how he had embraced the German officer in farewell. They released him when they saw his obvious inability to be a German spy.

That's the unusual story of Isaac Melamed, the victorious. He is no longer among us. I recalled the story because it gives us a wonderful example. If people can become friends during the war,

---

3. SMERSH (*Smert' shpionam* — "Death to spies"), the Soviet Army counterintelligence in World War II.

when they are on opposite sides, then why is that impossible during the state of humanity that we can call — albeit with sad irony — peace?

Moscow the She-Bear

There are various explanations for the origin of the word *Moscow*. The Scythian version gives Moscow as meaning the huntress. One Slavophile variant has *Moscow* coming from the word for "bridge," another from "swampy place." I am no specialist in etymology, and it is hard for me to judge who is right. But personally I like best the theory of the prerevolutionary scholar S. K. Kuznetsov, that the word Moskva is of early Slavic origin: "Maska" is bear, and "ava" mother, that is, She-Bear. This is the most poetic proposal, and it reflects the truth, because once upon a time there were deep forests where Red Square is, filled with entire colonies of those marvelous animals, unfortunately now disappearing. Bears exist in other countries, but for some reason the bear has been a symbol of Russia for many foreigners since a long, long time ago.

There is a bureaucratic Moscow, but that is not my Moscow. There is a Moscow of connivers, black marketeers, and speculators of all stripes, but that's not my Moscow, either. My Moscow is a working city, where new houses are built, cancer cures are sought, and paintings, poems, and music are created. My Moscow is a lyrical city of meetings under the clock and the click of dominoes in green courtyards.

This city does not offer an easy life, and much is lacking in it. But I've been in cities where the stores are full, and yet the table for guests is almost empty. Moscow is a city where the store shelves are sometimes bare but the table can never be empty when there are guests.

Born in 1147 out of the instinct for survival of a divided nation, Moscow became its long-suffering heart, the shield that protected Europe from the Tatar invasion, taking all the blows upon itself. Burned many times, it was reborn from the ashes. The ashes of Moscow, sticking to Napoleon's boots, were so heavy that the lover of glory barely managed to get his feet out of Russia. But Moscow suffered at the hands of its own tyrants, as well as of foreigners. A lot of Russian blood was shed by Russians in Moscow, and many freethinking heads were laid on Moscow's execution blocks. Those people, who died for freedom and whose shadows invisibly flicker among the green lights of Moscow taxis today, are inseparable from the eternal spirit of the city. Those shadows are also my Moscow.

Now when I walk through Moscow, I walk past my first kiss, my first hurt — and if there should be more pain, all I have to do is enter a glass phone booth and find the number of an apartment where I can go at any hour of the day or night, and get a cup of tea or something stronger, where they will heat up some cutlets, and give me money if I need it.

But I'd better hurry dialing that number, because a new, impatient generation is banging on the glass with a coin, a generation that has its own Moscow secrets.

Youth and Courage Are Sisters

SPEECH AT THE SIXTH WRITERS' UNION CONGRESS

June 22, 1976

YOUTH AND COURAGE are sisters. "Craven old age" does not sound very nice, but how terrible are two other words, set side by side, cringing and fighting the forced, unnatural combination — "craven youth." Sometimes one who is brave in his youth later loses faith in his youthful ideals, betrays them with shameful reasonableness and becomes a coward in his maturity or old age. But it is impossible to be brave in your maturity or old age if you were not brave in your youth. Our youthful courage, preserved and not betrayed by word or deed, is the only hope for victory over age and even death, because courage is victory over spiritual death and physical death.

When I speak of courage, I do not mean the courage of people who were duped by illiterate hopes for false ideals and who performed sometimes even heroic deeds in the name of stuffed idols. History puts everything in its rightful place and laughs bitterly, shaking its head over people who were subjectively honest but objectively wrong, for heroism in the name of false ideals is false heroism.

I am speaking of another courage, courage in the name of immortal ideals like equality, fraternity, liberty, the end of the exploitation of man in any form, including spiritual. I am not talking about exhibitionist courage, but modest courage that sometimes

does not even understand that it is courage — take the daily courage of our Russian women, who manage to work, then stand in
lines, bring up their children, take care of their husbands, and still
retain their eternal femininity and kindness — surely an exploit.
I am not talking about the animal courage needed to save one's
own skin, where the spirit is replaced by strength, by action without morality, but about another, true courage in the name of people we love or people we don't even know. That courage has
nothing in common with the philosophy of the superman, which
unfortunately has infected some of our young people today.
Superman's courage replaces the spirit with action, but how can
you call it courage to avoid spirituality and your own conscience?
It is simply a new zoological exploit of cowardice, flexing its muscles, made by bodybuilding, not by honest work.

For its time Christianity was a great civic courage, juxtaposing
its willingness for self-sacrifice to the spiritually empty and fat
Rome, collapsing but still strong. Later Christianity was distorted, perverted by the Inquisition, interchurch intrigues, turned
by priests of all kinds into a source of profit, speculating on people's naive faith.

Socialism is a distant great-grandchild of Christianity, which
inherited only some of its traits and which polemicizes with it,
sometimes fiercely, and which brought a new hope to humanity,
to be the new, striving thought of humanity.

We Russians, we Russian writers, speak the language created by
the pen of one of the most courageous men in history — Pushkin.

Pushkin was a bold citizen, a bold poet, a bold historian, a
bold editor. He was bold even in his lyric poetry.

> *I loved you so sincerely, so tenderly,*
> *As may God grant you be loved by another.*

This is a bold ethical postulate, which places love above personal
wish, above egoism.

God gives everyone equal ability in talent, but not in courage.

The artist must be bold in the forms of his works. The artist
must be bold as a philosopher. But for any boldness, particularly
in philosophy, it is necessary to know what came before — that
which we have as an inheritance from Marxism and that which

contradicted it, for in order to evaluate any phenomenon, it is necessary to know how it withstood the battle.

I heard an American graduate student (in philosophy) ask one of our young writers, "Tell me, please, what do you think about your philosopher Berdyayev?[1] Don't you think that his concepts, which your society does not accept right now, will eventually be acceptable?"

Our young writer, whom I will not name, could have honestly said, "I haven't read Berdyayev." Instead, he tried to cover up: "You're making a mistake in trying to pull our philosopher Berdyayev into your camp. He has recognized his errors and now is working in a different way." Luckily, the American took this as a joke, an elegant way of avoiding a real answer, since he couldn't imagine for a moment that the writer had never heard of Berdyayev and didn't know that he had died long ago.

How can such elementary illiteracy be possible?

I want to talk about some of our editors and the invisible censors behind their backs. I am astonished by them. They are Russians, heirs of the Revolution, and yet they're always afraid. Where does that cowardice come from, which doesn't take into account the historical courage of our people or its conquests? If there had been similarly craven editing of Korolyov's plans by the people in charge of our space program, Gagarin would not have been the first man in space.

I know of instances when an editor was fired for publishing something. But I have never heard of an editor being fired for not printing something. And that should become part of our journalistic ethics.

There have been cowards in every period of our country's history, but they remain only as pathetic shadows. But the people whose portraits hang on our walls and libraries were all bold men.

I want us to study our history more, to draw strength from it for our daily work in civic courage. What we learn from history will let us become historians, because the best of what we write becomes the living and bold history of our country.

---

1. Nikolai Alexandrovich Berdyayev (1874–1948), religious philosopher, contributor to *Vekhi* (Landmarks) and editor of the periodical *Novy put* (The New Path).

Tolerance *(1988)*

I CAN'T REMEMBER the first time I heard that profoundly Russian, tragically all-embracing word, *priterpelost*. But it came to mind of late.

"Forgive the present, Yevgeny Alexandrovich, but it's a precious thing nowadays," said a distant relative as she put a sack of sugar, almost impossible to find, on our May Day holiday table. This was in the seventy-first year of Soviet power, this was over forty years after the war! And suddenly I caught myself happy with the small domestic predatory joy of obtaining, which for so many of us substitutes for any real joy of existence. The woman who had brought the sugar sighed and said, "Look what we've come to. . . . And it's all the fault of our damned *priterpelost*. . . ."

I couldn't put it any better.

The word isn't found in Dal's dictionary of the Russian language, but it does give a verb of the same root: "The smith's hand was habituated to fire [*priterpelas'*]." The verb expresses respect for patience. But when a woman asks another, "How are things going with your husband? Is he still drinking and beating you?" and the other replies, eyes lowered, "It's all right, I've gotten used to it," there is no respect for her patience in that at all, but only complete depression, a sense of no way out, an oppressive force of habit.

There is patience and tolerance worthy of respect — the patience of a woman suffering in labor, the patience of real creators at their work, the patience of those who suffer for truth, the patience of people under torture who will not name their friends. . . . But there is useless, humiliating patience. A lack of respect for one's own patience that turns into civil wrath — that is the resurrection of a personality or a nation. It is horrible when disrespect for one's own patience turns into numb *priterpelost*. There can be no self-respect there! How can we respect ourselves if we allow such disrespect for ourselves every day? Every line, every shortage is the society's disrespect for itself.

We're used to blaming the society's shortages on others, in particular, on the government. Now, thank goodness, we have begun speaking not only of Stalin's personal guilt, but of the guilt of his entourage for crimes against the people. I am not an adherent of panicky rapid renaming of all cities and streets, but I still don't see why, for instance, the name of Zhdanov,[1] who humiliated the great Leningraders Akhmatova and Zoshchenko, cannot be removed from the portals of Leningrad State University, and why the innocent city of Mariopole has to bear that shameful name. And whenever I walk down Kalinin Prospect[2] in Moscow, I think of the days when the "all-Union elder" was handing out medals at the Kremlin while his wife, accused of being an "enemy of the people," was squashing lice in the seams of prisoners' shirts with a piece of glass, as an eyewitness described it. But let's be honest and admit that it was not only the ruling clique that was guilty before the people, but the people themselves as well, who

1. Andrei Alexandrovich Zhdanov (1896–1948) was the spokesman for cultural Stalinism. His attacks on the poet Anna Akhmatova and the prose writer Mikhail Zoshchenko and on "formalist" composers like Shostakovich were the ugliest examples of the power wielded by the state in the arts under Stalin. In 1988 the critic Yuri Karyakin began a campaign to remove the reviled name of Zhdanov from cities, streets, and Leningrad University. The Crimean city of Zhdanov (scene of the popular film *Little Vera*) was among the first to go back to its original name of Mariutoll.
2. Mikhail Ivanovich Kalinin (1875–1946) was the formal head of state when Stalin was General Secretary of the Communist Party. His wife was arrested and sent to the camps. Kalinin Prospect in Moscow is a wide modern boulevard that was cut through the crooked and picturesque alleys of the Arbat, a historical neighborhood. It is so incongruous and artificial that Muscovites call it "Moscow's gold tooth."

allowed the clique to do whatever it wanted. Permitting crimes is a form of participating in them. And historically, we are used to permitting them — that's *priterpelost*. And it's time to stop blaming everything on the bureaucracy now. If we put up with it, then we deserve it. According to Dal's dictionary, to tolerate also means to indulge. Tolerating is indulging, participating.

Let's take a seeming "trifle," the disappearance of sugar. This is, of course, correctable and perhaps by the day this is published the problem will be resolved. But whose fault is it? The Central Committee? The Council of Ministers? Of course, they are at fault, too. But aren't you and I? Isn't the Party? Aren't the people? Today we've come to tolerate the disappearance of one item and then another. Of course, how can we be surprised at the tolerance of the disappearance of such relatively minor things when just yesterday we put up with the disappearance of so many people. And so a major scientist disappears from life, committing suicide at the peak of his powers, and we are afraid to speak up as a nation and ask, what happened to him, why did we lose him? This *priterpelost* to silence about causes leads to repetition of consequences.

Let us at least get down to the causes of why sugar is a pathetically precious gift on the Day of International Solidarity of Workers.

The new leadership, as opposed to previous ones, is sharply aware of the key role of statistics in the national economy. Without hiding their heads in the sand, our leaders were the first to take a fearless look into the eyes of numerical truth about alcoholism and its consequences; they gasped. A harsh, radical decision was taken.[3] But the justified emotions were not supported, unfortunately, by a long-range, well-worked-out plan. They made a decision from the heart, but it was rushed.

The duty of leaders is to serve the people. But the people

3. The antialcoholism campaign instituted by Gorbachev in 1987 backfired. Like Prohibition in the United States, it created a criminal bootlegging underground, led to hoarding and shortages of any form of alcohol (from alcohol spirits used in hospitals to cologne and shoe polish) and anything from which moonshine could be made (especially sugar), and increased the illness and death rate among people who drank whatever they could get their hands on. It also created a budget deficit. And it was the beginning of Gorbachev's loss of popularity in the Soviet Union.

sometimes forget that their duty is to help the leaders. Why did our lauded public opinion not help the administration with counsel not to rush, why didn't it insist on an elementary sociological analysis, on public discussions of ways to combat alcoholism, before the measures were undertaken? The appearance of discussion was organized in the old way, fishing for supporting voices.

Sometimes I think bitterly: what if the April Fool's issue of *Pravda* published a Party and government resolution calling for a campaign against sobriety? I'm sure there would be "faithful soldiers of the Party" who would immediately organize "large meetings of the workers in support of this 'historic decision.' " A national "Drunkenness Society" would be formed and it's quite possible that among the founder and leaders would be a "reformed" temperance leader, just as some of the leaders of the present-day "Sobriety Society" are allegedly reformed alcoholics. The words "abstainer" and "morally steadfast" would become anti-recommendations in character references for travel abroad. The brave highway-patrol inspectors would enthusiastically start taking away the driver's licenses of all drivers who did not reek of vodka. I can imagine the peer-show trials of nondrinkers, the denunciations of Party members observed amorally drinking mineral water in restaurants! . . . This absurd phantasmagoria is unfortunately all too easy to imagine. I am convinced that if the same April Fool's issue proclaimed me or anyone else a spy for the country of Riki-Tiki-Tavi (say), there would be lots of people who would support that with patriotic fervor. Oh, how deeply rooted is our society's tolerance of turncoats, chameleons, who are ready to cut their consciences to suit any resolution coming "from above." But they don't respect the top, either, and are ready to sell out anyone who falls from the top.

What is the value of a writer who under one party leadership pretends to share its conservative views and under another its ultraradical ones, and now, just in case, pretends to be carefully, calculatedly middle-of-the-road — somewhere between Andreyeva's article in *Sovetskaya Rossia* and the criticism of that article in *Pravda* (who knows which way things might turn?).

Sometimes there are people who sign collective letters in support of perestroika with a secret hope that perestroika will fail.

The first method of slowing down perestroika is sabotage in the guise of support.

The second method is stifling it with embraces.

The idea of fighting alcoholism, correct in principle, has been stifled by delighted embraces and ruined by distorted, hypocritical enthusiasm, instead of people's supporting a serious national consideration of the serious chronic disease of our society. Chronic diseases are not treated by impulsive surgical intervention. Many of our campaigns and reforms collapse because we substitute homegrown social surgery for long-term constant social prophylaxis.

Parisian construction workers take a lunch break on the joists of the Eiffel Tower, washing down their traditional bread and cheese with a light red wine, and just imagine, they don't fall off, and they're not dragged down by their feet by any union or party organization with accusations of amorality. The long-living Caucasian tribesmen also drink, not "white lightning" or other home brews, but natural, pure wine, and they don't fall off their mountains into ditches. I believe that prophylaxis of alcoholism must not be done through puritanical policing but by a general elevation of the culture.

A bottle of white lightning can poison a man. A bottle of good wine can be a good dinner companion. But our wine production was automatically curtailed by ruthlessly chopping down precious vineyards. Alcoholism that is a socially dangerous condition must be treated punitively. But who has the right to take away from a man who is not an alcoholic his right to a mug of beer after work, his glass of natural wine or champagne?

All the founders of Marxism-Leninism loved beer.

Pushkin loved champagne.

But why did the entire nation become suspicious of alcoholism and after other humiliating lines have to queue up for more hours?[4] There were a few crazy instances of expulsion from the Komsomol for serving champagne at weddings. Some movie

4. The hours when vodka could be sold were severely cut back, and the shortage naturally created longer lines of shoppers.

theater managers, half-crazed by the public enthusiasms, cut out the scene from *Man's Fate* where the Soviet soldier drinks a glass of vodka as a sign of his scorn for the Nazis. Actors had better not repeat Pushkin's line, "Let us raise our glasses and bring them together!"

The reason is our tolerance of mindless execution of all decisions.

But this is only apparent execution. Mindless execution is sabotage of the new thinking. There have been positive results: an end to white lightning, fewer drunkards lying around on the streets. But not only time and mental health are destroyed in lines; people are destroyed too. The first harsh measures were a positive shock therapy. But you can't have daily social shock therapy — the society's nervous system will collapse, revealing many unexpected ulcers. Babushkas who sell a couple of places in line a day make as much as a PhD. A bottle of vodka in a nighttime taxi costs as much as twenty-five rubles. The government prices are very high as it is, but everyone who makes a profit on any shortage keeps adding to the price. We have enough solid shortages without adding a liquid one to it. This has a horrible effect not on the drunkards themselves, but on their wives and children, who go hungry in order to pay for the booze.

The campaign against alcoholism has been turned into a campaign against legal vodka, legal wine, legal beer. State vodka and wine, which have dropped significantly in quality over recent years but are still more or less quality-controlled, have yielded to moonshine made out of the devil-knows-what, including lotions and callus removers. This will have and already has had horrifying genetic repercussions. What will a child be like conceived under the effects of antifreeze? Even Salvador Dalí's surrealism would consider farfetched such scenes as people smearing shoe polish on pieces of bread, people getting high on bug spray in a plastic bag over their head, people seeking nirvana in the smell of airplane glue.

I admit it, chilled to the bone one night in Kamchatka, I had a shot of the local moonshine made from tomato paste. The next day my feet were swollen with arthritis so painfully I wanted to howl, and the doctor who gave me a hydrocortisone injection made an accurate diagnosis: "Our famous tomato brew."

I think that the best beer in our country, equal to the Czech, is brewed in Providenia Bay in Siberia, but hypocritically its production is being cut back to a minimum, as it is in other cities. As a result, last year the local military band played its marches on November 7 to the percussive rhythms of exploding three-liter jugs of home brew, which made neighboring Alaska shake. The most popular people in the North are ones who have raw alcohol: helicopter pilots and doctors. You can get a sable skin for just a bottle of alcohol. But pure alcohol is a rarity, like Courvoisier, throughout the country. Think how much valuable working time our doctors must waste having to write prescriptions for the simplest mixture if it contains even a tiny amount of alcohol. Alcohol or vodka compresses may no longer be prescribed. How can we be surprised that sugar is suddenly scarce? It was bound to disappear. And shouldn't society as a whole, you and I, and not just the government, have foreseen this?

Society needs not just farseeing people but also foreseeing people.

The only democratic society is the one that feels that it governs in its entirety — from bottom to top — and is not governed by the top, awaiting its commands and then blaming it for all mistakes. Personal craven irresponsibility is what hides behind toadying and mute obedience. The development of the creative initiative of the masses is incompatible with a tolerance for initiatives only from above. Forcible nagging to be socially active with its nauseating didacticism has led our society to an ironic passivity. A tolerance for one's own passivity, suppressing embryonic, potential positive energy in many talented people simultaneously, creates a nourishing medium for the negative energy of active scoundrels. Passivity's capitulating slogan is: "I'm just a little person; what can I do?" But if you justify your cowardice by saying you can't do anything, then you can't complain and you can't whine either. Don't extend your hand for a handout if you can't make it into a fist! Enough of the endless letters and protests "upward"; it's time to move on to letters and protests "down" to ourselves, against ourselves. The murderers of perestroika are among us. We are killing perestroika with our civic temerity, our waiting by the sidelines to see which side wins. . . .

A major journalist came to see me yesterday, confused, nervous. "You have a good instinct. . . . What's going to happen at the Party Conference?" He was wrong about my instinct. I used to have a good instinct, but it's gone. Many times I had assumed the best, but the worst happened. My instinct's ruined: I still hope for the best, of course, but just in case, I assume the worst will happen. I hate that about myself, but what can you do! I'm not alone — there's a multitude of instincts like that around, banged on the head by history. But this is what I replied to my guest: "What will happen? The way you and I are will determine that. . . ."

Perestroika will be whatever we will be.

If we are halfway, we'll have semiperestroika.

If we rebuild with rotten camp boards, perestroika will collapse.

If we all pull the blanket toward ourselves, perestroika will freeze.

I'm not a non–Party person in relation to perestroika — I'm in the perestroika party. There are quite a few non–Party members of the perestroika party. But we must recognize the bitter truth: many Party members are not in the perestroika party. If a Party member supports or semisupports attempts to turn history around as a justification or semijustification of the crimes of Stalinism against the people, as a new mudslinging campaign against names just recently rehabilitated, as a demand to gag glasnost, he shouldn't hide behind ideological interests. What is done in the name of protecting one's slipping cushy armchair isn't ideology, it's cusheology.

Between the properestroikers and the antiperestroikers, unfortunately, is a large group I'd call the "oy-kers." They're the ones whining constantly about the lack of sugar and other things but not lifting a finger to stop those who want to kill perestroika. They want an improvement in life-style, but reducing civic feelings to a consumer whining can lead to a situation in which the life-style will remain unimproved, as in the tale of the fisherman and the golden fish,[5] a broken trough from which even pigs can't feed. It is time people understood that there are not two separate perestroikas — one material and one political. Without defending democracy, there's no point in demanding democracy.

. . . And that's how our *priterpelost* took an edifying turn in an individual but sufficiently pathetic instance, when on May 1, 1988, to the sound of perestroika slogans on Red Square, I received a rare gift — a sack of sugar, as if the war were still on . . . an exhausting war . . . a war not against someone else, but against ourselves. . . .

2

In 1955 the Theater on Malaya Bronnaya was rehearsing a production based on my poem "Bratsk Hydroelectric Station." There is a section in the poem that begins:

> *Russia's patience is famous,*
> *It is heroic.*
> *Russia was mashed like clay with blood*
> *But it put up with it.*
> *And to the barge hauler, shoulder worn by the strap,*
> *and to the plowman, fallen in the steppe,*
> *it whispered with maternal love,*
> *the eternal, "Patience, my son, patience."*

When I performed the poem, I usually read it with a sacrificial-romantic enthusiasm, awed by the long patience of our people, which I saw as a heroic exploit. And suddenly, the marvelous actress A. Sukharevskaya read this part with a sarcastic and accusing tone, which astonished me.

> *I can understand how Russia bore*
> *Cold and hunger for so many years,*
> *And the inhuman cruelty of wars,*
> *And the burden of unbearable labor,*
> *and spongers, who lied to the limit,*

5. The folktale of the fisherman and the golden fish was retold by Pushkin. A grateful golden fish grants a fisherman his wish for setting it free. The man's wife keeps upping her demands, from riches to being the tsaritsa and so on until the fish tires of her greed and leaves her back where she started, next to the broken trough in the couple's yard.

and all kinds of treachery and deceit.
But I can't understand: how did it stand
its own patience?

I usually read the last two lines with breathless compassionate awe, but Sukharevskaya read them angrily, outraged by patience as yet another of our country's disasters. The actress understood the poem better than its author.

"Patience will crack a rock," the old folk saying goes. Three hundred years under the Tatars, three hundred years under the Romanovs developed both heroic patience, which blew up into popular revolts, and servile patience, *priterpelost*. The first Russian revolution, which unfortunately is not called that in any of our textbooks, was the emancipation of the serfs. But Russia was the last European country to free its serfs, and it plunged into socialism from sovereign feudalism, almost completely bypassing the experience of bourgeois democracy. The bedbugs of feudalism and servility moved inside wooden trunks from village huts into communal apartments. Many bosses behaved like "red feudal lords," taking away not only the peasants' land but their passports, too, which really smacked of serfdom. Violating Lenin's precepts on voluntary collectivization, the forced collectivization was a crude mockery of the slogans "Land to the peasants" and "All power to the Soviets." The promised gates of paradise turned out to be a trap. After the harsh treatment of peasants branded as kulaks, who were sent off to hell, the next wave of mass cruelty, the fake trials, seemed a normal manifestation. The level of tolerance went up.

Tolerance gradually developed for many things — repressions, arbitrary taxation, forced signatures, the image of "the best friend of Soviet body builders" [one of Stalin's titles], the removal of the best seeds, the transformation of churches into vegetable storehouses, to the iron curtain, to the humiliation of scientists, composers, writers, and whole movements and even branches of science, for instance, cybernetics. The best people were pruned away. It was like a nightmare in which a gang decided to kill all the Thoroughbred horses and wandered through the stables at night with axes. Horses as a breed survived, but many of them turned out to be horses with the psychology of mice. We need much more to be able to restore our human breed, which has suffered such losses. Servile blood today does not need to be squeezed out drop by drop, but scooped out by the bucket. We must not allow ourselves to tolerate our own patience. *Priterpelost* is the main obstacle to perestroika.

Pasternak wrote these lines:

> *Farewell, woman challenging*
> *Infinite humiliations!*
> *I am the field of your battle.*

Priterpelost is capitulation before "infinite humiliations."

Mutual humiliation is a handful of vipers tossed into many families. The vipers of boorishness and crudeness crawl out of these apartments onto the street, into the subways, curling up on the desks of secretaries and counters of saleswomen.

Our everyday life has turned into "infinite humiliations." First we humiliate ourselves to get an apartment. Once we get an order to move in, we cry with prerenovation humiliation when we see it. We humiliate ourselves, hunting in the jungles of commerce for wallpaper, faucets, toilet bowls, latches, and the sight of a Yugoslav lamp fixture or a Romanian sofa bed brings fireworks to our eyes, like the eyes of a tiger that has sunk its claws into an antelope. When a child is born to us, we humiliate ourselves to obtain day care and kindergartens, finding pacifiers, crawlers, disposable diapers, tights, carriages, sleds, playpens. We humiliate ourselves in stores, beauty parlors, tailor shops, dry cleaners, car-repair garages, restaurants, hotels, theater box offices and Aeroflot counters, repair shops for TVs, refrigerators, and sewing machines, stepping on our pride, moving from wheedling to arguments and back to wheedling. We spend all our time trying to get something, begging, pleading; we are pathetic petitioners, nagging and annoying "the powers that be." Sometimes it seems that everyone in our country exists merely to service the service industry.

It's humiliating that we still can't feed ourselves, having to buy bread, and butter, and meat, and fruit, and vegetables abroad. Coupons and rationing in many regions is our great shame.

It is humiliating that we still can't dress ourselves well and chase after foreign goods. The clothes of many of us are like a geographical atlas. But all the Cardins and Burdas won't save us. We have to manufacture clothes and shoes that will not make Soviets ashamed to wear them.

It is humiliating that we still don't have enough medicine to treat our people. It is painful to see war veterans coming to a drugstore and wearing all their medals and orders, to be more convincing, and still be told that the medicine prescribed for them is not there. It is horrible to see mothers, like wounded birds, darting from drugstore to drugstore with prescriptions for their children, and the druggists looking down in shame. A shortage of medicine is betrayal of human life.

The shortage of books is humiliating — a betrayal of the human spirit.

The shortage of computers is humiliating — a betrayal of modern technological thought.

The system of residential permissions is humiliating — it is an artificial way of forcing people to live in certain places, despite the fact that the Constitution guarantees freedom of movement. But with the geographical inequality of distribution of elementary goods, this system — alas! — is a salvation, otherwise Moscow would turn into a city of twenty million with supplies equivalent to those of long-suffering Yaroslavl.[6]

The system of travel abroad, not in line with the Constitution, is humiliating, despite all the promises for simplification. The gates should be opened wide for anyone who wants to leave forever with the exception of the few connected with security work. It is humiliating to hold people by force. But you can't call those who leave enemies! And if they haven't insulted the homeland in any way, they should be able to come back to visit or return for good. Why shouldn't all citizens of the USSR be given a Soviet foreign-travel passport good for, say, three years with the right

6. Yaroslavl, a city of 600,000 people on the Volga, northeast of Moscow, is being used as an example of the tragic situation of suburban cities. Under the centralized administrative command system, all the regional cities around Moscow turn over their allotment of meat and other goods to Moscow. Then their citizens come to Moscow to shop for goods that are unavailable in their hometown, thus stripping Moscow's shelves and creating a vicious cycle.

to travel on business, for tourism, or to visit relatives. A Soviet passport in hand should be recommendation enough to travel.

The most horrible thing is when we, humiliated by someone, start to humiliate someone else for cheap compensation. Humiliating others is a terrible addiction.

Glasnost is a declaration of war against "infinite humiliations." Glasnost is war for man's social dignity. Man has the right to like the music he wants, to dress as he likes, to wear his hair as he likes.

The pluralism of socialist glasnost is an inculcation of tolerance. But it must not turn into *priterpelost* for any form of humiliation of man by man.

The antiperestroikers are trying to represent our still young but maturing glasnost as a discrediting of the achievements of socialism. Nevertheless, glasnost itself is an achievement of socialism. *Pravda* correctly posed the question of the culture of discussion. Squabbles in the style of a communal kitchen are harmful to our progress, yes. But we should not be against open discussions. Points of view should be made clear and not disguised. That is why it is good to air various points of view on today's social process, including Petr Proskurin's thesis on "necrophilia" in publishing long-banned works, and Yuri Bondarev's thesis of the need for a new Stalingrad in our ideological front.[7]

In that sense we must be grateful for the publications of Dmitrii Urnov's article on Pasternak's *Doctor Zhivago*. The author of the article, just appointed editor in chief of the theoretical journal *Issues in Literature*, crosses off the novel from a political and artistic point of view, daring to call even the poems from the novel "a stylization of the poetry popular in those days" and to compare

7. Petr Proskurin, a writer with right-wing tendencies and chairman of the Cultural Foundation of the RSFSR, scornfully referred to the publication of long-banned works by now-deceased authors as "necrophilia." He later explained that he thought the word meant something else.

Yuri Bondarev (born 1924), a writer best known for his works on World War II, considers perestroika and glasnost a threat to the Soviet Union he knows and loves and compared perestroika to the Nazi attack on Russia. He said the only thing that could save the USSR now was another Stalingrad, the battle that turned the course of the war and led to the eventual victory over Nazi Germany. The reference to Stalingrad was also shocking because it was perceived as a not very subtle positive reference to Stalin.

Dr. Zhivago with the immoral renegade Klim Samgin.[8] The article says this about Pasternak's beloved hero: "Dr. Zhivago should have been pushed up against the wall and shoved into the corner." The article creates a strange impression — as if it was a speech given at the Writers' Union meeting to expel Pasternak and published thirty years later. No, the times when writers and their creations were put up against the wall are over, and I hope forever. The rehabilitation of Pasternak and many other unjustly defamed citizens of our society is irreversible and will not turn into a re-rehabilitation. We cannot give up this great achievement of glasnost — our spiritual perestroika.

Spiritual perestroika and economic perestroika should be mutual guarantors. Unfortunately, economic perestroika is severely lagging behind. But like glasnost, it is being discredited, hobbled, scared off, worn down. In economics, as in literature, there are "sacred cows" who pretend to be defending the national interest and are actually defending only their own. Today glasnost must help the economy. And tomorrow, if glasnost is in trouble, it will be helped by the mighty shoulder of the new economy. Without personal initiative, without major individual efforts, we will not be able to move forward either in glasnost or the economy. And, in Mayakovsky's words, while the "stupid penguin hides its fat body in crevasses," glasnost, like the stormy petrel, "like lightning," will awaken the civic conscience of the people.

In English there is a word, *image*, which has a political and poetic meaning. Every presidential candidate in the USA has a team of psychologists, sociologists, and politicians who work on creating his image. Every political system and every country also worries about its image. Of course, a cleverly constructed image can be just makeup or even a mask hiding ulcers.

The iron curtain between East and West for many years created an image for our country that was both attractive and frightening. The exploits of our people in the war against Hitler added an aura of heroism to that image. Khrushchev's thaw added glimmers of hope for mutual understanding. The horrible truth about Stalin's

8. The hero of Maxim Gorky's unfinished novel *The Life of Klim Samgin* (begun 1925), whose life involves forty years of Russian political upheavals but who never commits to a single ideology.

camps, the arrests of dissidents, the abuses of psychiatry, and exile of Academician Sakharov, our troops in Afghanistan — all that, lined up and blown up by certain reactionary elements in the Western press, worked to destroy the heroic aura, bringing our image to an Antichrist "empire of evil." However, thanks to the peaceful initiatives of our country in nuclear disarmament, glasnost, and democratization, that Antichrist image has been shattered.

We don't need makeup or a mask on our face to impress foreigners or to make them like us. Of course, I would like our country to be liked by humanity, not through lies, but for the truth it brings to the world. But most of all, I want our country to like itself. We love it, we are proud of its cultural and revolutionary traditions. But not all traditions are good. And *priterpelost* is a bad tradition that must be rejected as being incompatible with perestroika.

⸎ A Nation Begins with Women (1989)

THE FIRST IMAGE for all people, for humanity, is the still-blurry face of the mother leaning over the infant's body. The child is pushed into the world from a woman's body and the reason for the first cry is that he wants to go back inside his mother. A mother is a child's first homeland. That is why the two concepts are so naturally combined — Motherland. The famous World War II poster proclaiming "Your Motherland Is Calling You!" worked not only politically but lyrically, emotionally, for it touched the most hidden strings of the heart. A nation begins with women.

Pasternak said this of women: ". . . I am indebted to them all." This unpaid debt of each of us begins with the first drop of mother's milk, the first tears we make a woman — our mother — shed, the first kiss, the prayerful touch of your wife's hand on your brow when you are sick and feverish. In moments of danger a man's beloved becomes his mother. A woman's feeling for defending a man is so strong that women are much braver than men.

One of my first memories: 1937. I am four. Both grandfathers have been arrested. Mother and I with a parcel wrapped in cloth stand in a long, long line on a street with the lovely name of Sailor's Rest. Half snow, half drizzle. A blue-gray fog and in it,

the backs of heads of woman, after woman, after woman. All with
parcels. Just women. Not a single man. The men were afraid. The
women were not afraid to make inquiries, to bring parcels. All of
them — even the wives, and the fianceés, and the daughters —
turned into the prisoners' mothers.

The Revolution announced the emancipation of women. But
when they took away the passports from the kolkhoz men, did
the kolkhoz women get to keep theirs? Mukhina[1] was a marvelously talented sculptor, but when I look at that gigantic metal
couple — worker and kolkhoz woman — I am oppressed by the
thought that the monumental giantess never had a tiny little passport. In the villages women were enslaved once again by a new
landowner, the state, and in the factories by a new factory owner,
the state. The law "who does not work, does not eat" seemed to
include women. Nowhere was it written that motherhood was
also a job. Housewives and mothers practically disappeared; they
were like white crows, an alien class element. Even poets sang not
of woman's fragility, helplessness, passion, and tender love, but
woman's physical strength, political maturity, labor indexes, and
heroism in overcoming hardships.

Women were not raised to equality with men, but reduced to
it. During the Saint Bartholomew's Nights of Stalinism the wives
and daughters of "enemies of the people" had to endure much
suffering and humiliation. In her astonishing book *Journey into
the Whirlwind*, Eugenia Ginzburg writes about the seventh train
car, loaded with women, "enemies of the people," headed into
the depths of camp-laden Siberia: "Underwear will be changed
only for the heavily menstruating," the head convoy guard announced solemnly. "The rest can only be roasted. They'll roast it
in the disinfection chamber while you're washing and then you
put it back on. It won't be too attractive, but at least you won't
catch anything. . . . " How many thousands of centuries of civilization separate this monologue, not at all nasty, even rather
good-willed and sympathetic, from Pushkin's "I loved you once:
my love perhaps may still be there. . . ."

1. Vera Igantyevna Mukhina (1889–1953), a sculptor best known for her monumental
work, *The Worker and the Female Kolkhoznik*, placed at the entrance to the Exhibit of Economic Achievements Park in Moscow and shown at the beginning of Mosfilm Studio movies.

Olga Berggolts's[2] child was kicked out of her belly. Marina Tsvetayeva,[3] despite her request, was not hired as dishwasher at the writers' dining room in Chistopol, and she hanged herself in Elabuga.

While the nation's screens showed Lubov Orlova and Marina Ladynina playing life-loving Soviet women ennobled by labor, millions of real women were breaking their backs in poverty-stricken kolkhozes, mixing concrete with their feet, having babies in barracks that were not much better than the ones in the camps. There were the women on posters — the pilot Valentina Fruzo-dubova, the cotton picker Mamlakat Nakhangova, the beet grower Maria Demchenko — but the accurate picture of the ordinary Soviet woman existed only in the heartbreaking *chastushka*, or street ditty:

> *I'm both horse and bull,*
> *I'm both the woman and the man.*

The privileged state of the "Soviet high society" ladies was special — it was serf privilege. The singer V. A. Davydova-Mchelidze, who was close to Stalin, recalled how the driver of her car asked her to intercede with Stalin on behalf of his dekulaked father. After she tried, she never saw the driver again. Stalin took sadistic pleasure in tormenting his comrades in arms, declaring that the wives of Molotov and of Kalinin were spies and arresting, just in case, the wife of his faithful assistant, Poskrebyshev.

Women pilots, women partisans, women military doctors and orderlies, and women in the rear were a great women's army, equal to the men in destroying the Nazis. But even the wartime heroism of Zoya Kosmodemyanskaya, who cried out "Stalin will come!" when the noose was around her neck, did not soften the tyrant's heart when it came to our long-suffering women: they were just female cogs in the machine. After the war it was the village women who hauled Russia out from under on their backs, while the state ruthlessly took away their seeds for the next har-

2. Olga Fyodorovna Berggolts (1910–1975), a Leningrad poet.
3. Marina Ivanovna Tsvetayeva (1892–1941), poet. *See* "Poetry Can't Be Homeless: Marina Tsvetayeva," pp. 300–309.

vest. In a country where women can get Heroine Mother medals, nobody thought that the best reward would be the right not to go to work but to stay home and bring up the children.

We had a movie called *Member of the Government,* but actually there were no women in government. Ekaterina Furtseva was the rare exception. She was rather resourceful in helping Khrushchev run the Central Committee Plenum where he won against the Molotov, Kaganovich et al. group. However, Khrushchev followed the tradition of doing away with those who helped his rise to power and he demoted Furtseva from the Presidium of the CC and made her only Minister of Culture. Kalatozov and I, in her office one day, were shocked to see a military communications man come in without a by-your-leave and clip the wires of a "hot line" phone and carry it out under his arm. Furtseva bit her lip painfully at this crude insult. Those people didn't even think that she was not only a former member of the Presidium but, first of all, a woman.

The antiabortion law that reigned for so many years was not only a mockery but a killer of many women who were forced to seek illegal back-street abortions with old midwives or all kinds of charlatans. Several generations were brought up in the abnormal separate-sex school system and this led to a worsening of the alienation between men and women.

There were attempts to free women from heavy physical labor: for instance, women were no longer allowed to work in underground mines. The famous female pumpers of mining folk-song glory receded into the past. But men refused to do their hard work for the same low pay, and the salaries had to be increased.

I wonder: why were women paid less for so many years for exactly the same work? Women's salaries nationwide are only 60 percent of men's even today. Is it because men's work is harder? Or that men occupy most of the high-paying jobs? I think that the main cause of low pay for women is the totally unfounded male sense of superiority — male chauvinism.

Part of my first election-campaign platform, printed in *Ogonyok,* was a proposal banning females from hard labor. I got numerous letters that deeply affected me with their tragic hopelessness: women wrote that hard-labor jobs were the only ones that paid well and that such a ban would be catastrophic for them.

Yet the Soviet working woman has not one job, but three. The first is in the workplace. The second is that of standing in line. And the third is that of the children, house, and kitchen.

Sovetskaya Rossia of April 23 published interesting information, that Austrian women do housework that is worth 350 billion schillings a year. Cleaning, laundry, ironing make up 130 billion. Kitchen work is 60 billion.

Who will ever calculate how much the housework of Soviet women is worth? And how much does that horrible, exhausting, nerve-racking job — standing in line — amount to?

A few years ago I was in the capital of East Germany. I dropped by a small store not far from the hotel. I didn't need to buy anything, but I was following my purely Soviet consumer curiosity. The store was not a chain or a hard-currency place; however, it had about twenty types of sausage — salamis, glazed, smoked, liver, veal, hunters', and so on. . . . Suddenly I heard something fall to the floor. A young woman was lying unconscious. Her hairdo, dress fabric, beige sandals, and many other factors that defy description told me she was a fellow Soviet. I had only read about fainting in nineteenth-century novels and had never seen anyone pass out. The young woman came to whispering, "Why? Why?" as I helped her. When she was back on her feet, I took her to a nearby café. What had happened to her? What was implied by her question, "Why? Why?" She was from the Altai region, where she drove a tractor and a thresher and had no complaints about her salary. Her bonus for a job well done was a trip to East Germany. Seeing the abundance of sausages, cheese, and everything else, easy to get, no lines, she was stunned. "What does it mean?" she said. "We won the war, they lost. It's not that I mind that they live well. . . . But why do we live so badly? Why?" With a sigh I thought, thank God she came here and not to West Berlin first, where there is a store with at least five hundred kinds of sausages.

Really, why do we live so badly? Why?

Academician Shatalin writing in *Ogonyok* gives a horrifying figure: the country's unsatisfied demand is over seventy billion rubles.

Of course, men suffer from the unsatisfied demand in trade, too. But women bear the brunt of it. After all, they're the ones who have to keep "making do." Many foreigners are amazed by how well Soviet women dress now. If only they knew how much wheeling and dealing each article and detail involved. They are also delighted by the hospitality and culinary talents of our women. But it takes so much effort to get all those things that are placed so beautifully and generously on the table! Women shop for the house, the children, the husband, and only then for themselves. And just try to buy at the same time and the same place some sausages, detergent, disposable diapers, razor blades, and some inexpensive but not disgraceful shoes. Every Soviet woman should get a full pension for just this constant work as supplier. And why haven't we gotten a one-year maternity leave with full salary yet?

While lagging desperately behind economically, we managed to burst into the front ranks of the world in the divorce rate. Why? The aggravations of daily life lead to the mutual murder of love. When there is a room of one's own for everyone, then there is a place to run during an argument, to keep from exploding. But what if there is nowhere to run, because you live in one room? And what if your in-laws are squeezed into that one room, too? A recent sociological survey shows that many Soviet women list difficulties (hers or his) with in-laws as a reason for divorce.

One of our ladies in public life announced that we did not need any imported dresses — for we would never learn to make our own if we did. She may have been wearing a Soviet-made dress during the television broadcast, but it had to be a designer original. Women don't care whether dresses are Soviet or foreign as long as there are more than one for every three women, as long as they are attractive and, one would hope, inexpensive. So let's stop the fake patriotism in discussing domestic production — let's have products that are no worse than foreign goods. And until we do, don't skimp on hard currency; buy up goods so that our women can dress well, so that they can be fashionable while they are young enough to enjoy it. Haven't our women earned the right to dress beautifully? To dress their children beautifully? Yet we men still dare to lecture them on how they should look and behave, our long-suffering women.

The few of our women in public life, despite all my respect for them, could hardly express all the problems of the women of the USSR. We need an association of Women for Women's Rights. We need women in all levels of Soviet power and state. Nastriddinova[4] made it, but this has no effect on all the other women. We don't have a single woman minister of the USSR, not a single woman editor in chief of a national newspaper. Like a rebuke, on March 8, International Woman's Day, *Pravda* published the photographs of five women who are heads of state.

Of course, the point isn't in having token women. Unfortunately, there were many token females at the Nineteenth Party Conference in 1988, and the women did not give a single bold, statesmanlike speech.

The conversations of some of the women delegates in the corridors of the conference boiled down to complaints about the lack of a special store for the delegates. I don't blame these honest workers — milkmaids, crane operators, cotton pickers — who came from areas where infants' wear, baby soap, or a pair of women's boots can't be found for love or money. But why were they delegated to the Kremlin conference, when they barely understood that a serious political battle was going on for their future and that of their children?

The list of People's Deputies of the USSR shows that there will be a few women deputies, who are perhaps even good producers, but are they politically able to handle this responsible legislative role? Many fine women candidates could not get through the "dragon's teeth" of the local commissions. For instance, I was struck by the marvelous environmental and moral programs of Cherkasova in the Lublinsk Region and Usova in the Mytishchinsky Region, who were not elected. But Alla Yaroshinskaya, beloved in her native Zhitomir, could not be stopped by the local bureaucracy.

I hope that the women deputies will band together to bring

4. Iagdar Sadykovna Nastriddinova (born 1920), Uzbek Party figure.

their best and the brightest to the forefront. It's possible that peasant or worker women could be among those leaders. But they should move beyond class narrowness, which has harmed us so much in the past. Women from the intelligentsia might be able to defend the interests of milkmaids, crane operators, and cotton pickers just as well, or sometimes even better, than they could themselves.

We men must cease feeling our unfounded superiority and condescension toward women in society. Enough bouquet bribes on March 8 and cake handouts on birthdays. We need perestroika in our attitude toward women. A nation begins with women. Can a nation be respected if it does not respect its women?

Religion As Part of Culture (1986)

IT'S TOO EASY of late to be considered part of the intelligentsia. It's enough to have a university pin on your lapel, and that makes you unarguably cultured. If we counted the people with higher education, it would look as if our country were flooded with intelligentsia. But is that really the case? How many people graduate from colleges not because they were interested in a profession but because "their parents decided"? How many get in through pull or pressure, whose grades are overlooked on admissions or graduating exams? . . . The problem is that the country is flooded with the unprofessional.

An unprofessional doctor with the nicest personality is a potential murderer. In one sense any unprofessional is a murderer. An unprofessional writer murders innocent paper, an unprofessional economist murders national funds, an unprofessional builder murders construction materials, an unprofessional environmental engineer murders rivers and lakes, and an unprofessional lecturer murders our time.

But narrow professionalism is not culture either. You can be an average doctor or engineer, but if your interests do not go beyond your professional circle, you're still only a technician and not an intellectual. It's impossible for a person of limited mind to become an outstanding doctor or an outstanding engineer. Only people with a high level of multifaceted culture can perform qualitative revolutionary changes in their own work and in history in general.

The sad evidence of a low level of culture is the success of cheap commercial films, junk songs, gooey pseudopoetry, and cleverly concocted and readable novels. True culture is taste that won't let you bite dubious bait. Taste like that can't be artificially added. Real culture is a knowledge of the experience acquired throughout the existence of mankind. This experience consists of history, folk wisdom, philosophy (including a knowledge of religion), science, and art. Let's be honest with each other — could many of our graduates pass exams in these five subjects?

During the play *Dictatorship of Conscience* at the Lenin Komsomol Theater, playing, it would seem, to an educated public, an actor asks the audience, "Who was Andre Martí?" Usually, the audience responded with silence. Yet Hemingway wrote about Andre Martí, and Hemingway is one of our most-read foreign writers. What an astonishing lack of correspondence between the hundreds of thousands of photographs of the author in apartments all over Russia and a knowledge of his work. Or try to start the quote from Pushkin, "The less we love a woman," and 90 percent of our fresh-baked intellectuals, eager to show off, will say, "the more she likes us." Yet Pushkin wrote "the more easily she likes us." The gigantic lines to attend exhibits of some rather questionable artists who seem almost like inventors to naive audiences are evidence that people don't know the original sources — starting with the Russian artists Nesterov and Roerich. Ignorance of original sources leads to dependence on very dubious sources.

The fashionable look of a cross outside a blouse or shirt bespeaks an elementary ignorance of what the crucifixion was and not religious fanaticism. And what's more dangerous — an ignorance of religion or religious fanaticism? Perhaps the two phenomena are closely connected and we're just not trying to understand that. When our inventive television puts on variety shows on Easter eve to distract young people from going to church and observing the processions — more beautiful and poetic than any public gathering — I see only our weakness in that. All the attempts have failed to create a ritual in our wedding palaces to rival the beauty of the sacrament of marriage. Sometimes people have a church wedding or baptize their children not out of "religious fanaticism" but because it's beautiful. Churches attract many, not only the devout, because the architecture enchants and the faces of saints painted by folk geniuses are more impressive than the stony faces on honor boards in factories and offices.

The source of morality is culture. But religion cannot be dropped out of the experience of morality — positive and negative — since its history is inseparable from history per se.

Let us recall that in the Roman Empire, Christianity played a definitely revolutionary role: no wonder the proselytizers of the ideas of "Thou shalt not kill" and "Love thy neighbor as thyself" were torn to shreds by the emperor's lions. Let us not forget the cruelties of the Crusades, the bonfires of the Inquisition, the bloody hypocrisy of those who perverted the postulates of Christianity. But did that happen only to Christianity? Think of the Gulag, the genocide in Cambodia, when the Pol Pots declared "red terror" against their own people. We must not confuse the postulates with their perversions.

The Constitution in our country speaks clearly about freedom of religion. Our church is separated from the state and that is just. But nowhere in our laws is it written that the state and atheism are inseparable. Atheism should be a voluntary phenomenon, not an imposed one. Atheism must be one of the manifestations of freedom in our society, just like religion, and not a manifestation of violence. Now our state spends incredible amounts of money on restoring churches turned by "proletcult barbarism" into vegetable warehouses and cow sheds.

Some atheists defend their atheism with boring dogmatic rhetoric: "Our atheism is based on a scientific worldview and it is as unshakable as that worldview." You can't polemicize with any dogma if the polemic is based on more dogma. It's such boring atheism lectures that send young people to take a look at Easter processions.

The Bible is a great monument of culture. To this day I cannot understand why the state publishing house published the Koran but not the Bible. Without knowledge of the Bible our young people cannot understand much of Pushkin, Gogol, Dostoevsky, and Tolstoy. All of the early Mayakovsky is scattered with biblical metaphors. The Bible costs huge amounts in rare-book stores and on the black market. If atheists want everyone to become atheists, how are people supposed to do it without knowing the Bible? A worldview should not be a closed philosophical system built on nothing. A worldview must include all the moral striving of human thought in the name of humanity, including the best of Christian morality. For a society to develop, it must be able to sum up and to filter, but nothing valuable from the experience of human thought must be discarded.

Religion that served social oppression was justly called the opium of the masses. But can we forget that during the war against fascism our church collected enormous funds for our common victory? Can we forget that the archbishop of Canterbury Cathedral, Hewlett Johnson, was one of the founders of the peace movement?

The primitive division of the world into believers and atheists as the unclean and clean, as proposed by antireligion extremists, is beneath all criticism, even if you base it on scientific materialism. One atheist, a Professor Kryvelev, writes with illogical vulgarity, "Morality is not only not contraindicated in atheism, it is an organic part of it." Does he mean that atheism is a guarantee against immorality? If it were only so! Unfortunately, many so-called atheists were thieves, picking the national pocket, bureaucrats, toadies, avengers, tattlers, political chameleons and in no way better than those religious leaders who fleece their simple-minded flocks.

Atheism by itself is not a source of morality. The source of morality is culture. The culture of human behavior. The culture of conscience, which does not need scientific diplomas. The culture of the soul is perhaps uneducated but it instinctively feels where lies the truth and where falsehood. But when instinctive love of truth is combined with education, this source of morality cannot be muddied by any pseudotheories — neither religious fanaticism nor proletcult barbarism.

I'm not calling on people to break their foreheads against the floors of churches. The source of morality cannot smell only of incense or the dust of archives. The source of morality is first of all life itself and people themselves, a many-faced but single god consisting of those who fight to free people from fake idols. Not believing in anything is worse than false faith.

Improper Upbringing

(1989)

A Country Begins with the Airport

STANISLAVSKI used to say that a theater begins with the coat check.

A country begins with the airport. Sometimes, even with the cabin of a plane.

Last year I was returning on Aeroflot from Thailand. My seatmate was a union activist, a Thai carved out of politeness, like a statuette of ivory. The first thing he did was look for the earphones and channel control, usually found in the armrests of all airlines of the world, except for our Aeroflot. In foreign planes, as a rule, you have five channels: symphonic, opera, jazz, country, and rock, and on long flights, a movie. In other words, if you're going to die, it might as well be to music.

When the Thai gentleman asked the stewardess with plaintive politeness, "Where's the music?" she proudly turned on the loudspeakers, like in our trains, and in every section of the plane blared: "But why, but why, why was the light green. . . ." It was only after an Indian lady with a sleeping child complained that the "green light" was turned off. They also turned out the lights — all over the plane. My seatmate, who was hard at work on his lap-top computer, sought the overhead reading light in vain. "Individual lights were not planned for this plane," the stewardess announced with inexplicable patriotic pride. The Thai managed: he took a small flashlight out of his briefcase and illuminated his keyboard.

The layover at Delhi airport was like a visit to a colorful fair. Despite the midnight hour, the souvenir shops were open and the pleasant but not too pushy salespeople invited you into their shops. They had everything — wooden and bronze Buddhas, and fabrics that looked like the wings of the Firebird, and VCRs, and about fifty kinds of Indian tea. . . .

When we landed in Tashkent a few hours later, the scene at the airport was different. Everything that should have been open was closed. We sensed that we had entered a closed zone even in the air — as soon as we had crossed the border. It was night, but through the silvery blue haze, like scattered beads, lights of lonely *kishlaks* [Uzbek villages] glimmered below. My Thai, despite his businesslike demeanor, must have been endowed with a feeling for beauty and immediately pulled out his Minolta to photograph the phosphorescent miracle of the night. But the vigilant hand of the stewardess covered his lens. "Photography over the territory of the Soviet Union is forbidden," she said sternly and finally. The Thai hurried to put his camera back in the case. Yet it's so ridiculous to ban photography from a plane, since you can read license-plate numbers through special optical equipment on satellites.

All the bureaucracy's attempts to impress foreigners are useless, because the very first step in our country frightens them with blockheaded forbiddance and revolts them with the low level of concern for people. My seatmate cringed when the border guard who met us on the tarmac in Tashkent transit airport regarded him with piercing eye, as if he knew the man had a microfilm under his capped tooth revealing the secret plans for Uzbekistan's irrigation system. The passengers, huddled together in fear, moved into the bowels of the Tashkent airport on creaking escalators. There were piles of garbage everywhere. The Thais, who had been taught from childhood that Soviets were robots stuffed with propaganda and who stuffed others with it, hunched their shoulders as they went past identical posters of Lenin — of which I counted twenty. The peeling walls were also hung with Aeroflot's self-praise: "Soviet aviation carries peace and friendship on its wings and helps the development of political, economic, and cultural ties between states with different social systems." The restaurant and bar were closed. There was no souvenir kiosk. Stands were filled with primitive propaganda literature, which made the Thais pull in their heads like turtles. An exhibit of faded photographs, "The privileged class of Soviet society," with nauseating lack of conviction was trying to show the aristocratic life of the Soviet proletariat.

My Thai came back from the toilet and whispered shyly, "I think the administration should be told that they've run out of toilet paper." Naive man — they never had any in the first place. When I told the sleepy cleaning woman, she sniffed vaguely, disappeared, and soon returned to the toilet with an armful of crumpled newspapers full of calls for perestroika. At last, a sleepy waitress appeared, pushing a rolling table with glasses half filled with a mysterious tea-colored liquid. When asked what it was, she replied succinctly: "A drink." The children of the third world mostly avoided it — in their so-called backward country it is considered elementarily unhygienic to serve open drinks, just as in their backward country I never saw newspapers instead of toilet paper.

When we were returning to the plane, my Thai, who thought he had been checked enough, tried to get through the control point with his briefcase. No way. The powerful arms of the Aeroflot representative, who looked like a bar bouncer in drag, grabbed his attaché case for inspection. When he tried to explain something in English, he was shoved in the back. "Go on, go to the holding cell. . . . Babbling like that — go figure it out. . . . Why don't they learn our language before coming around here?" My Thai was terrified that they would take away his attaché case, and when they gave it back, he was overjoyed in a very Soviet way, with a grateful, humiliated smile. It never occurred to the Aeroflot representative that she was the one who should know at least one foreign language, working as she did in an international airport.

And it didn't occur to her that "holding cell" was a camp term.

Have you ever thought about how much there is of camp life in our everyday "free" lives — all sorts of holding cells, lines for this and that, as if for prison chow, enforced herding into groups, humiliating searches, physical and spiritual, chiefs and gangs, visible and invisible barbed wire. . . . When I rebuked the Aeroflot woman, "Why do you behave so rudely?," she yelled in outrage, "What do you mean rudely? What am I supposed to do, crawl on my belly in front of them?"

There are people who consider politeness to be humiliating and rudeness as preservation of their personal dignity. That's how they are brought up — impolitely. That's why even in the eyes of guests from the "poorly developed nations" we look like a nation of poorly developed politeness. But perhaps what happened at the Tashkent airport could not happen in the capital? Here's Sheremetyevo-2, the main air gates of the country. Have you ever noticed that there is nothing to sit on in the lobby? It's most likely because they don't want people sleeping on the benches the way they do in Kazan Station, spoiling the radiant impression of the USSR. But people do sleep there. Right on the marble floors. Lots of them, when there's bad weather. Bad weather is not a purely Soviet phenomenon, but for some reason, they sleep on the floor only in our country. The hotel space is several times less than it should be. "It's all right, they'll manage," they say with a gloating grin about foreigners. But the foreigners have to make do only temporarily, while we have to make do all our lives. And who created that life for us? The foreigners? We did it. Our rudeness toward foreigners stems from our rudeness to one another. And that rudeness keeps on exposing us, right from the airport.

The plane landed at Sheremetyevo. Sometimes you have to wait a half hour for the stairs. When the stairs are brought, you then have to wait for the bus. On the stairs is the inevitable border guard, a double of the one who scared my Thai in Tashkent. This border guard doesn't check anyone or anything — he just peers into faces with meaningless vigilance. Then we see several glassed booths with border guards who check passports. Usually most of the booths are empty and the passengers bunch up at one or two, immediately creating lines. The young guards in the booths may be very nice guys, but they feign grim hostility and sometimes demand that passengers take off their hats and ask questions that have been answered in the exit applications. Never once did I hear one of these guards of the state border ever say, "Welcome home!" "Have a good trip?" or at least smile in a human way. Are they forbidden to do that or something? Yet the border guard's face is the face of the country.

The border guard reluctantly returns your passport and you enter the baggage-claim area. You can calmly sit down on the nonmoving conveyor belt — you'll have to wait at least an hour. When the belt does start moving, pay no attention to the announcement boards — Bangkok luggage may end up on the belt for the Montreal flight and vice versa. There are about ten times fewer porters than are needed. That means there should be carts, right? You're expecting too much from Aeroflot, too busy with carrying peace and friendship on its wings. I once almost died of shame seeing a group of Canadian old ladies struggling with their bags. Thank God, our sailors returning from Singapore were right there and we helped the old ladies.

All civilized airports of the world have two exits — for those with something to declare and for those who feel they have nothing to declare. The professionalism of customs inspectors lies in selective inspection, based on information or intuition. Our customs agents inspect almost everyone, with the exception of members of delegations, and then not always. As a result foreigners can begin their adaptation right in the airport to observing our Soviet lines, and returning Soviet citizens undergo de-adaptation from a lack thereof in capitalist countries.

The customs regulations are astonishing in their arbitrariness, pickiness, and occasionally outright stupidity. My translator, Nina Bouis, came to spend a week to put finishing touches on her English translation of *Fuku*. They took her translation at customs, saying that they needed a week to check (!) it. But she was gone by the end of the week. A Kafkaesque situation. And this happened not in the period of stagnation, but now, during perestroika. Quite recently on the Helsinki-Moscow train, the Finn in my compartment had his copy of *Time* confiscated, even though it had a very positive article on Gorbachev in it.

In all economically rational countries, duty is imposed on items that can be bought in the country you are entering, so that you don't undermine the economy. But we do it just the other way around — you pay duty on things we don't have. At first glance, this might be perceived as combating black-marketing. But actually it simply raises black market prices. Why is there duty on video and audio cassettes, which can't be found in any of our stores? Why is there duty on computers, if the head of state calls for computerization and our domestic computers aren't worth a damn?

The customs regulations handbook — which I managed to hold in my hands once after persistent demands — is jabberwocky, with all kinds of bosses' bugaboos written in and crossed out, often not the fault of the agents themselves at all. Just two years ago I saw a famous actress, on her way to an international film festival, weeping in humiliation at the airport. Her earrings had practically been pulled out of her ears — not allowed. Now the Draconian ban on bringing out personal jewelry has been lifted, but who knows what new humiliations they will come up with tomorrow.

Passengers spend about three and a half hours upon arrival in Sheremetyevo — about as long as a flight from London to Moscow. Three and a half hours of humiliation by crowding and confusion. The last time I saw my Thai, he was stuffing shirts and socks, that someone had pawed through, back into his suitcase. His eyes were filled with the sadness of submission and something new — the habit of humiliation.

From Tsarism to Cerberism

For all the hassles, the foreigner is a privileged person in our country. It's funny and sad that two categories are united by their privileged status: deputies and foreigners, as if all deputies were foreigners and all foreigners, deputies. Otherwise how do you explain separate lounges, separate ticket counters, and separate buffets in airports for deputies and for foreigners? But the Soviet deputy's privileges end in the face of the hard-currency bouncer who stands immobile at the door of the Beriozka store, where our ruble is no longer valid. Our ruble is eligible for membership in Pamyat, because it is so ultrapatriotic that it does not sell itself to the enemy. It's a bitter paradox to see that docked liner named for our great poet Alexander Blok turned into a valuta [hard currency] restaurant where Russians with their rubles are not allowed. The chocolate selection called Pushkin's Fairy Tales has been available only in Beriozka stores for years. But can you imagine an American store called Sequoia that refuses Americans and their dollars and caters only to foreign currency, like the yen? Our attitude toward foreigners has long been of two minds: spyphobia and valutomania.

Recently I had a call from a neighbor, a People's artist of the USSR, who told me that all the residents of house 2/1 on Kutuzovsky Prospect were being evicted so that they could sell the apartments to foreign companies for valuta. Can you picture a memorial plaque honoring the star of the world-famous revolutionary film *Chapaev* next to a sign proclaiming some crummy Flybynight Import? According to legend, there was a French king who could not force his baker to move out. After our vigorous protests, the Moscow City Council was forced to retreat like the French king, but how humiliating was the whole idea of evicting your fellow countrymen, who are expected to put up with anything just to make some valuta!

Why do they call for a rule of law and at the same time humiliate right and left, giving us mocking lessons in lawlessness?

We began building socialism on the scheme of serfdom. Forced collectivization is economic uneducated absolutism. Mockery of the best minds of Russia is ideological uneducated absolutism. Serfdom gave rise to an overseer subclass — the Cerberuses. The chains of tsarism fell apart but unfortunately so did the chains that held the Cerberuses. Becoming a Cerberus is a tempting prospect for a cur who is willing to bite anyone he is sicced on, and even kill him, for a bone. Cerberuses of the prerevolutionary formation were handled by the serf owners. Cerberuses of the new formation were handled only by the fear of each other in the pyramid structure of the Cerberus hierarchy. Not only was Beria Stalin's Cerberus, but Stalin himself was a Cerberus who depended on other Cerberuses. It was dog eat dog. Under Cerberism that consisted of mongrels made good, medals were awarded for lack of breeding. The times of bloody Cerberism are over. But the Cerberuses are long-lived. Lack of breeding doesn't die. It turns into devilish breeds. Dostoevsky's *Devils* is becoming more and more timely.[1]

Immunity from Cerberism is provided by a moral and cultural upbringing. But Cerberuses, like man-eaters, devoured the carriers of morality and culture for being carriers of immunity. The lack of breeding in our upbringing is the breeding medium for Cerberism. We are all suffering from the daily barking, the daily biting of one another. Is there at least one Soviet citizen who has never been bitten by a single Cerberus?

The *dezhurnaya* floor ladies in our hotels are a metaphor for a Cerberus society. Many years ago I saw them throw out Sviatoslav Richter's things from his deluxe suite in Irkutsk, where he was giving a concert. "Who is this Richter guy!" bellowed the ignorant hotel director. "The head of the Bratsk hydroelectric dam construction, Naimushin, is coming and I need the room!" Nodar Dumbadze, the Georgian writer and People's Deputy, was not allowed to spend the night in the Moskva Hotel when he forgot to move his deputy's badge from one suit jacket to the one he was wearing. The tense atmosphere of camp zones reigns in our hotels, where the doors are manned by Cerberuses with gold galloons on their uniforms and a past as camp guards. One time I went to the National Hotel in Moscow with a former camp inmate and was stunned by his almost warm reunion with the former major in the sentry guards who had now moved on to a higher-paying job — coat check at the restaurant. Intourist's inflexible policy of exclusion is baloney, for all the restaurants and bars are filled with prostitutes, black marketeers, and the trade mafia. The privileges of exclusion turn into the very lucrative privilege of elective

1. In *The Devils* (1872, also known as *The Possessed*), Dostoevsky showed the dangers of revolutionary politics and the manipulation of groups.

inclusion. The most thriving republic in our country is the "restaurant Switzerland."

Some workers in OVIR, the visa and passport agency, behave like the doormen of our state borders, pretending to be mysteriously unapproachable when what they want is a bribe to soften their patriotic vigilance. And don't the ideological excluders behave the same way, watching like Cerberuses that the "wrong" people, books, ideas, and inventions don't get in? Externally this political safeguarding may look like puritanical fanaticism, but behind the doors guarded by the shoulders of the ideological bouncers, there is the same bedlam as in the Intourist departments.

There is personnel Cerberism, too. Sometimes it has an international agenda covered up by chatter about internationalism. Around 1963 an editor considered progressive, a professional international expert, replied to my request to hire a recent Literary Institute graduate, a young Jewish girl. "Old man, those horrible anti-Semites are picking on us as it is. . . . You have to understand that we're over the quota at the journal already."

"What quota?" I was stunned. "Are there instructions on a percentage for Jews?"

"Of course there isn't such an instruction, but . . . But it does exist."

"Where is it written?"

"In the air, old man, in the air," the editor said and rushed off to a meeting of the Soviet Peace Committee.

The main principle of personnel Cerberism is in not letting in so-called ungovernable people and in selectively letting in the governable — that is, those who obediently twist and turn with the general line. It is these governable people who have governed our country right up to the brink — both moral and economic. Cerberean panic has engulfed certain regional committees now that ungovernable candidates have been nominated. The Cerberuses didn't even think of barking — at least for form's sake — at the anti-Semitic insults hurled at the candidates. But they did manifest their Cerberean vigilance in tearing down announcements of meetings with the candidates, in papering the houses with voters who have their instructions, in dubious vote counting, in not letting in representatives of the press and the public to the elections. Cerberized democracy is a cerbocracy.

It wouldn't be fair to ascribe Cerberism only to bureaucrats, who see themselves sentimentally as Saint Bernard lifesavers. In our families, stores, and streets you hear more and more Cerberean growling at one another, the Cerberean click of teeth. We are all bitten by one another.

Recently, as I was late for a performance, I hopelessly tried to hitch a ride on Academician Oparin Street, near the Center for Mother and Child, where I had been visiting my wife. At least fifty cars dashed by without even slowing down. I got in the middle of the street and made a cross with my arms over my head — an SOS. But the cars swerved around me, driving up on the sidewalk. I was near the hospital — something more serious than being late for my own reading could have been wrong. But the answer to my plea for help was a splash of mud in my face. And I thought suddenly, do I always stop when I drive past someone with his arms out for help?

Haven't I, in a different guise, in a plural form, sat behind the wheels of cars splashing mud in my own face?

Where Do Cynics Come From?

Cerberism is the product of our moral impoliteness. A society brought up in morality would not allow Cerberuses, whose place is on a chain, to put people on a chain. Our upbringing is impolite. The main goal of decerberizing our society will be accomplished by changing our rearing of children. The teaching of morality must begin with rearing the teachers properly.

What can a teacher teach if he himself does not follow the moral laws he teaches to his students? The teaching of morality by immoral people is turning education into a factory that stamps out cynics. There's no need to shake our heads and mutter in outrage — where do those cynics come from? From our bosom. We cannot blame the "corrupting influences of the West" for the mass cynicism that we have faced and recoiled from in horror — could that be our face, genetically repeated in the faces of our children?

There is a whorish teaching of immorality, when corrupt teachers try to recruit still pure souls, turning them into the newly corrupted and then take the most "talented" students and turn them into future teacher/corrupters. Immoral teaching usually tries to appear as the only morality. Isn't it immoral to consider a person a cog in a state machine, or to hammer officious "musts" into people's heads, or to consider the class struggle to be more important than human values?

We would be oversimplifying the problem by thinking that this teaching of immorality came from evil intentions on the part of the teachers. Many of them were simply moved by "holy simplicity," teaching children how to throw kindling on the bonfires for heretics. The hurried canonization of former heretics and the branding of former saints into evil sorcerers has led many young people to cynicism. Let's not rush into identifying youthful self-protective skepticism with cynicism, though. This kind of skepticism often masks a thirst for high ideals, mixed with a fear of being fooled by the ideals, of falling for the mocking bait of promises.

Haven't we adults, once children who were tricked many times, fooled our children with promises to "pass and surpass," "to live under communism," and so on? Haven't we sent them off with bands playing to the so-called great construction sites, where our children skinned the palms of their hands on frozen metal, laying the "rails of the future," which sank the very next summer into what turned out to be not very permanent permafrost? Haven't we compromised the teaching of history by fawningly changing the center of the victory in World War II first from Stalin's study to the parts of the front visited by Khrushchev and then to Brezhnev's hometown region Malaya Zemlya? Haven't we with rushed ingratitude cut Khrushchev out of newsreels showing him with Gagarin upon his return from space? Haven't we reached new heights of hypocrisy when publishing anniversary articles about outstanding figures of the Revolution who were killed by Stalin by not even mentioning the year of their death — 1937 — because our children might still guess that these people did not die in their beds? Haven't we taught our children to bite their tongues and not say "too much," thinking that we were saving their future instead of destroying it? And yet that "too much" was the glasnost that we were stifling with the best of intentions. Haven't we sent our children off to Afghanistan, cravenly hiding our parental pain instead of turning it into public opinion that could have saved our children? Haven't our children seen us change eternal ideals like whores wanting to please successive customers of ideology, and hurriedly modifying ourselves to their tastes? Just recently didn't our children laugh in front of the TV, watching the barely functioning grandfather Brezhnev award himself more honors? And yet didn't we force those children the next morning to write compositions about the grandfather's antischolarly and science-fictionlike memoirs, which received the Lenin Prize, and were fabricated by high-placed literary ghosts?

We are Gepettos who carved cynics out of wood, instead of Pinocchios. We can't blame the textbooks. A teacher, even tragically deprived of textbooks for modern history, can be a living textbook for his students. It's wonderful, if he is a truthful one, and frightening, if false.

Tact in Regard to Nationalities Is the First Sign of Belonging to the Intelligentsia

Over a hundred years ago Tolstoy noted in a letter: "I'm more and more interested in publishing books for the education of Russian people. I am avoiding the word 'for the people,' because the point is that there be no distinction between 'the people' [narod] and 'not the people' [nenarod]."

As we see, the greatest Russian intellectual showed tact in regard to nationalities, social shyness, and did not consider that he had the right to monopolize patriotism. Some of the members of Pamyat and their literary inspirers should learn such tact from Tolstoy. The "nationalist" division of our population into "the people" and "not the people" is no less tactless than the social. Tact regarding nationalities should be inculcated in school. The scandalous incidents of not teaching the national language in schools are an insult to national dignity.[2] I'd also like to say that

2. Supplemental language courses had to be organized privately for children in the Baltic republics, the Ukraine, and in other ethnic regions where Russian was the only language offered in public schools.

bad teaching of Russian is equivalent to destroying it. Respect for one's own language is part of national dignity.

No less important than personal and national dignity is international dignity. A man who praises only his people and scorns others does not even notice that he is lowering his personal and national dignity by doing so. A sense of national supremacy actually demeans your own people and not others. Both great-power chauvinism and narrow, egoistic nationalism that negates the enormous positive contributions made by Russians to world history are examples of low social culture. We must preserve the purity of our languages, the beauty of our national cultures, the uniqueness of our native lands, the characteristics of our customs and beliefs together, not in alienation, separatism, and juxtaposition. There is no nation that is fatally doomed to being the enemy of another for all of history, even if they had once shed each other's blood. All peoples have the same enemy: wars, catastrophes, the difficulties of daily life, lack of trust, lack of freedom, bureaucracy. Isn't that enough? Why must we create enemies of one another?

Sometimes the spark that starts passions is not even hatred but elementary lack of tact regarding other nationalities. During the Days of Soviet Literature in Abkhazia,[3] in the ancient village of Chlou, a writer and even editor of a Komsomol journal suddenly burst out and said, "Look how many famous writers from all over the Soviet Union have come to our tiny Abkhazian village. I was in the USA recently — could you imagine American writers in such an impressive array going to a reservation of almost extinct Indians?"

This lack of tact almost led to an unpleasant conflict; it was prevented by the inherent tact of the elderly Abkhazians, whose silver cartridges jerked and trembled over their hearts, but who said nothing.

---

3. Abkhazia is a small republic on the Black Sea coast in Georgia. The traditional costume for male Abkhazians is a black military uniform, tightly belted, with a sword and dagger, silver bullet cartridges across the chest, and tall soft calfskin boots. In the general move toward independence in 1989–90, as part of the disintegration of the USSR, Abkhazians had several armed skirmishes with Georgians (who in turn had declared their independence of Soviet rule).

National dignity lies in national tactfulness. Perhaps such tact is the first sign of belonging to the intelligentsia?

Anti-intellectualism Is Antipopulism

I was ashamed to see the cheap bazaar cursing matches of the election campaign trying to pit the people against the intelligentsia.

Our intelligentsia is the long-suffering child of our people. Our intelligentsia is the defender of the people.

The journal *Novy mir,* headed by the populist intellectual Alexander Tvardovsky, defended the interests of the deceived and abused Russian peasantry much more than the bemedalled, silent Stakhanovites of the fields, who presided at the Supreme Soviet and obediently voted for everything proposed from the tribune.

Pitting the people against the intelligentsia is pitting the people against its defenders. Anti-intellectualism is antipopulism. The militant anti-intellectualism, first expressed in the person of the ancien régime Pobedonostsev[4] with his owl wings smelling of mothballs, and then in the person of the new régime types wearing butcher's aprons spattered with people's blood, had no shame in dividing up the nation as it saw fit into the people and not the people. After individually separating Leo Tolstoy from the church, anti-intellectualism moved on to mass separation from the people of such outstanding intellectuals as Vavilov, Chayanov, Platonov, Bulgakov, Tabidze, Charents, Mandelstam, Akhmatova, Shostakovich, and Pasternak.

The most terrible part was that the school was brought into this separation. Out of a breeding ground of the intelligentsia it was being turned into a party for destroying the intelligentsia, which proceeded along with the destruction of the most talented peasants, workers, and Red Army commanders. Stalin's system tried to turn our universities and institutes into an incubator of Cerberism out of a cradle of civic spirit. Fortunately, it was not completely done.

---

4. Konstantin Petrovich Pobedonostsev (1827–1907), an archconservative official and director general of the Most Holy Synod of the Russian Orthodox Church, consistently opposed liberal reforms.

Our education was given a terrible blow — physically, since many brilliant teachers were killed in the camps and prisons, and morally, since the surviving teachers were doomed to a spiritual ambivalence between bloody reality and the demands of the education system. In effect it was teaching in a camp.

However, despite these inhuman conditions, the Karbyshevs[5] of our education, frozen alive by instructions, nevertheless continued to perform the exploit of bringing up the human in people. I bow low to these teachers for bringing up the people who later saved humanity from fascism and for keeping alive the hope in those bloody or simply vile times for the nation's eventual salvation by itself through glasnost and democracy.

But next to the noble teaching of morality, both our schools and our press still harbor tendencies toward teaching immorality that tries to disorient our society.

For instance, in issue eight of *Molodaya Gvardiya* for 1988, we find this passage: "Let them tell us when Mandelstam's work played a significant role in the literary process. When did it reach the broad masses of the people and reflect its real interests and hopes?"

This rhetorical figure of neo-Zhdanovism is immoral because the poetry of Mandelstam, who was killed in the camps, was banned for a long time and physically could not "reach the broad masses of the people."

In number twelve of the journal *Moskva*, another critic insults another classic of our poetry in passing: "A certain section of critics, realizing that an authoritative ancestor is needed in order to reanimate the poetic avant-garde, are actively 'pumping up' Pasternak." Isn't this teaching immorality? Isn't this anti-intellectualism, when once again those who know little insult the great poet who was insulted unfairly more than once? Aggressive anti-intellectualism most often comes from those who are not quite intellectuals.

The banner of Saint George the Dragon Slayer should not be

5. Dmitri Mikhailovich Karbyshev (1880–1945), Russian war hero and lieutenant general, was tortured to death at the Nazi Mathausen camp. He was stripped naked, water poured over him, and left to freeze.

used by the anti-intellectuals. Instead of using Georgii Pobedon-osets, as he's known in Russian, they should have a banner with owl wings, representing Pobedonostsev.

Shame Is the Engine of Progress

A teacher is a writer who writes living people instead of books. A lying teacher turns into a mass producer of future liars. Bad children, like bad books, cannot be released in large runs. The release of good people and good books in too small a run is a threat to the genetic pool. All shortages are antihumanistic and therefore unjustifiable. But one of the most antihumanistic short-ages is of books.

Let's say I'm a wino. And suddenly I see the light and want to become educated. I'm in the mood to commune with world cul-ture, damn its eyes. I'm drawn to Montaigne, pardon my French. Some mysterious force is driving me to La Rochefoucauld. But at the bookstore, the girls just laugh at me. One deigns to talk to me. "I had a book lover from Anadyr — and he gave me a sable skin for Teilhard de Chardin. So, Mr. Red Nose, I'll do you Montaigne if you do me a pair of Italian boots." How can I do her a pair of Italian boots if first of all, I'm not Italian, and sec-ondly, not a cobbler? Well, how's a simple Soviet alcoholic going to get in touch with world culture?

I'm joking, of course, but it's laughter through tears. There is a vast difference between a person brought up on *The Eternal Call* and one brought up on *The Foundation Pit*.[6] Zamyatin's *We* and Orwell's *1984* are textbooks of antitotalitarianism. *One Day in the Life of Ivan Denisovich, Life and Fate, Kolyma Tales*, and *Journey into the Whirlwind* are textbooks of history.[7] But these books are still hard to come by. Today's book shortage is the castration of the future's heart. D students in morality played hooky from great books.

6. Anatoli Ivanov (born 1928) is an immensely popular writer of pulp fiction. *The Eternal Call* is one of his best-sellers. *The Foundation Pit* is by Platonov. *See* "The Proletariat Does Not Need Psychosis: Andrei Platonov," pp. 310–329.
7. Solzhenitsyn's *One Day in the Life of Ivan Denisovich*, Vassily Grossman's *Life and Fate*, Varlaam Shalamov's *Kolyma Tales*, and Eugenia Ginzburg's *Journey into the Whirl-wind* each depict life in the camps.

There is a pseudoliberal idea that students who get bad grades should be promoted anyway. I'm afraid that this idea is being used experimentally on adult *nomenklatura* men, who deserve D's in ideology and get promoted to the next class, to putting out fires or, vice versa, from putting out fires to ideology. The *nomenklatura* boxes are filled with overage D students, who never read or will read *The Brothers Karamazov*.

The struggle against the D-rank *nomenklatura* should have begun in school, because the embryonic tyrants start there, and if they grow up, they can stifle fledgling glasnost and democracy with their sturdy hands.

In order to bring up a new generation in the understanding of glasnost as being as necessary as air for the development of the personality, rather than being a temporary gift from above, the teacher must be a personality himself — that is, a person with his own face, and not a face in which every feature has been pre-scribed and approved by the State Education Commission. For teachers, as for people's judges, there can be no orders from above, except the highest order — to preserve the people's interest and their own consciences.

No one brought so much heart to Marxism as the mediocre people who tried to inculcate it. Students in schools and colleges should be reading the whole world's philosophy, and not a cas-trated version, including the history of religion. In no case should literature and the humanities be dropped from the curricula of technological schools. Otherwise we will lack a harmonically de-veloped intelligentsia. We must double the hours devoted to for-eign languages and not promote those who do badly in languages. In today's world, a person who does not know at least one foreign language, as a key into the rest of the world, does not have the right to consider himself adequate. We must remove all barriers to exchanges between our teachers and students and the rest of the world. The new thinking is impossible without global think-ing. The combination of the three dignities — personal, national, and international — is the trinity of human dignity.

We must teach children, who are not personally responsible for the mistakes and crimes of the past, to have the courage to accept the historical guilt. If they do not feel historical shame, they will become adults who could repeat these mistakes and crimes. A comfortable avoidance of responsibility for the past turns into an avoidance of responsibility for the present and future. That is also an improper upbringing. The education in a country determines what its people are like.

Who's Stronger in This Painting? *(1988)*

I HAVE A PAINTING on the wall of my dacha in Peredelkino. No matter who comes to see me, the visitor is hypnotically drawn to that painting. Some like it from first glance, others have to think about it. Sometimes it elicits raptures, sometimes it shocks and even frightens.

The painting is called *Birthday Party with Rembrandt.* In dark crimson swirls of blood, or wind-whipped fires, sit two artists, born the same day, July 15, but one of them, Rembrandt, in 1606 in Leyden, the other, painter of this work, Oleg Tselkov, in 1934 in Moscow. Both are holding glasses filled with red wine, or the flames of history. The Russian is bending toward the Dutchman and whispering conspiratorially into his ear, or perhaps asking something, not simply, but in an insulting, pricking way. A daring but not very merry devilish gleam twinkles in the eye of the Russian, imbued with the terrible superiority of knowing everything that happened on the planet after Rembrandt's death. There is a scary power, an ability to survive in that Russian artist, who had gone through the school of store lines, communal kitchens, overcrowded trolleys, the school of fear of the nighttime knock on the door, the school of Khrushchev's screams at artists, the school of the bulldozed art exhibit under Brezhnev, the school of not being allowed to travel abroad, of unexhibited and unsold paintings, the school of endless exceptions, bans, and threats.

Rembrandt in Tselkov's painting is no longer the man on whose lap Saxia smiled so charmingly, facing all future generations with his will and genius, but the dying Rembrandt, celebrating his last birthday with the strange Russian artist transported in time by Woland's [in Bulgakov's *Master and Margarita*] magic. This is the Rembrandt no longer struggling for fame, but who has won it and despises it. This is the Rembrandt who survived old age and poverty with as much dignity as he had youth and money. This is the Rembrandt who had forgiven life for everything it had taken from him and for everything it had given him. This is the Rembrandt who had not stooped to slyness but who had not rejected simple peasant cleverness.

I've asked myself many times: who is stronger in this painting? I've asked my guests. I believe the best reply was Gabriel García Márquez's: "Both are." A Georgian poet who chose to remain anonymous gave a pretty good answer, too: "The one whose glass is lower is the stronger." The older artist holds his glass lower in the painting. But the sad thing is that almost none of my guests (with the exception of a few foreigners and Soviet art specialists) recognized the painter; they asked me to repeat the artist's name when I told them: Tselkov.

Tselkov was one of my two or three closest friends. I could go to his home without calling first at any time of night or day — alone, with a friend, or with a large group. One night we left his apartment and went swimming in the canal in moonlight, as if to bid farewell forever to our youth and to one another: Bella Akhmadulina, Vassily Aksyonov, Bulat Okudzhava, the young Japanese woman, Yoko, Oleg, and I. Some inexorable fate separated me from some of them, but not from Oleg. He had the great gift of maintaining friendship. The secret of that gift must lie in tolerance of others' opinions, different from your own. In that sense Tselkov is more like the Rembrandt in that painting than like the Tselkov painted by Tselkov. He never gave advice or lectured, and he never asked for advice. He had that rarest quality — the ability to take on another's pain and the ability to confess. He could help when you were in need and not be envious when you were fortunate. Struggling with poverty all his life, he did not count other people's money and managed without his own quietly and almost elegantly.

Oleg and I traveled many thousands of kilometers by motor boat along the Vilyui and the Aldan rivers. He was funny in his urban fears of and delight in Siberian nature, and he was always touchingly loyal and when necessary, a fearless comrade. The first two years after his departure, unexpected for everyone including himself, I caught my car instinctively trying to head for his place in Orekhovo-Borisovo until I remembered that Tselkov was no longer there. It's eleven years now that he hasn't set foot on the Moscow streets he loved with his whole wanderlusting heart. They weren't quick enough to recognize him here, but they've managed to forget him. He is remembered only by his relatives, personal friends, and a few professional artists and collectors. Never interested in politics, he lives in France with a "political refugee" passport, which however does allow him to travel freely the world over and exhibit, exhibit, and exhibit his work. Everywhere, except his homeland.

Last year the Italian publishing house Fabbri published a gigantic color coffee-table book devoted to Oleg Tselkov, as part of their series "Leading Twentieth-Century Masters." Very few living artists were worthy enough to be included. What has happened then? Why did our country allow itself the criminal "luxury" of stealing from itself Tselkov and many other artists — at rough count approximately two hundred? This didn't occur in the Stalin years, but after the Twentieth Party Congress. We are all responsible for this. Of course, the Stalin years were the cradle of a historically unprecedented national robbery. So many generations were deprived of the Russian avant-garde — Kandinsky, Malevich, Filonov, Goncharova, Larionov, Tatlin, Tyshler, Lentulov, Rodchenko, Melnikov![1]

The iron curtain between two systems became a wall between

1. The artists of the Russian avant-garde, who had hailed the Revolution as the proper medium for their heady experiments, soon found themselves to be politically incorrect in the oppressive culture of the Stalinist Soviet Union. Hundreds of banned canvases were stored in museum cellars. Several generations of Russian artists and art lovers were not allowed to see seminal works by artists who continue to influence twentieth-century Western art but left almost no mark in their homeland.

two cultures. Akhmatova, by her own admission, learned only accidentally and very belatedly that Modigliani, the unknown Italian who courted her in Paris, posthumously had become enormously famous. In 1962, Chagall told me when I was visiting him in France that he wanted to die in his homeland and give all his paintings to it — and all he wanted was a modest house in his native Vitebsk. Chagall gave me a monograph about him inscribed to Khrushchev: "To dear Nikita Sergeyevich with love for him and our Homeland." (Chagall made a typo and corrected it; he had "for the sky" [*k nebu*] instead of "for him" [*k nemu*] at first.)

V. S. Lebedev, Khrushchev's assistant, who had never heard of Chagall, refused to give the book to Khrushchev. "Jews, flying yet," he commented in annoyance about the reproduction of two lovers kissing and floating near the ceiling. Lebedev, who — and I must give him credit for this — helped the publication of my poem "Heirs of Stalin" and Solzhenitsyn's novella *One Day in the Life of Ivan Denisovich*, was irritated and even frightened, with good reason. Attacks on artists by Khrushchev and his entourage had turned into attacks on writers, and on the freethinking intelligentsia in general. But the limitations on art always loosened much more slowly than on literature. Nothing changes as slowly as the habit of visual stereotypes. Even in the most "thawed" times Camilla Gray's book on the Russian avant-garde was confiscated by our inflexible customs agents. The moral castration gave rise to an artistic and even stylistic castration. Unusual artistic form was perceived as anti-Soviet content.

But the iron curtain rusted at last and through its holes with sharp, dangerous edges seeped people and books in both directions. Unfortunately, original paintings done here went that way, and this way came only reproductions of Salvador Dalí, Max Ernst, Joan Miró, and many others. Recently at the Sotheby auction, when I saw canvases by Rodchenko, Drevin, and Udaltseva and talented works by our young, still living artists who had been ignored by the state purchasing commissions at home, I heard the auctioneer's mallet and fantastic prices sounding an alarm. On the one hand, it's good that Russian art will be seen in other countries and that young artists thanks to the money falling from capitalist heavens will be able to work peacefully, without hustling for daily bread. But still, I felt cats scratching my heart. Why couldn't we buy these works ourselves? It smelled of national self-robbery to me. But let's return to Tselkov.

He says that no one steadily taught him art as a child. But one day the artist Mikhail Arkhipov spoke at their Pioneer summer camp and astounded Oleg with colorful tales of the life of artists, of painting, and its sacred role. The impressionable youth spent a sleepless night and realized that he was also an artist. Oleg was accepted at the Surikov Art School. His mother recalls: "He was given a stipend at the school, twenty rubles a month." For a fifteen-year-old boy and within the modest budget of a family of mid-range office workers, this was actually a lot. But Oleg was stripped of the stipend because of the first two works he turned in at the winter session. One disgraced painting depicted a concentration camp. Hopeless, submissive faces looked through the barbed wire. The painting was accused of pessimism, of moving away from socialist realism, of being overly tragic and realistic, of being overly tragic in depicting camp life, because there was no hope in the people's eyes based on the nearing Soviet troops. The second work was a composition: a lone soldier playing a guitar at a small dock on a foggy, misty morning. The director called in Oleg's father and interrogated him: how could his son develop such depressed feelings, who were his friends, was there an older artist among them who was a bad influence? His father was surprised. 'Why?' he asked. 'You see — there's no sun! Just clouds, damp, gray . . .' "

"That was the first emergency in my life," Oleg said. "But it was also my baptism. I began as an artist after that incident."

This is the atmosphere in which Oleg Tselkov and his peers, young artists, grew. When Oleg graduated, one of the supervisors of the Surikov school looked over his diploma exhibit and stamped his feet and shouted, "I won't allow this!" Nevertheless, Oleg decided to go on to college, where, naturally, he was not accepted. Some of his early works have chalked 2's (the equivalent of American D's) on them. Tselkov was unexpectedly supported by a pillar of official painting of those days, B. Ioganson. His letter to the Minsk Theater Institute reads: "I recommend Oleg Tselkov as wonderful material for a future artist. . . . He is a marvelous painter and I am certain that he will justify my hopes." Ioganson was consistent in this case. A year after Tselkov was expelled from Minsk (for "formalism"), he helped him get into the Academy of Art in Leningrad. But when Tselkov had his first-year exhibit, some Chinese students wrote a collective protest against it for being a "corrupting bourgeois influence." Where are they now, those Chinese artists? Did they perish back in China, where they might have seemed "too bourgeois" to the rampaging crowd of infantile executioners, the Red Guards?

Tselkov was expelled from the Academy. He was helped out by the brilliant director and artist Nikolai Akimov, who took Oleg into his course at the Theater Institute. It was then, in 1957, when Boris Slutsky and I were giving a joint poetry reading in Leningrad, that Slutsky introduced me to my future best friend with a joking seriousness: "Oleg Tselkov, perhaps a future genius." Tall, handsome, dark-eyed, and curly-haired, the youth stood with casual indifference leaning a shoulder against the door frame of Kirill Kostsinsky's apartment, a popular literary hangout in Leningrad. There was something of Dolokhov [in *War and Peace*] about to walk to the window in Tselkov's pose. But as opposed to Dolokhov, Tselkov never mocked others and like a real man of art he had a childlike curiosity about people and life. We became friends at first glance.

Until I had met Oleg I was an admirer of Glazunov.[2] In 1957 there was a sensational exhibit at Central House of Workers in the Arts of this unknown Leningrad orphan, married to the granddaughter of Benois, banished from the Academy, and who was said to sleep in the bathtub of the widow of Yakhontov when in Moscow. After the endless Stalins, after the mighty kolkhoz women with just as mighty sheaves in their pithecanthropine

---

2. Ilya Glazunov (born June 10, 1930) shot to stardom as an artist with his enormous, posterlike canvases of crowds combining historical and religious figures. At first considered anti-Soviet, he is a well-rewarded official portraitist, who is now expressing nationalist, conservative political leanings. Alexandre Benois (1870-1960), grandfather of Glazunov's wife, was a turn-of-the-century artist in Saint Petersburg and co-founder with Sergei Diaghilev of the *Mir iskusstvo* movement. He died in Paris. Vladimir Yakhontov was an extremely popular reciter of poetry on the stage.

mighty arms, came the enormous eyes of children in the Leningrad blockade. Dostoevsky's tormented face, the tragic image of Blok among the swinish faces in a restaurant, a modern boy and girl, waking up in a city resembling a ghetto, chimneys spewing out something cruel and all-devouring behind the metal bars of their bed. One winter evening Glazunov and I carried his paintings out of the dormitory of Moscow State University, where they were hidden, pushed them through the bars of the massive cast-iron fence with cast-iron seals of the USSR on it, and loaded those paintings into my peeling Moskvich, while streams of melting snow pelted the glassed-in face of Ksyusha Nekrasova. Could I have guessed then that the oppressed and degraded artist Glazunov would soon become the unofficial official artist of the Ministry of Foreign Affairs and would speak of the long-suffering Russian avant-garde in a condescending manner?

They began deriding Tselkov when he was in grade school. By 1957 they had rolled out the heavy artillery — the academicians. For instance, Academician Yuon's article listing the renegades from socialist realism mentioned today's chairman of the board of the Artists' Union USSR, A. Vasnetsov, Yu. Vasilyev, K. Mordovin, E. Neizvestny, and O. Tselkov. The following opinion was expressed at a plenum of the board of the Artists' Union: "O. Tselkov's still lifes are a very bad fakery à la Cézanne" (*Sovetskaya Kultura*, June 4, 1957). Tselkov's former "godfather," Ioganson, renounced him.

But almost simultaneously the young artist's paintings were given a very different evaluation by a man who had been Picasso's friend and knew a thing or two about art. It was Pablo Neruda, who had seen only two of Tselkov's still lifes at a young artists' exhibit in Moscow. He sent Oleg a letter with the line, "On your artistic path you look like a truthful realist who has his own expression and poetry. Bravo!" The revolutionary Turkish poet Nazym Hikmet believed in Tselkov immediately and asked him to design his play, *The Sword of Damocles*, at the Satire Theater. I think that Hikmet saw reflections in Tselkov's work of the great avant-garde that he had been lucky enough to see in the twenties in the Moscow of Mayakovsky and Meyerhold.[3] This reflection drew Kirsanov, and Lilya Brik, and Katanyan[4] to Tselkov's work. Not long before her death Anna Akhmatova, who did not spoil artists with her appearances, visited Tselkov's apartment.

Tselkov was accepted by the Artists' Union, in the theatrical section. But no official organizers bought his work. If not for the constant support of his parents, who never lost faith in him, Oleg would not have lasted. But his first buyers appeared at last. They were very young actors, artists, journalists, and physicists. The watershed for his "buying reputation" was the moment when one of the most famous collectors of the Russian avant-garde, Costakis, bought some of his canvases.

Tselkov's first major work sold abroad was *Group Portrait with Watermelon,* which I described in my narrative poem "A Dove in Santiago." "With enormous, predatory knives, their steel thirsting for blood, for now the watermelon's, and not a victim's, thirteen conveyor-belt faces, swinish slits for eyes, posing like the mafia, are frozen over the first crimson wound, from which bewildered seeds spew forth." The painting was bought by Arthur Miller, visiting the USSR, who later wrote with highest esteem of Tselkov.

I once saw the Mexican artists Siqueiros and Guttuzo greedily asking Tselkov what he used for his paintings. Oleg casually turned over the canvases, and on the backs were the composition of the paints and varnishes. The two old wolves of painting copied everything down, like schoolboys. This was the highest professional recognition.

From still lifes, which were somewhat influenced by Cézanne, Tselkov slowly and powerfully moved to a series of individual and group portraits of conveyor-belt, robotlike people, born of an age of the smashed atom and electronics, the age of Dachau, Gulag, and Hiroshima. These people are scary, but nevertheless

3. Vsevolod Emilyevich Meyerhold (1874-1940), avant-garde theater director, staged all of Mayakovsky's dramas. He was arrested for "formalism."
4. Semyon Isaakovich Kirsanov (1906-1972), a poet close to Mayakovsky. Lili Brik was Mayakovsky's mistress and inspiration of many of his poems. Vladimir Katanyan was a poet who worked with Mayakovsky in LEF (*Levyi front iskusstva,* Left Front of Art).

sentimental; completely human impulses are not alien to them, and their automated psychology hovers on the border between fascism and childish savage naïveté. This type is international, for they can be found as easily in New York as in Lubertsy. The series was impressive, its heritage coming to some degree from Malevich's *Women with Yokes* and some of Léger's images. But the genealogical tree of these fellows grew out of reality, and it was that realism that frightened the "fighters for realism." Actually these "fighters for realism" were abstractionists, for their subservient paintings depicted a nonexistent, abstract Soviet life. These "fighters for realism" persecuted Oskar Rabin, an artist who lived in a barracks in the town of Lianozovo and depicted barracks life with terrible realistic simplicity. When the "art historians" with volunteer police armbands launched their motorized attack on the famous art show in an empty lot, Rabin managed to leap up on the blade of the bulldozer at the last minute, balancing on the edge with his rescued painting. That's how many of our artists lived — standing on a knife edge with their paintings.

The artist Yuri Vasiliev served in the air force during the war, was shot down, survived miraculously, and joined the Party. After the war he first worked, like many students, in the sickly sweet pastry style of realism. But honor and glory to him for being one of the first Russian Soviet artists to return to the forgotten, besmirched traditions of the great avant-garde. Vasiliev moved to a realism with fantasy and visions, creating an atomic Leda lovingly caressing a jet plane, and Slander, a monstrous metal woman, chewing and swallowing people. Having exposed slander, he was accused of it. Members of the Moscow Artists' Union party bureau appeared at his door to check the ideology of his pictures. Like the folk hero Ilya Muromets up from his stove bed,[5] Yuri Vasiliev stood in the doorway with his small children and his wife and with a loaded carbine in his hands. He said that if they dared cross his threshold without his invitation, he would kill his children, his wife, and himself. That's what lay behind

5. Ilya Muromets was a *bogatyr*, a mythical Russian hero. Paralyzed, Muromets rose from his bed atop a Russian stove when his country needed him.

Yuri Vasiliev's happy smile in the newspaper photograph of his opening in Japan.

The artist Mikhail Chemiakine was tossed into a mental hospital [for his dissidence], and when he made astonishing, realistic pencil sketches from life, he was accused of "distorting the image of Soviet mental institutions" and of being a psychopath.

Sculptor Ernst Neizvestny, a military scout, unit commander, posthumously awarded medals (they thought he had been killed), a man whose back is full of shrapnel, was insulted by Khrushchev, who shouted at him, "Take your passport and get out of here!" Did that head of state guess that it would be this sculptor, who valued the release and rehabilitation of so many innocent people as being more important than personal injury, who would create the monument over his grave? Without giving it any thought, they called Neizvestny an abstractionist. After a special dinner for the intelligentsia at the House of Receptions, the surveillance officers, straining, brought out his sculptures and set them up on the government table, still covered with grease spots from the lamb shashliks. Suslov's desiccated inquisitor's face showed behind a sculpture depicting a camp boy with a mouse in his hands. The victim in bronze and the ideology chief looked like a unified architectural ensemble. The hell with abstractionism! The instinctive fear of appearing ignorant was directed against the realistic depiction of the era. The cat knew whose meat it had eaten, and it wanted only innocent milk on its whiskers, instead of meat, in its pictures. But why did they also persecute abstract art (you would think the most politically safe style)? Abstractionism was feared because they imagined within the stormy splashes of color, like a conjurer's trick, lay a demeaning portrait.

An aggressive misunderstanding provokes a feeling of fear in oneself. Ignorance does not want to admit that it does not understand something. Ignorance instinctively hates the object of its misunderstanding, and creates an image of the enemy out of it. Oleg Tselkov found himself in the field of aggressive misunderstanding. He himself had never been aggressive, never had hunted for publicity-creating scandals that try to use a political spicy sauce to make yesterday's dried-out meat loaf, in which real meat may have spent a night but without creasing the pillow, into something more appetizing. Oleg always loved his homeland, its art, without accepting the face of bureaucracy as the face of his homeland.

He was too busy working on mastery of his art to bother with calling foreign correspondents to tell them ahead of time when he would be "subjected to repressions" yet again. Tselkov did not fit any stereotypes, did not belong to any groups, did not take part in political actions, yet everyone respected him and took his opinions seriously. Probably some people thought him the secret leader of all underground artists. The logic came from the criminal world: "If everyone respects him, he must be the chief." There was plenty to respect. Tselkov is a man of rare good will and broad tastes. He once spent an entire evening telling me rapturously about the Peredvizhniki, or Wanderers, as they were known, and said that Serov's *Troika*, with peasant boys pulling an icy barrel on a sled, is one of his favorite paintings.[6] I never heard another artist have so many good things to say about other artists. Tselkov has a rare quality — confidence in himself that does not turn into arrogance. It is the confidence of a master, who knows his work. Real masters simply don't have the time for envy and hatred.

Tselkov, who loves literature, is the least literary artist of all the figurativists I know. Color is three quarters of the content of his canvases. But the attacking juiciness of his color contained a political threat too. His first show at the House of Culture at the Kurchatov Institute opened in 1965, and the organizers got into a lot of trouble. They were forced to repent publicly their ideological immaturity. In 1970 the House of the Architect organized a one-man show for Tselkov. The show set a world record — for short-livedness. It was shut down in fifteen minutes. Someone, waving a red card under the nose of the frightened director, de-

---

6. The Peredvizhniki, or Society of Wandering Exhibitions, was a group of artists who quit the Academy of Arts in Petersburg in order to paint "realistically." They organized traveling exhibitions, to bring art to the people. Valentin Alexandrovich Serov (1865–1911) joined the Society in 1894. He is one of the greatest exponents of Russian realistic painting.

manded the lights turned off, the public thrown out, and the paintings removed. The next day Tselkov was expelled from the Artists' Union for self-willed (!) organization of the exhibit.

I hurried to help my friend — to Minister of Culture Furtseva. It was she who had permitted the song "Do the Russians Want War?," which had been banned for a half year from the radio for allegedly "demoralizing our troops." Furtseva was in a kindly mood this time, too.

"What if we drop by this Tselkov's studio right now?" she proposed with energetic democracy.

"Better not, Ekaterina Alexeyevna," I said with a sigh. "It will be harder for you to defend the artist once you've seen his work."

Furtseva thought it over and called up the Artists' Union, feigning authoritarian ire. "This expulsion was too hasty, and it could turn into a political error," she said into the telephone in the ritual lexicon and winked at me.

Tselkov was reinstated. But what had changed in his life? He still had no official sales, and that was a tragedy for Tselkov, because he is not an internal artist but a museum one. His paintings feel cramped in private houses. Tselkov was not being shown — except for a collective show of unofficial artists, which was paradoxically forced into the Beekeeping pavilion at the Exhibit of Economic Achievements and ridiculously surrounded by numerous cordons of police. Tselkov showed his most tragic and controversial canvas there, *The Last Supper,* bordering on rebellious blasphemy and depicting Christ and thirteen apostles as robotlike conspirators against humanity. But perhaps that is how he saw the last supper of the Antichrist?

His paintings were stacking up, unshown. The sense of prospects was lost. That was the scary part of the swamp of stagnation — it sucked people into despair. Many talented people became pessimists, and the talentless optimistically forged ahead.

Tselkov did not want to move abroad — he wanted to visit. In 1977 he received an invitation to France. One of the heads of OVIR [the passport and visa office] then promised him a two-month visa. Tselkov's wife asked me to keep an eye on their apartment, talked me into giving up a prewar edition of Maupassant to pay off an OVIR clerk who took rare books as bribes. With aching heart I gave up the book. And suddenly the usual OVIR hassles began. The Tselkovs were called in by their benefactor, who said with a sad face, "You see, it's like this: either now and forever, or never." That's a horrible word, "forever," especially if it is joined to the word "homeland." Many, and not only artists, would never have left if they had not been forced to make such an inhuman choice — now and forever or never.

Tselkov, my best friend, was leaving. Did I have the right to ask him not to do it? What could I offer him — an exhibit on Kuznetsky Most,[7] the purchase of his paintings by the Tretyakov Gallery? What right did I have to take away his opportunity at last to see the Louvre, the Prado, the Metropolitan, the Tate Gallery, the Uffizi? But why should he have to pay such a high price for seeing those great museums — the loss of his homeland? Why, when the most talented young artists before the Revolution were given fellowships and sent to Italy and France so that they could study the masterpieces in the original?

Tonya Tselkov burst into my house just before they left, all in tears. A special commission under the Ministry of Culture demanded that Oleg pay twenty-two thousand rubles in order to bring out his own paintings. Oleg had never had so much money at one time in his life. The Artists fund gave him a certificate showing that in the fifteen years he was a member of the Artists' Union he had earned 4,500 rubles. They used to sneer at his paintings, "They're not worth a kopeck!" And now the state, which had never bought a single picture from Tselkov, decided they were worth something, but only with that damned departure "forever."

Old man Rembrandt had had his troubles, but in his worst dreams he could not have imagined this customs surveillance over art.

I hurried to see the deputy minister of culture, Yu. Barabash, and told him something like this: a marvelous Russian painter was

7. Kuznetsky Most is a Moscow street that holds both the Artists' Club and the Artists' Union exhibition hall, both prestigious galleries. The Tretyakov Gallery is a museum based on the collection of the prerevolutionary patron of the arts Pavel Tretyakov, who began buying art in 1856.

leaving. Who knew how his life would turn out and how history would turn out. Why insult him with this fee, as if purposely trying to turn him against his homeland, sadistically breaking the threads that tie him to the culture whose son he was. Barabash had a reputation as a cruel, dry man. To his honor, he understood my argument and helped. The next day the twenty-two thousand magically changed into two thousand.

Moreover, they bought several engravings for exactly two thousand rubles, so that he left practically for free. But forced emigration is never free for the artist or for society. They both lose something irreparably.

It is torture to leave, torture to live far away without hope of return or at least a visit. His wife told me that when Oleg was falling asleep at night, she quietly wept into her hands in fear. To Oleg's honor, he did not stoop to political bustles or to profiting from his "émigré" status. He did not waste his time and gave himself one day off, his "museum day," he called it — Friday. In Paris there are seven hundred picture galleries — lots to see. He painted a lot and grew as an artist. Just recently he has developed a smokiness, a softness, and he has returned to tender still lifes from his conveyor monsters. His "marchand" is Eduard Nakhamkin, a former economist from Riga, who has several galleries of Russian art in the USA. Times have changed, and Nakhamkin regularly comes to the USSR, buying paintings, and inviting our young artists to exhibit.

Materially Oleg lives very well and is grateful to France for giving him shelter. After a long and exhausting battle with OVIR, I got permission from them for his parents to travel to Paris a few years ago to visit him. Oleg is watching the changes in our country with enormous interest, not falling into a rosy euphoria, but not stooping, like some, to hostile ill-wishing. Almost everyone changes abroad — for the better or the worse. Oleg astonishes me in that he has not changed in character at all. He has been in many countries with his shows and he has never complained of homesickness aloud — though sometimes he'll say, "Oh, how I'd like to be hunting woodcock somewhere near the village of Luzhki. . . ."

But that horrible "forever" used by the OVIR benefactor still torments my soul. We've just marked the millennium of Christianity in Russia, but do we always remember its moral postulates that go beyond the framework of religion? If people speak out against bureaucracy, we should not ascribe activity against Russia to them.

Now is not the time for vicious unforgiving. Now is the time for bringing Russian culture back together.

In this article I tried to draw a detailed picture of what happened to Tselkov and a few other artists.

So, who is the stronger in this painting? The red-tape symbiosis of the arrogant Prishibeyev and the meek Akaki Akakyevich,[8] trembling with fear?

Or the daring wisdom of bringing our national culture back together? Or will all our artists who left tragically be able to return to their homeland only in their late eighties, the way Chagall did?

8. Prishibeyev is the arrogant officer in Chekhov's short story of the same name, and Akaki Akakyevich is the meek clerk who loses his prize possession in Gogol's story "The Overcoat."

PART IV

Brief Excerpts from Selected Prose

The Poet's Role in Society

¶ From an interview with *Ogonyok*   (*1987*)

WHAT DID THE POETS of the sixties bring into our lives?

First — a radically anti-Stalinist direction. On this, despite our individual differences, we were all agreed. Second — the detabooing of all topics that had borne a written or unwritten taboo. Third — a disgust for cheap patriotism and nationalistic limitations. Fourth — a new poetic language, which included fresh assonance in rhyme, new rhythms, fearless use of contemporary "unpoetic" words. Fifth — the expansion of poetry audiences to sports palaces and squares. And sixth — the triumphant entry of Russian poetry into the international arena.

It is not true that we were "allowed" many things. We fought for our rights. The democratization of poetry began before the democratization of life. The only advertising we had in our early youth was abuse. But we had to pay dearly for that advertising.

We broke into the fortress during a social cataclysm, when there were breaches. We continued waging war inside the fortress, sometimes in lone battles, hearing the shots of our comrades on some distant street. The breaches were artfully sealed, cutting us off from young people. They began to dig a moat around the fortress, so that the next generation could not come to our aid. We were dead tired, running out of bullets and strength. Foreign helicopters circled overhead, throwing down rope ladders in an inviting gesture. But only those who had lost hope scaled those ladders. Perestroika is the child of those who did not lose hope.

From the novella *Ardabiola*   (*1981*)

Yevtushenko's science fiction novella, Ardabiola, *centers on a man seeking a cancer cure.*

WHAT IF THERE ARE psychological carcinogens? Why can't our suppressed thoughts be carcinogens, for instance? The ancients called cancer "bile disease" — the disease of a gloomy sense of life. Can't pessimism be cancerous?

No one knows what that optimist's face looked like when he was alone. Often those who pretend to be optimists are actually eaten by worms. Cancer, it seems, is an infection. But it's easier for an infection to get through a body that has a weak psychological defense. And what if exhaustion is a carcinogen? Every infection is a poison. Nature is wonderful, it has an antidote for every poison. But sometimes the antidote is scattered in various places — it has to be fathered, put together, figured out in terms of what goes where. Nature figures itself out through our minds.

It's not necessary to wear a cross on your chest. What's important is that it be inside you.

Is there anyone in history who had time to do everything? Everyone who died didn't have time for something. Christ didn't have time to make everyone brothers. Hitler didn't have time to throw all the Jews into his gas chambers.

Why is there so much rudeness, elbowing aside, and pushing? Life is hard? Is that an excuse? Why make a hard life even harder? We must not forget that we are people, human beings.

If a yogi can lie on a bed of nails, then anyone can. You just have to concentrate. If Abkhazian men can live to be one hundred fifty, everyone can live that long. You just have to know how to live. We know very little about ourselves and our powers. First we must learn how not to get sick. And then we must learn not to die.

From the novel *Wild Berries* *(1981)*

Wild Berries, Yevtushenko's first novel, was nominated for the Ritz-Hemingway Prize for best novel published in English in 1984.

PEOPLE MUST be reminded that they are part of a nation. War reminds them, but the price of that reminder is too high. Literature reminds them. Literature is a reminder to people that they are part of a nation and to humanity that it is humanity.

.

Tsiolkovsky put it wonderfully: "All our knowledge, past, present, and future, is nothing compared to what we will never know." That's not sad. That's marvelous. When there is an infinity of the unknowable, then knowledge itself can hope to be infinite. Mankind has that hope, too, because man is knowledge that knows itself. The highest reason of the universe is not something separate from man. Man is part of it. Perhaps the main part. Thus, if we get stupider, the highest reason gets stupider too. . . . Knowledge by itself can be heartless. There is something beyond infinite knowledge — infinite heart.

Every Russian is a collection of all of Dostoevsky's heroes in one.

No father can ever teach his son to be a genius. That is not taught. But if the father is not a scoundrel, he can at least teach his son not to be a scoundrel.

 From the screenplay *The End of the Musketeers* *(1988)*

The End of the Musketeers has not been filmed yet. Yevtushenko has directed two films based on his screenplays, Kindergarten *(1985) and* Stalin's Funeral *(1990).*

I AM A SIMPLE MAN and do not understand politics, but I figured out a long time ago that the state usually considers its best people enemies. Friendship is also a state, and don't worry, that state I will not betray.

The system needs people like a liquid that takes the shape of whatever vessel it is poured into.

All power comes not from God but from the devil. Power cannot be improved, just as the devil cannot be improved.

 From *A Precocious Autobiography*

A Precocious Autobiography by the twenty-nine-year-old Yevtushenko appeared first in Stern in 1962. Its first publication in the USSR was in 1989 in Nedelya, the weekly supplement of Izvestia.

ON MARCH 5, 1953, an event took place that shook the country — Stalin died. It was almost impossible to imagine him dead, for he seemed such an integral part of life to me.

Everyone was stunned. People had been taught that Stalin thought about all of them, and they were lost without him. All of Russia wept, and I did too. They were sincere tears of sorrow and, perhaps, tears of fear for the future.

At a writers' rally poets read poems about Stalin with sobbing voices. The voice of Tvardovsky — a big strong man — trembled.

I will never forget how people went to see Stalin's coffin.

I was in a crowd on Trubnaya Square. The breath of the tens of thousands of people pressed against one another, rising above the crowd in a white cloud, was so thick that it reflected the swaying shadows of the naked March trees. It was an eerie, fantastic sight. People entering the flow from behind pushed and pushed. The crowd turned into a terrifying whirlpool. I saw that I was being carried toward a traffic light. The pole moved toward me inexorably. Suddenly I saw the crowd squeeze a young woman against the pole. Her face was distorted by a desperate cry, which could not be heard above the general screams and groans. The crowd pushed me against the girl, and I could feel the crunch of her bones against the pole. I couldn't hear it but I felt it with my own body. I shut my eyes in horror, unable to bear the sight of her wildly bulging, child's blue eyes. And then I was swept away. When I opened my eyes, the girl was gone.

She must have been crushed underfoot. Now a man was pushed against the traffic light, grimacing, arms extended as if in crucifixion. I realized there was something soft under my feet. It was a human body. I scrunched up my feet and the crowd carried me away. I was afraid to put down my feet for a long time. The crowd grew thicker. I was saved by my height. Shorter people suffocated and died. We were crushed from one side by the buildings and on the other by a row of military trucks.

"Get rid of the trucks! Take them away!" came shouts from the crowd.

"I can't, I don't have instructions!" the young blond militia officer shouted from the top of a truck, almost weeping in despair and frustration. People, pushed against the trucks by the wave of the crowd, smashed their heads on the edges of the trucks. The trucks were covered with blood. And suddenly I felt a powerful hatred for everything that had given rise to that "no instructions," when people were dying because of someone's stupidity. And at that moment I thought of the man we were burying, for the first time with hatred. He had to be guilty of this. And it was that "no instructions" that created the bloody chaos at his funeral. From that moment I realized that there was no point in waiting for instructions if people's lives depended on it — you had to act. I don't know where I got the strength, but energetically working my elbows and fists, I tossed people aside and shouted, "Make chains! Make chains!"

No one understood. Then I shoved people's hands into other hands, using the most horrible swearwords from my geological expeditions vocabulary. A few strong men began helping me. And people understood. They began holding hands, forming chains. The men and I continued our actions. The whirlpool quieted down. The crowd was no longer a beast.

"Women and children into the trucks!" shouted one of the men.

And women and children floated overhead, passed from hand to hand, into the trucks. One of the women being passed was hysterical, thrashing and shouting. The police officer patted her on the head, muttering soothing things. The woman shuddered a few times and grew still. The officer took the cap from his fair head, covered her stiffened face, and bawled like a baby. But I saw the whirlpool farther up ahead.

The guys and I pushed our way there. Using curses and fists, we organized people into chains in order to save them.

The police began helping us at last. Everything calmed down.

For some reason I really didn't want to go to Stalin's coffin anymore. I took one of the men who helped make chains, bought a bottle of vodka, and came back to my house.

"Did you see Stalin?" my mother asked.

"I did," I said taciturnly, clinking jelly glasses with the guy.

I didn't lie to my mother. I had seen Stalin, because all that had happened in fact was Stalin.

That day was a watershed in my life, and therefore, in my poetry.

I realized that no one was doing the thinking for us anymore and perhaps even that no one had been doing it for us before. I realized that I had to think for myself, think and think some more. . . . I don't want to say that I had instantly comprehended the entire degree of Stalin's guilt just then. I continued idealizing him slightly for some time afterward. Many of Stalin's crimes were still not known then. But for me, one thing had become clear: an enormous number of problems had developed in our country and not taking part in their solution would be a crime.

 From various articles

I STARTED OUT as a lone wolf cub. As a child and teenager I had no peers who wrote like me and I was always drawn to my elders. But when I was suddenly and miraculously accepted at the Literary Institute in 1952, even though I lacked school records, I began writing in a completely different way, thanks to my peers' saving irony toward my homemade rhyme juggling. O! what a precious feeling — fear of your comrades' opinion! How much that fear gives you, how many diseases it cures — first and foremost, conceit! I was pelted by a hail of healing friendly jibes, and I gradually recovered from a case of newspaperese. I can say this without idealized exaggeration: we were forged in a love of poetry, combined with a love of each other. Our milieu had no envy, no sarcasm, no back-stabbing or back-patting, which is typical of many young people now.

Stalin's death united us even more, because we wept together and rethought things together as the curtain slowly lifted from the past and put us face to face with tragedy and crime. On the day of Stalin's death one of our teachers, the poet A. Kovalenkov, was arrested. Vladimir Sokolov and I were shocked and discussed it, trying to find traits of the "enemy" in him, as the rules of our upbringing demanded, recalling certain things he said that now, after his arrest, began to seem suspicious. And suddenly Vladimir Sokolov said harshly and angrily, "What bastards we are. Instead of this we should go see his wife . . . share her grief. . . ."

And that's what we did. A few months later, Kovalenkov was released. Life was changing. The hypnosis of Stalinism was gradually weakening. The first class the year after Stalin's death was very different from ours — much more relaxed, more radical: Bella Akhmadulina, Yuri Kazakov, Mikhail Roshchin, Yuna Morits. The word "we" expanded. A. Surkov, then Secretary of the Writers' Union, came to the institute and in his speech attacked the first antibureaucratic swallow — Dudintsev's novel, *Not By Bread Alone*. He shouted, pointing at a freshly whitewashed wall, "There, you see, there's a spot on that basically clean wall. If we, like Dudintsev, rub our noses just in that spot, it will always seem dirty to us. . . ." Roshchin, still very young at the time, calmly countered Surkov's argument while the rest of us applauded, "Yes, but if you step back too far from the wall, you won't be able to see the spot at all." Surkov left, muttering angrily that the Literary Institute was a hotbed of nihilism.

One shouldn't exploit ugliness any more than beauty — it has nothing to do with the aims of art. Appearance is an accident of nature, while inner beauty is a not-accidental miracle.

Forgery is written with someone else's blood or with red-colored liquid. This kind of forgery can even be talented and affect somebody's tear glands. The French call this "sentimental blackmail." But, as Baratynsky[1] said, such a muse is like "a perverted beggar, begging with another's infant in her arms." . . .

There are born forgers in art. They will always exist, alas. But that is not as sad as a talented poet forging his own emotions. The thought "I'll just do this now, when I'm in a difficult position, and then I'll do a bang-up real poem" is deceptive. The hand grows accustomed to forgeries, and it develops a fear of the real, like the fear of signing your own death warrant. Yet the history of literature shows that writers sign their own death warrants when they are alive and begin fearing themselves. A clever survival becomes death, and a tragic death can turn into immortality. Is it worth being clever?

And there are also such sad cases as when a real work is perceived by contemporaries as being a forgery. For instance, *Eugene Onegin* was called "soap bubbles blown by a fanciful imagination." A literary verdict can turn around against the critic. People should be more careful in their sentencing.

Inner culture is the best vaccination against the epidemic of indifference. Inner culture is the guarantee of eternal youth. You can't go far on pure emotions, the fragrances and colors of first impressions, if the instinct for life is not supported by a knowledge of life. Time slips out of unwise hands, even if those hands at first have the grip of youth.

*   *   *

1. Yevgeny Abramovich Baratynsky (1800-1844), poet.

A poet must combine three qualities. The student — unyielding rebellion seeking a storm; the monk (symbolically speaking, of course) — dedication and a chronicler's impartial evaluation of events; and the warrior — fearless readiness to defend what you believe and preach.

I began my literary life at a time when our art was sick with gigantomania. Pompous films with casts of thousands at an electric power plant, poetic cycles on the Don River or on virgin soil constructed on the principles of plasticine monumentalism. I was a child of my times and had the same illnesses with it — thank God, I had the measles of gigantomania in my literary infancy rather than as a grown-up, though there were some long-term complications. But it seems to me that lately our art in general and our poetry in particular has caught a new disease, no less fraught with complications, and that is "tininess," and Blok's advice "to think about the big" takes on great urgency. A kind of fear of historical space, spiritual space, has occurred in art. Unfortunately, some critics, instead of being thoughtful healing doctors fighting this disease, actually support the tininess of intentions.

Western poetry has had a number of significant poets of a "hermetic" direction. We never had it in Russian poetry. Russian poetry from the very beginning of its existence took on the function of conscience of the people. That function is impossible without pain, without compassion. But poetry, like medicine, is trying to be painless. Yet in the words of Herzen,[2] "We are not physicians, we are pain."

Hurrying, as we all know, does not help poetry. But there is the hurrying that comes of wanting to speak your mind before you are killed, because tomorrow may be too late to speak out.

* * *

2. Alexander Ivanovich Herzen (1812–1870), writer, founder of the liberal journal *The Bell.*

We worry too much about using great praise when talking about living poets. A sober, seeking person will not be ruined by praise, while a frivolous person can have his head turned even by abuse.

It is fair to call disrespect for the historic monuments of antiquity spiritual vandalism; it is just as fair to call scorn for man's complex contemporary problems spiritual vandalism, since today is the ancient history of the future.

A true poet is a special kind of surgeon who is given the moral license to open up the body of the era only by his fearless opening up of himself.

I recommend translating only those poets who are better than you or your equal. Then the benefit is mutual.

Poetic daring is sometimes understood as the use of confusing metaphors, knockout rhymes, rhythmic supermodern cacophony, or, just the opposite, "simplicity courageously juxtaposed to modernism," which is actually worse than theft. Poetic daring is sometimes understood only as the ability to punch someone in the face.

But real poetic daring begins not with ruthlessness toward traditions, not with ruthlessness to the violators of those traditions, in fact not with ruthlessness directed outward, but with ruthlessness toward oneself.

Wandering in elegiac mists has never saved anyone from getting mixed up in dirty deals.

A verse that is too masterfully crafted can sometimes be insulting in terms of someone's pain, and in many cases I prefer a lack of professionalism to an excess of it. Perhaps the occasional lapse in one's ability is a manifestation of a higher level of mastery, since mastery is inseparable from moral tact.

Some poets decorate every poem like a Christmas tree, weighing down the meaning with glass balls of metaphor, cotton wool of sentimentality, garlands of delicate rhymes, so that you can't see the tree. There is another strength — unadorned, unornamented.

Being a poet is more than knowing how to write in rhyme. Poetry is a quality of the spirit that raises a master above a craftsman, a person above an almost-person. As a child I used to like to visit the tiny shop under the stairs of the invalid cobbler of Zima Junction. The material he received from his clients was pathetic: tarpaulin boots worn on the inside folds, canvas shoes on wooden heels, shoes on worn rubber soles. His repair materials weren't much better: old automobile tires, the tops of boots that had given up their souls but were still good enough to patch other barely living boots. And his white matchstick nails were so neatly cut and lined up in the old candy tin, and the waxed thread smelled so delicious and dependable, and the awl made magic so fiercely and carefully in his crooked and thick yet marvelous and light fingers, that this too had the poetic quality of a master who overcomes his circumstances — that is, who transforms the reality that appears before him in the shape of ruined shoes.

Western sociologists inform us that only 20 percent of people earn their salaries by doing what they love. If that is true, how miserable is the other 80 percent of humanity, forever denied the incomparable joy of creativity — a joy that makes a person in any profession a poet. Many young poetry writers, hoping to become poets, think that the secret of greatness is in mastering technique and hope to increase their mastery, forgetting to enlarge their own souls. What use is a master of metaphor if he is indifferent to people, who needs a jeweler of fine epithets if the lace jabot of his uniform hides a chest without a real human heart, what good is a smith of resounding rhythms creating a shower of sparks on the stage when he is a coward and is afraid to defend a comrade in distress? You can't grow your own soul to help the cowardly — you might grow it too big and it will be inconvenient or ridiculous, like Cyrano's nose.

There are poets who fill their poems with thunderous sounds of industry, the booms of battle explosions, the bravura hissing of peacocklike fireworks, but when you read their poetry, it is like silent films: lightning bolts jump over the pages, but you can't hear real thunder.

There are poets who constantly proclaim that they speak in the name of the people. If you look closely, you feel sorry for them — they are so alone. There are other poets: they speak more about loneliness than about the people, but if you look closely you will see that they are the ones who speak in the name of the people.

Poems about death test a poet's talent no less than poems about love.

I often get letters from beginning poets who ask, "What qualities are necessary to become a real poet?" I never answered that question, which I considered naive, but now I will try, even though that may be naive, too.

There are five such qualities, I suppose.

First: you must have a conscience, but that is not enough to become a poet.

Second: you must have a mind, but that is not enough to become a poet.

Third: you must have courage, but that is not enough to become a poet.

Fourth: you must love not only your poetry, but other poetry, but that is not enough to become a poet.

Fifth: you must write poetry well, but if you do not have the other four qualities, that is not enough to become a poet.

Poetry, according to the famous adage, is the self-consciousness of a nation. "In order to understand itself, a nation creates its poets."

Being banned had created a special aura for some poets and their first publications ruthlessly destroyed the phosphorescent mists of legend.

*   *   *

There is this falsely beautiful phrase: "No one owes anyone anything." Everyone owes everyone else, but especially poets are in debt.

To become a poet requires the courage to declare yourself a debtor.

A poet is indebted to those who taught him to love poetry, because they gave him a feeling for the meaning of life.

A poet is indebted to today's poets, his comrades in the workshop, since their breath is the air he breathes, and his breath is part of the air they breathe.

A poet is indebted to his readers and contemporaries, because they hope to tell about their times and themselves through his voice.

A poet is indebted to his descendants, because someday they will see us through his eyes.

We have the expression "pangs of conscience," why not "pangs of memory"? Art is a bed of nails, not a soft couch. Art is humanity's main memory. No one who flees memory is a real person.

I don't like the word "poetess." I immediately picture something ethereal, rustling fake wings, and writing insipid nothings in a gilt-edged album. Let's agree to call women who write real poetry poets, for a master is a master, and there are no handicaps in art for gender.

Many poets actually declare a striving for the high-flown, forgetting, obviously, that the high and the high-flown are different things.

I understand that the desire for the high-flown is a reaction against an intentional degradation of the language. But why trade one extreme for another?

Poetry is feeling the earth with a bare foot.

A young writer without the intention of saying something that no one else has ever said is unnatural. There are no people in the world who have nothing to say. Every new person in humanity has his own unique secrets of life, and each and every person has something to say for the first time. If you can get to your own soul, you'll find your own words. Imitators are simply weak-willed people who could not get to their own souls either out of cowardice or laziness. Inside every person, be it a dry-cleaning clerk, a general wreathed in laurels, a janitor or a cosmonaut, a peasant woman or a ballerina, lives and most often dies at least one potentially great book of his life, where everything is unique. Even the life of a dyed-in-the-wool bureaucrat is unique in its own way, as the evolution of an innocent creature kicking in its mother's womb into a dehumanized, paper-pushing thing. But we have yet to have *The Confession of a Bureaucrat*. And that's too bad. It would be edifying. Sometimes the most marvelous people become tongue-tied when they talk about their lives, getting mixed up in secondary matters, and even if they are brilliant raconteurs they make their lives unbearably boring once they set pen to paper. Fortunately, there are good memoirs, but with rare exception they are those of celebrities, while the dry-cleaning clerks and the janitors do not write their memoirs.

The argument between the Slavophiles and the Westernizers lasted a long time, but practice resolved the issue its own way. Without imitation, without mimicry, Russian classics imbibed the best of the West, transformed it in the crucible of Russian conscience, and then conquered the West with Tolstoy, Dostoevsky, and Chekhov, determining for many years ahead the development of world literature.

This is the story of the publication of "The Heirs of Stalin." When I wrote the poem after Stalin's body was removed from the Mausoleum, I spent a lot of time in different editorial offices. Even Tvardovsky at *Novy mir* said (sarcastically, of course) to me, "You know, why don't you just hide that anti-Soviet stuff in a desk drawer and don't bring trouble down on your head."[3] He

3. Alexander Trifonovich Tvardovsky (1910–1971), poet and influential editor in chief of the literary journal *Novy mir* (1950–54), had published Solzhenitsyn's *One Day in the Life of Ivan Denisovich*. "The Heirs of Stalin" expressed concern that the simple removal of Stalin's body was not enough to remove Stalinism from Soviet society.

used the word "anti-Soviet" knowing that was the likely label they would use.

I began publishing the poem in the only way available to me — with my voice. I read it for the first time in a television studio. The reaction was the same as after my first reading of "Babi Yar." Dead silence. The first sounds afterward were not applause but the scrape of chairs as people left the hall. About fifty left in protest.

I continued reading the poem for several months in various halls. Tvardovsky predicted accurately that the poem would be called anti-Soviet. It was called this by Sobolev, chairman of the Writers' Union of the RSFSR [Russian Republic]. At a meeting he said, "Look how far the anarchy has gone! Yevtushenko is reading anti-Soviet poetry from every stage, spitting upon the memory of Comrade Stalin and all the years of Soviet power."

What could I do? I went to my old friend, the editor of *Literaturnaya Gazeta,* Vladimir Alexeyevich Kosolapov, the man who had printed "Babi Yar," to ask his advice. He suggested showing the poem to Khrushchev. But how was I to do that? Kosolapov helped there, too — he gave me the telephone number of Nikita Sergeyevich's aide, but asked me not to use his name.

I called Khrushchev's aide and, unexpectedly, he agreed to see me immediately. Later it turned out that he knew my work well, was a fair photographer, and had a unique collection of pictures of Khrushchev. I can still see one of them: Khrushchev listening to a nightingale. Besides which, the aide had been a student of my grandfather, Rudolf Yevgenyevich Gangnus. My grandfather, besides teaching school, gave mathematics courses at the Party higher school (I believe that's what it was called). The aide asked me to make a few changes: add two quatrains on Turksib and Magnitka [two major construction projects, of a railroad line in Asia and a metallurgy plant in Siberia, that were endowed with great symbolism in the early years of socialism] and replace the word *Homeland* with *Party.* I didn't think he was right, because the theme of the first Five-Year Plans was in the poem as it was, and the two additional quatrains made the poem too heavy. And from my point of view the word *Homeland* was more appropriate.

But in the interests of having the poem published, I agreed. He said, "But, Yevgeny Alexandrovich, don't rush, I'll give it to Nikita Sergeyevich at a convenient moment."

Several months passed. I went to Cuba. The Cuban crisis came. The world hung by a hair. [Soviet President Anastas] Mikoyan flew to Cuba. He arrived in the only airplane allowed to cross the blockaded airspace (by agreement with the Americans). He had come for negotiations. And at a reception in his honor, Mikoyan chatted with Fidel Castro, mentioning in my presence that a few days before his arrival in Cuba *Pravda* had printed Yevtushenko's poem "The Heirs of Stalin," and that it would be good to publish it in Cuba. He handed Castro the newspaper. Mikoyan apparently thought that I knew all about it and was rather shocked to see me practically tear the newspaper out of Castro's hands. I couldn't believe my eyes.

How did it get published? Mikoyan told me. Khrushchev was in Abkhazia visiting the chairman of a local kolkhoz. And that chairman told him of the illegalities that happened in Abkhazia in the thirties. The chairman wept and so did Khrushchev. And then he said that Stalin could not be justified, if he had done nothing else. And he had done so much more!

And at that moment the First Secretary's aide showed him my poem with the words, "Nikita Sergeyevich, I have a poem on that very topic written by Yevtushenko. May I read it?" So Khrushchev heard my poem for the first time along with Mikoyan and that kolkhoz chairman. He said, "It must be published immediately!" The poem was sent by plane to Moscow, to the editors of *Pravda*.

When it was printed, a group of workers at the Central Committee and the Moscow Committee sent a collective letter to Khrushchev with a complaint against P. Styukov, editor of *Pravda*, for publishing that anti-Soviet poem. They had no idea that it was Khrushchev himself who had sent the poem for publication there.

At a meeting of the Secretariat of the Central Committee Khrushchev used that letter as an example of outdated thinking. "If this poem is anti-Soviet," he said, "then what am I? Am I also anti-Soviet?"

This is the story of that poem, which might never have been published. The decisive role was played by a combination of circumstances and the will of an all-powerful leader.

I do not idealize our poetic generation. We all wrote — and occasionally still do — bad poems, hurried, with lapses in taste, and sometimes ones we are ashamed of. We did not perform only heroic deeds, but were sometimes afraid and made compromises. Sometimes we kept silent, and that was a compromise. But still, the poets of our generation were the first to speak out — before Solzhenitsyn, before Sakharov, before the human rights movement.

There are poets of a special type — simultaneously hidden and defenselessly open. That kind of hidden openness is instinctive self-protection in the battle with the censors. Willy-nilly, censorship forces you to be subtle and metaphorical.

Futurology is always inaccurate in some sense — sometimes fortunately, sometimes not. The utopias of Thomas More and Campanella, idealizing the future, obviously have not come to pass. But neither did the vicious 1984 described by George Orwell. It turned out to be easier to guess about the future achievements in science, in the case of Jules Verne, than to picture its military application — for instance, spy satellites or Star Wars. But Alexei Tolstoy, who described laser weapons in the hands of the global adventurer Garin, did not foresee that the laser could be used for good in medicine.

Ever since Hiroshima, futurology has centered on nuclear catastrophe. This led to political opportunism as well as sincere but weak works of literature. But real art was born as well, going beyond alarmist posters. In cinematography, the first powerful film of this sort was Stanley Kramer's *On the Beach,* which was shown only in the creative union clubs, unfortunately. The American television film *The Day After,* which shows our planet destroyed by nuclear catastrophe, was a sensation. It is weaker artistically, but very acute.

My childhood memories include the Soviet prewar film *If Tomorrow There Is War,* which radiantly depicted our lightning-fast victory if the fascists were to attack. The movie was belatedly criticized after our severe lesson with millions of casualties. Did that film, along with other manifestations of insouciance, prevent us from preparing properly for the war? Did it have a weakening effect not only on its "ordinary viewers" but on the people who had it made?

While our art is correct in not taking the path of "nightmarizing" the future, we sometimes take the other extreme, and avoid discussing those horrors that await us in case the threat of war stops being a poster symbol and becomes a reality. Sparing our countrymen's nerves may turn into moral unpreparedness. Optimism unprepared by knowledge or forewarning can lead to the most pessimistic results. Let us note that many of our movie audiences avoid films about the last war, preferring commercial entertainment. The unwillingness to know the suffering of the past, the unwillingness to be prepared for the possible suffering of the future weakens and destroys today's civil courage and tomorrow's multifaceted courage.

My favorite writer when I was nine was Maupassant, and I gulped down with great delight the love adventures of Georges Durois [in *Bel-Ami*], who elegantly opened the doors of high society with the curled tips of his mustache. I did not understand then that Georges Durois was a miserable man, deprived of the gift of loving. Connoisseurs of love do not know love.

Who hasn't experienced this: you're coming home late at night. Dead tired. Filled with disgust for the world and yourself. And suddenly you see two young shadows in a chaste embrace, as if there is no lust, no cynicism, no blood, no filth in the world. Even if there were only two people in the world who loved each other, we would not have the right to lose faith in the possibility of love.

Why are true love and tragedy like two convicts chained together? Because love is such perfection that all the imperfection of the world envies it and tries to stifle it.

*   *   *

Love and art are equal — for they are the only ones who conquer time.

In northern Russian villages to this day they use the old "I pity you" instead of "I love you." Someone created the ridiculous idea that "pity demeans." Pity demeans only those who don't know how to pity others.

Long, long ago, I was walking down Gorky Street alone around three in the morning, under swirling snowflakes, when I stopped dead in my tracks. Coming right at me out of the blizzard was Pasternak. He had his hand on the arm of a blue-eyed woman just returned from distant parts, her cheeks reddened by the wind and joy, in a white down scarf, and he walked sideways a bit ahead of her, so that he could see more than her profile, all of her, and he kissed the snowflakes from her face, and laughed like a boy. He was sixty-five then, if I'm not mistaken.

Some readers have this sniffing attitude toward love poems: they want to read lyricism as material for gossip about the poet's personal life. When I published "I've stopped loving you . . . " my wife got phone calls from outraged strangers, who said, "He's made a laughingstock out of you before the whole country." When I wrote the poem "Masha," a respected old poet actually waved his cane over my head and claimed that I had compromised not only the poor girl but her mother, too, an honest writer. Incidentally, to my regret, there was nothing between us. Most noble was the brother of the heroine of my poem "From Desire to Desire." After a reading that he attended, I asked him which poem he had liked best, with a nervous glance at his strong biceps. He smiled and said, "Unfortunately, I liked the poem dedicated to my sister."

If you see people with a dry, haughty look or, on the contrary, with a smutty, nasty look, ask yourself: did they ever love anyone? And while you're at it, ask yourself: have you ever really loved?

PART V
Beyond Borders

§ *The Price of a Fantasy*

(1987)

"DO YOU KNOW how much this 'fantasy' cost?" I was asked by a Brazilian woman of about sixty, sadly and proudly smoothing her snow white lace dress. In that fantasy dress the woman looked like an ebony sculpture hidden in a huge glowing chrysanthemum. The lace, like whipped cream, covered the heavy flesh. Her body was gasping after the carnival parade, and her dark wrinkled hands with infantlike pink palms were opening the mother-of-pearl buttons of the constricting dress. The woman sat on the grass, her white shoes off, blissfully moving her stiffened toes and her bare feet, which had stood so long in line for a chance to dance, and had danced so much that they could no longer hold up their exhausted mistress.

But this woman could at least still sit and talk, while other women in their fantasy dresses, who had just been dancing with her, were sprawled on the grass, fast asleep. The field behind the sambadrome, covered with wild grass, looked like a battlefield littered with the dead bodies of white flowers. Here, in the field, it was almost dark, and the occasional passing car's headlights were reflected in the metal-framed glasses of the woman who was talking with me. The sambadrome — a gigantic stadium built especially for watching the carnival — shone brightly in the distance, roaring with delight at the parade, and other middle-aged women were dancing there, in fantasy dresses, glowing with the expensive joy of looking happy for at least a half hour, before falling down in exhaustion back here. They call women in these dresses *bajanas,* that is, women from the province of Bahia, but at the carnival in Rio their dresses are merely stylized to look as if they came from that region, and most of the *bajanas* are actually from the slums of Rio, the *favel.*

"This fantasy cost me two thousand cruzado," the woman said. "My husband makes eight hundred, nine hundred a month, and only when there's work. He does whatever comes along: dockworker, painter, garbage man. When there is work, he does not drink, but when there isn't, he sometimes does. He drinks on credit, and then he has to pay it back. So it's hard. And we have five children. Don't think I use his money for the 'fantasy.' I earned it myself; it took a whole year. And just imagine — I didn't have enough for the buttons. It was almost carnival time. My husband started drinking. I went to the neighbors, but no one had a cent. One neighbor offered me money, but not for nothing. Son of a bitch. He had bothered me when I was young, and now he's old and I'm old, but his pride is still bothering him, I guess — he wants to make me a sinner even in my old age. A woman helped me out — she took the buttons from her old, rotting wedding dress. Nice buttons, eh? Of course, I don't have enough money, so we'll have to sell the dress after the carnival. Maybe I'll be able to get half price."

"Are you going to make a new one for next year?" I asked, astonished by her simplicity and frankness, of which usually only children and the very strong are capable.

"Well, and how else, senhor?" She was sincerely surprised by my question. "What would Brazil be without a carnival?" And then she asked her own question, "Did you notice me at the sambadrome when I was dancing?"

"Yes, yes, I did. You were wonderful," I hurried to say and then thought that maybe I wasn't even lying. With my press pass dangling on my chest, I sort of danced to the sounds of samba on the sidelines of the *pasarella,* using two cameras, and sometimes moving into the midst of the moving, dancing flow, from where

I was plucked unceremoniously but fairly by the guards, to keep from being underfoot. I think once through my lens I saw her or a similar face with glasses in a copper-wire frame, and eyes like black stones washed by the sea, young eyes generating such maidenly radiance that it seemed to wash away the treacherous wrinkles. Now, after the carnival wildness, the lines had returned, the body had lost its lightness, and weariness came like a hangover after the feast of sound and colors. The next day the routine would return, care for the children, arguments with her husband, getting money. It was far to go home and there was no transportation, and her rubbery legs would not get her to the favel sticking to the sides of the hills. The windows in the favels also glimmered that night, but the favels resembled a dim glow, enviously looking down at the diamond necklace of the carnival lights in the big city. And the black daughters of the favels, transformed once a year from Cinderellas to princesses under the projector lights of the *pasarella,* lay exhausted on the grass, having left the kingdom of light, music, and applause, and I thought that their dresses were going to turn back to rags at any moment.

I went back into the sambadrome, and the carnival drew me into its foamy, bubbling whirlpool. The carnival begins long before carnival. Every samba school prepares a new song. First the beat of the song's theme is established. Then the lyrics and music are written — usually by amateur poets and composers. In Rio there are sixteen regional samba schools and each prepares about five thousand dancers and singers. When the songs are written, the lyrics are learned with the music. Poverty still not dressed up in fantasy, unemployment still not disguised by peacock feathers, they learn the songs with their whole bodies, rehearsing and holding little pieces of paper with the words. Musicians play the drums on the smoky balconies of the dance halls, increasing the rhythm until the dancers are in ecstasy, as if around a campfire somewhere in the jungles of Africa. At rehearsals they settle on a final beat and on the voices and movements. The words are an amazing *batida* (a blended cocktail) of high-flown sweetness and a dash of stinging salt.

Here are a few sample lyrics:

São Clemente,
Full of cops,
Full of thieves,
Full of sorrow.
There's no tomorrow.
Life is a deathly somersault.
We're the kings of the asphalt.

I'm sick of being tricked
I'm sick of demagogues.
I'd like to fill
My belly, for I'm hungry still.

The rehearsals end. Helicopters cruise over Copacabana beach, pulling advertisements for carnival. Hotel prices double. Journalists crowd the doors of carnival headquarters to get accreditation. Tickets are scalped. And in the favels women are sewing their dresses just so that they can get out of their semihungry quotidian life for a short time under the lights of the *pasarella*. They line up for the parade. What an array of costumes: Jesuses with fake beards and glittering white wings, mulatto women from the tobacco factories dressed as the Statue of Liberty — about a hundred of them, each with a battery-operated torch — Mickey Mouses, and fabulous monsters. But the most beautiful are the *bajanas*. Middle-aged, and some simply old, they spin in blissful oblivion, using the samba for revenge against their irretrievably lost youth. Brazilians dance so beautifully, they use every throbbing sinew in their bodies. The carnival parade began around eight and ended around nine the next morning.

As a nation the Brazilians represent a unique mixture of Indian, Portuguese, and African blood, but the carnival tradition came from the African villages from which the colonialists took their slaves. Humiliated, bound by visible and invisible chains, the children of African tribes superstitiously kept their only freedom, the freedom of song, and the only human right, the right to dance. The rhythm developed from the swing of axes, oars, machetes, out of the genetically encoded tom-toms of their homeland, lost forever. Carnival, which filled the streets like floodwaters, was gradually channeled into the sambadromes and industrialized. In the provinces that did not work, but the old-timers of Rio complain that carnival used to be more spontaneous and populist. Carnival is expensive only for those who make their own costumes. But there is a new and intriguing profession — carnival businessmen. They say every carnival brings at least 300 million cruzados.

One left-wing Brazilian writer called the annual carnival "the national narcotic." Of course, despite this extreme opinion, he was under the head-spinning spell of the samba during the carnival, and his whole body — shoulders, hips, and feet — unconsciously moved to the music, despite the resistance of his critical mind. He was the one who said to me, "We Brazilians expend so much energy on the carnival that we don't have any left for revolution. The only way there would be a revolution in Brazil is if the government bans carnival."

Yes, it is true that no government ever risked trying it. On the contrary, they tried to make the carnival serve a political end, by distracting people from politics. Carnival is used as an advertising billboard to hide the favels. During periods of dictatorship the fantasy dresses, swirling in the samba beat, became a live curtain to hide the prisons. Behind the clouds of those dresses, as if behind a smoke screen, former Nazis, with plastic surgery and forged papers, quietly sat on their remote jungle haciendas, sipping Munich beer, whose foam was the breeding ground of fascism. Just before the carnival, Latin American newspapers were full of a sensational report. An Argentine businessman was offering material for a gigantic sum allegedly proving that Hitler and Eva Braun had quietly lived all these years in Argentina and had died only the year before. Apparently, this was a hoax, like the Hitler diaries. But there were so many fascist criminals who were thought dead and turned out to be alive! Yes, the woman from the favel paid a high price for her "fantasy" dress. But what was the cost to humanity for the bloody fantasy of so many tyrants, executioners, and enslavers, most of whom did not pay with their lives? . . . Think how much Stalin's grim fantasy cost our people!

Not far from Brazil, the Paraguayan dictator Alfredo Stroessner continued his prolonged political carnival for many years. During the Pope's visit to Chile, Pinochet dressed up in a carnivallike snow white uniform to match the Pope's robes, and tried to look like an innocent lamb. Sweet, exhausted woman from the favel, you have the right to your fantasy, because you're the only one who has to pay for it. But what right do those who imagine themselves the makers of history have to their fantasies, for which innocent people must pay, losing their freedom of choice, of conscience, no longer their own masters.

The day after the carnival the sun rose over Rio, a blinding golden disc. The sun's rays picked up the spangles that had fallen from the costumes, and the trampled masks, and fishermen pulled nets from the sea filled with fish that sparkled like decorations from the carnival. Only the huge statue of Christ, arms spread above the city from the pedestal of a mountain peak, was wrapped in fog, and he appeared and vanished, and above his head flew Boeings and Caravelles, and it seemed that they had spangles from the carnival stuck to their wings.

And despite the warnings that I could be robbed or killed in the favels, I went with two Brazilian friends to the hovels from which white clouds of fantasy dresses came down to the valley, today melted like dreams. At the entrance to the shantytown stood a police car, and the guardians of the peace, armed to their teeth, looked at us as if we were mad. But I've never feared poverty since childhood, and I always feel comfortable with slum dwellers, always safer than in some literary restaurant where you can be stabbed with a knife of insult at any moment and for no reason. The favela's elder walked with us along the hills sprinkled with little houses made of plywood, or old planks, or the richer ones out of mismatched brick and stone. I was struck by how even poor people tried to ornament these crooked streets with paper garlands and liven up their wretched hovels with flower beds. People were friendly because they could tell we had neither the tourist's indifferent curiosity nor any evil intentions, and the children followed us in droves, banging bamboo sticks on wooden pails and tin cans, as if they were drums. Two little girls ran home to change into their carnival clothes. The girls looked like two live spangles from yesterday. They beckoned to me, sat down next to a lopsided, listing fence, and showed me a magic grass, called *dormidera* ("sleepy grass") here. If you just touch it, it curls up in self-defense, protecting its brief green life. The girls touched the grass with their fragile fingers and sang, *"Dormi, dormi, dor-midera"* ("Sleep, sleep, sleepy grass").

"Would you like to see our princess?" one of them asked. "But I have to get her permission. You can take her picture."

We went to a tiny, almost toylike, shanty made of crate wood, half grown into the ground. The girl looked in, whispered a bit, and then said, "The princess permits."

I looked in and saw a young black woman sitting on a pile of rags in a crate house about two yards wide and a yard high. The woman was breast-feeding a tiny, sweetly slurping creature, and she smiled so shyly, and at the same time proudly, that the sun, peeping in through the tiny windows, seemed eclipsed for a moment compared to her majestic, embarrassed smile, deep inside the Virgin Mary shelter.

"Does she live here?" I asked the girl, carefully shutting the door.

"No, she has a house up there. . . . But she hides here when her husband gets drunk and beats her," she replied simply, like an adult woman.

"Why do you call her 'princess'?"

"Didn't you notice?" the girl asked in surprise. "She's not like everyone else. She really is a princess."

Then we met a girl of about seventeen, who wrote poetry, it turned out, and she invited us to her shanty and gave us coffee with such dignity and innate style, and she was so lovely with a rose tucked into the heavy black wave of her hair, and with deep eyes, carefully attending to every word of her guests, that I began persuading my bachelor Brazilian friend, Carlos Emilio, to marry her. She was thirsting to be faithful to the someone she would love, and I thought with pain about how that someone might start drinking and beat her, taking out his rage and frustration with his damned life, and beat her into a corner, like the black princess.

Then I played soccer with the Brazilian kids, and when I managed a goal, and a ricochet one at that, I was as happy as a kid — and why not, this was my first (and only) goal made in Pelé's homeland. And then I was taken to see the "mother of the favels" — a strong tall woman with penetrating eyes, who saw all your sins. She maintained a tiny and amazingly clean chapel, and in it she gave advice and diagnosed illnesses.

She didn't even want to examine me.

"Everything is fine with you," she said firmly. Maybe she only said it to make a guest happy? Thanks for that, too.

How did it happen that the favels have the reputation of being grim slums, where the air is imbued with killing, where no foreigner ever gets out alive?

The elder shook his fist wrathfully as he answered my question.

"Did you see the police car outside? The one on duty. Pretending to preserve order. But if you could see how they burst in here sometimes — but in several cars, not one — and pretending to search for stolen goods they rob us. They stole Amalia's only treasure, her TV. She's an old woman. At night cars come from the city and dump bodies of the people they killed and robbed down there in the big city. They want to blame all the crimes they commit on the favels. They say that all the people who live here are loafers and thieves. It's no fun being without work. Try to find a job, especially a steady one. Some start stealing because they have hungry mouths to feed. But the real big thieves judge the little thieves — thieves out of misfortune. . . .

"Of course, things are getting a little better. The new city authorities have opened schools where the children get breakfast and lunch. So now parents are sending children to primary school, eagerly, when before they sent their children to Copacabana — to beg from foreigners. Now that children are fed at school, there are fewer beggars. Why do you think seventy percent of Brazil is illiterate? Because the children have to earn their own keep — the parents can't feed them."

But the favels of Rio seemed almost paradise to me when I saw the favels on the water in Salvador. Ruins covered with rusty metal barely stood on poles, like thin, desiccated legs, over stinking mud. We walked along the shore, followed by hungry children in rags, asking for nothing. The scariest poverty is when you don't even have the strength to ask for anything. The air was filled with such toxic fumes that I couldn't breathe after an hour. Yet the people who live here breathe that air from infancy. We continued on our way, but a kindly old woman stopped us.

"You can't go farther," she said. "The favels start up there."

My God, she didn't even consider these pathetic huts on poles over concentrated sewage to be a slum! The real favels, she felt, were where there wasn't even a pathetic imitation of houses, but only tents without floors, with roofs of pieces of tin. It's awful when people are brought to a condition in which they cannot understand that they are miserable. I had traveled four thousand kilometers by car through Brazil, and that was just a tiny part of it. It is one of the most beautiful countries in the world, reminding me of Georgia in the mountainous areas. The power of open space overwhelms you, the harsh majesty of the cliffs combines with the tender, soft curves of the valleys, and the trembling flames of the flamboyant trees' red torches embrace with the gigantic purple spirit lamps of the bougainvillea.

Latin America sometimes reminds me of a beauty being raped on a dark night by drunken, bestial bandits.

Among the crazy, ambitious, and criminal fantasies there is a great fantasy of human brotherhood, a world without borders, without bureaucrats, without exploitation, without wars. This fantasy may have cost more than any other. It may be the only fantasy worth that price. But its price will be justified only if that great fantasy comes true.

Divided Twins (1988)

I WAS FLYING in a Soviet border patrol helicopter over the Bering Strait in November 1987 — over that narrow strip of water between America and Russia. There were ice floes in the strait — large ones and small ones, some resembling polar bears, some marble sculptures by Henry Moore. The helicopter was flying rather low, and I noticed a tiny dot below, zigzagging, leaping, halting. "A sable," said the pilot, lowering his binoculars. "Must be off to visit his relatives in America."

The sable must have gotten into trouble when the current broke off a piece of ice and carried it out to sea. But the sable didn't give up, and jumped from floe to floe as they approached. It was the dance of a free creature fighting for its life, a dance between two social systems, a dance between two potential nuclear strikes. Sniffing the wind, the sable could probably smell, among the ocean scents of iodine and the fur of walrus and reindeer, the steely taste of the traps hidden in the snow and the dangerous oily aroma of the guards' guns — on both shores. The sable, of course, did not know that the border guards belonged to two completely different worlds — both sides' guards were equally dangerous to the sable, they were just wearing different uniforms — but the sable knew perfectly well that either group would gladly skin it — on either shore.

The strip of water between America and Russia was just water to the sable, not a border. Borders do not exist for whales, as they salute both shores with white fountains of spray, or for walruses, as they lie majestically on the ice. Nature does not recognize the borders we humans erect. By inventing borders and then honoring them, we betray nature. Inventing state borders is a violation of moral borders.

Why is it that in folk songs of all nations and all ages people express the desire to become birds? Because birds know no borders. People are mortally envious of animals for their freedom, and probably that is why we try to deprive them of it by forcing borders on them — be they the barriers of a zoo, the bars of a circus cage, or the transparent but still prisonlike walls of an aquarium. People insult their one God-given planet with impassable fences (which Robert Frost described with such bitter irony) — with barbed wire, with iron or newspaper curtains. This division, the separation of the earth's surface, turns into mutual verbal and physical cannibalism. Our lack of knowledge of each other is like that of a blind sculptor, dangerous in his aggressive naïveté, who creates figures of so-called enemies.

The wall between the two Berlins became a horrifying symbol of the twentieth century. But people's longing to connect is greater than their fear of each other. We have genes not only of fear but also of a childlike desire to "sniff" each other, to rub against each other's fur.

Capitalist "punks," with hair like cocks' combs and with red metal stars attached to their torn jeans, regard the so-called neutral zone from the wooden observation platforms in West Berlin. Socialist "punks" wildly applaud the rock and roll that comes over the wall, which is not so impenetrable after all.

The Bering Strait, where the lone sable made its way leaping from ice floe to ice floe, is the Checkpoint Charlie of the North, and its watery neutral zone is also not without danger. They say that almost all the prisoners who tried to escape from Stalin's camps to America were either turned in by the Eskimos and Chukchi (who were paid in gunpowder and bullets) or froze to death or drowned in boats riddled by the machine-gun fire of the border patrol.

Of course, during World War II, American aircraft flew across Alaska and Siberia to Moscow. (In one of them was Lillian Hellman, who fell in love with a Soviet pilot — he later disappeared, and we can guess to where.) I was living in my Siberian hometown of Zima Junction in those days (about three hundred kilometers from Lake Baikal), and the planes sometimes landed in our small airport. Americans paced our wooden sidewalks, their bright yellow high-topped shoes squeaking, and gave us chewing gum, which we thought was candy.

The favorite foreign actresses of our childhood were Vivien Leigh and Deanna Durbin. But the Russian-American honeymoon ended soon after the victory, and the Cold War iron curtain came down over the Bering Strait. Only the most daring Eskimos found holes in it, or drilled them, passing the border zone under cover of thick fog to visit their relatives. To this day you can find an American Winchester in a *yaranga* [fur tent] on the Soviet side or a bottle of Soviet vodka, marked Petropavlovsk-on-Kamchatka, in an igloo on the American side.

I found an empty bottle just like that in 1966 in Point Hope, in the igloo of an old Eskimo widow. The bottle hung from a rope in the corner with a candle in its mouth that burned with a flame trembling religiously. The old woman said that she used to have an Orthodox icon in that corner but had sold it. She said that now she prayed to the empty bottle, because it was a gift from her relatives on the other side of the strait.

It is paradoxical and sad that on the American side many wooden Russian churches have survived, while not a single one has on the Soviet side. Those precious architectural monuments were destroyed by our ultrarevolutionary nihilism. The Cold War, which turned us into "enemies," destroyed the historical ties between the twins — Alaska and Siberia. That was against history and against nature. The unnaturalness of that fatal political separation, combined with an equally fatal geographical proximity, led to the idiotic act of cutting off water and air routes between Alaska and Siberia. Now, a resident of Fairbanks has to travel twenty hours via New York and Moscow to reach Bukhta Provideniia, which is twenty minutes away.

The eighty-six kilometers of the strait began to resemble a gi-

gantic, icy Sahara. Discovered by Russian explorers in the six-
teenth century and sold by the tsarist government in 1867 for $7.2
million, Alaska, though physically staying in the same place, was
torn away by a cruel hand from its blood sister, Chukotka, and
from all of Siberia.

The climate and the flora and fauna of Alaska and Chukotka are
so similar that to develop the natural resources or protect the
environment of one without consideration of the other is economically stupid. Once there used to be a Russian-American Company, created by our ancestors back in 1799, to do that. But all
this was gradually forgotten. Though they remained geographi-
cally unchanged, Alaska and Chukotka grew catastrophically farther apart. The divided twins floated farther and farther away,
and on their shores sables whimpered anxiously, standing on the
spines of whales.

In 1966 in Fairbanks, the local university poets told me their
dream — to chip in and buy a cheap used plane, repair it, and fly
off without any permission to visit the poets of Petropavlovsk-
on-Kamchatka. Shivers went up my spine when I pictured what
this lovely idea could lead to. In Alaska, my American friend
Albert Todd, a professor at Queens College, and I did rent a small
plane for a few days. The owner was a former military pilot who
had escorted transports of food to Murmansk during World War
II. He looked a lot like James Dickey, with a bull neck and beet-
red cheeks. He was sentimental, and during our flights he liked
to reminisce about the war, sipping from a tubby gin bottle.

Once, over the Bering Strait, he practically wept.

"Listen, Eugene, I really miss you Russian guys so much. We
used to drink vodka by the cistern in Murmansk. Let's go visit
your border guards for a couple of hours. . . ."

He wasn't joking. His hairy arms, like two gorillas, were already turning the wheel, and I barely managed to stop him, knowing that it was very unlikely we would be taken for peace doves.

In a bar in an Alaskan town, where soldiers from the missile
base danced with drunken Eskimo girls of fifteen and sixteen, I
met an American major who shouted in my ear over the jukebox
sounds of Elvis Presley.

"Eugene, have you ever been in the army?"

"Like Elvis was," I admitted.

"Then you don't know a damn thing about the army. You probably think that all professional military men are killers, but that's not true, Eugene. The professionals hate war even more because they know what a bitch war is. Let me draw you something on this napkin. Recognize it? That's your Chukotka. And here's your missile base, just like ours. And I'm certain that there are nice Russian guys there — just like ours. But we're aiming at those guys, and they're aiming at us. Understand? Does that make you feel good, Eugene? Not me . . ."

The major and I drank a lot. So much that I'm not sure whether what came next really happened, or whether I imagined it. Maybe it's half truth and half a dream that resembles the truth. I remember a rather wide blacktop road down which the major drove a jeep, swearing and drinking from a bottle. Large snowflakes swirled like butterflies in our headlights. The lights hit the childishly boastful road sign that's possible only in America: Secret Missile Base 1 Mile. You can't make that up! I remember that road sign perfectly. We drove inside a barbed wire fence. Pugnosed boys with acne saluted respectfully, heels clicking but eyes laughing — they could tell that the major and I had had a few.

We drove deep inside until our headlights hit a missile, resembling a shark that had just surfaced from the bowels of the earth instead of the depths of the sea.

The major, reeling, got out of the car, walked over to the rocket, and struck its side with the bottle. "May you never fly, bitch!" He drank, leaving some whiskey for me. Then he pulled out a Polaroid picture from a plastic sleeve in his wallet and showed it to me: a green lawn, a white cottage, a wife who looked like Doris Day (the majority of officers' wives look like Doris Day — even Soviet ones), three kids in baseball caps. . . .

Albert Todd, who was a witness to the start of our drinking but then went off to bed, now expresses doubts about my nocturnal visit to an American missile base.

"Forgive me, Zhenya," he said. "Of course our American secrecy is no match for the Soviets, but still, it does exist. . . ."

Nevertheless, Albert Todd went to bed and the major and I

didn't, and the more time that passes the more I both doubt this story and believe it.

I recalled it twenty-one years later, in November 1987, in Chukotka, when I flew along the Bering Strait in the border patrol helicopter and the lone sable leaped from ice floe to ice floe between America and Russia, reminding me a bit of myself.

The commander of the helicopter was what we call an "Afghaner," that is, a veteran of the Afghan war, and to tell the truth, I had some prejudices against him at first. Just recently I had been told a story about the murder of a bill collector in Moscow. The robbers shot him in the stomach. One of them asked, "Well, is it all right?" The other replied, "Fine. Just like in Afghanistan . . ." He was sure that the collector was dead. But the man lasted a bit, long enough to tell the police about this bit of dialogue. That's how they found the killers, our former "blue berets."

But this Chukotka Afghaner — a handsome man with a dreamy, bitter sensitivity, still young but already middle-aged — had an innate dignity and an astonishing storytelling gift. He was a professional who hated war, the kind the American major on the other shore, so close and yet so far, had told me about.

I asked him what had been his most frightening experience in the Afghan war. He thought, and said that it was when he was sent without any explanation from Kabul to Tashkent on New Year's Eve, and he had been certain that it meant at least a military tribunal. He didn't know for what, but an excuse could always be found. However, he was taken straight from the military airstrip to a hotel, given a room key, and, up in the room, he found a bouquet of flowers, orders from his commander to celebrate the New Year in the homeland, and a restaurant reservation. He obeyed orders and went to the restaurant, but he was unhappy and scared amid the laughter and congratulations, and his only thought was of his comrades, who perhaps were dying at that very moment for nothing.

He had been in Afghanistan several years ago, but he flew over Chukotka with that unceasing war in his heart, that war which will not cease inside him even when it does come to an end, God willing.

He had an astonishing sense of the beauty of nature, that

Chukotka Afghaner, maybe because he had come so close so many times to being killed. His own life, and everything he saw, was an undeserved and priceless gift. He and the American major would have understood each other perfectly, because the latter had come close to being killed in Korea many times.

I opened the helicopter window and photographed as we flew, my hands growing numb and my neck twisted at a bizarre angle. The Afghaner piloted the helicopter amazingly well; it felt as if he were turning Chukotka itself, with its incredible, piercing blue skies and its snowy hills that were shadowed even in daytime, when golden strands of sunshine rarely dropped through the purple clouds.

We were at a whale cemetery — exactly like the one I had visited once in Alaska, where the black rainbows of bones seemed like an architectural requiem for everything that finds even the oceans too small. We saw the skulls of polar bears, piled into a strange altar that was like nothing I had ever seen.

A white partridge, like a puff of frosty steam from my mouth, fearlessly sat at my feet, its beady eyes staring at me with curiosity. We went to a walrus rookery, and before we saw it, we smelled it — the harsh musky odor was powerful. About fifteen hundred walruses lay on the gravel in a single reddish-brown mass, their majestic, stalactitelike tusks shining. They looked like huddled hills. They were strong, and any one of them could have squashed a man with a camera who brazenly got within ten yards of them. If they all fell on me, I would disappear without a trace.

The walruses' genetic memory tells them that their most dangerous and treacherous enemy is man. A sentry walrus let out a warning bellow and the walruses headed for the water, their bodies billowing and raising dust. They were more mobile in the water than on land, which punished them with gravity. But once in the water, they felt safer, and curiosity replaced fear. Walrus heads with bright brown eyes bobbed in the waves. I had the feeling that a time machine had carried me to the beginning of the world.

And I remembered bitterly my 1963 trip on a hunting schooner in the Bering Strait, when someone set up a tape recorder on deck playing "Santa Lucia," performed by the celebrated Italian wunderkind Robertino Loretti. The sweet song attracted the denizens of the briny deep, and a seal's head with feminine, delighted, and curious eyes immediately popped up over the side.

Someone stuck a rifle in my hands and shouted: "Shoot!" I shot and what had just been alive, sentient, and radiant floated up dead, bloodying the water around it. The schooner went on without stopping. "We don't take the first kill," said the captain in response to the question in my eyes.

I had a similar experience when I killed a goose flying over the Vilui River, and, as God's punishment, the goose fell right into our boat into my hands. But that was just the start of the punishment, for the second goose circled above the boat that held his fallen brother for the rest of the day, crying, as if his cries could resurrect the dead. I almost stopped hunting after that. And I had never killed a man. What do people experience when they kill another person? Why don't they give up hunting men — why don't they give up war?

Of course, we musn't idealize love of animals — especially when it's just for show. They say Hitler loved cats and Goering loved dogs, which did not stop them from killing and torturing so many people. But cruelty to animals is training for cruelty to people. Recall the Spanish infante Philip, from Charles de Coster's *Till Eulenspiegel,* who placed live cats inside his harpsichord. Each key had a needle and when the keys were pressed, the cats meowed piteously. What did the infante's childish games lead to? The bonfires of the Inquisition, where he burned not his own pet monkey but heretics.

Soviet newspapers constantly criticize the USA for its propaganda of violence and cruelty. American newspapers criticize the USSR for violations of human rights — that is, for cruelty in the realm of the spirit. But here is the Bering Strait, separating our two countries, where there is the same number of incidents of cruelty to animals on both sides. The vicious slaughter of walruses, who are powerful but at the same time helpless and defenseless. The clubbing to death of baby seals, whose eyes fly out of their sockets and stick to the aprons of their killers. The skinning alive of dogs for hats, because the fur lasts longer that way. The shooting of wild deer from helicopters, the escaping pregnant does dropping their fetuses in terror, making it easier to run. The treating of domesticated deer like pigs, doomed to slaughter. The catching of fish with gill nets. The destruction of whales, which continues despite all public outcries and publicity campaigns. Do the whales commit mass suicide in order to awaken human conscience?

Listen to Paul Winter's "ecological jazz," where he mimics the songs of the whales, which sound like prayers to keep us from killing them! Could we really be practicing our cruelty on animals out of an instinct for preservation of that cruelty, which will be useful in a war against those like us? Wouldn't it be better to forget, to expunge the art of cruelty both toward animals and toward people from our genetic memory so as to lower the chances of mutual cannibalism?

Alaska and Siberia, the unjustly divided twins, could set a great example by reuniting. At the end of the twentieth century, hopes we had not dared to hope have appeared at last. The diplomacy of diplomats tricked us in many ways, but a new "citizens" diplomacy has appeared. This diplomacy has been extremely successful, just as the actions of partisans during wartime are sometimes more important than those of the regular army.

In 1987, an Englishwoman was the first person to swim across the Bering Strait, her body magically uniting America, England's prodigal daughter, with the semi-Asiatic, semi-European Russia. That same year an American ship first sailed from Alaska to a Chukotka port. That year for the first time Alaskan Eskimos officially set foot on Soviet soil. That same year residents of Kodiak in Alaska proposed a permanent exchange of people and ideas with the Chukotka city of Anadyr.

"The people of Anadyr and Kodiak have much in common. The most important is love for our cities and our hopes for a happy future for our children. We understand that in case of nuclear war everything we hold dear will be destroyed; that is why we would like to unite, to create communication bridges." That's what the citizens of Kodiak wrote to their Russian neighbors in Anadyr.

. . . The sable was still running along the Bering Strait, balancing on the ice floes and risking falling into the water. The sable had no idea that invisible bridges were being built on both shores. . . .

There used to be a song, "What about Siberia? I'm not afraid of Siberia. Siberia is part of Russia. . . ." The song was a response to all those who thought that Siberia was nothing but a gigantic snowy prison. But before there were exiles there, people ran off to Siberia seeking freedom. Those refugees became the conquerors of Siberia. They brought to Siberia a free spirit that could not coexist with the torture chambers of the Kremlin but that found space over the Ural Mountains. The seeds of European culture, of the aristocrat Decembrists, and the rebel Polish intellectuals fell on fertile soil in Siberia, plowed by the unruly Cossacks and peasants.

My ancestors had been exiled to Siberia for setting fire to their landowner's house, and it took them almost a year to walk to Lake Baikal in leg irons that chafed and scraped. Family tradition has it that my great-grandmother killed a tsarist village constable with a blow of her fist — she was a powerful woman. Both my grandfathers were revolutionaries, and both of them ended up in Stalin's Siberian camps after the revolution. They say that along the Kolyma River alone there were several million people in the camps.

But ever since my childhood I saw more than prisons in Siberia — for me it held a secret treasure house of freedom. There is truth in the saying that a man is nowhere as free as in prison. Where I grew up, in Zima Junction, the greatest crime was turning an escaped prisoner in to the authorities. If anyone ever did turn a prisoner in, he was soon found dead himself.

Another major crime in Siberia was not sharing. Not sharing a roof, some bread, or bullets or matches. During World War II Siberia fed millions of people evacuated from front-line cities and gave up its sons to the war. Moscow was saved by Siberians. After Stalin's death, Siberia's young people took down Stalin's camps with their own hands. The poet who was the first to call Stalin a murderer died in Siberia. The poet who was the first to once more call Stalin a murderer thirty years later was born in Siberia.

. . . The sable still ran from floe to floe. A close look revealed that the animal limped — the mark of an old trap. . . .

Zoya Nenlyumkina, the only Eskimo woman poet, is not running anywhere; she walks carefully, sideways, and performs actions that seem strange to outsiders. She came to my hotel in Bukhta Provideniia and read this poem written in her native Naukansky dialect.

Autumn.
A long, thick snowfall.
The raven cries out:
Brrrrother.
Me?
You?
And a half-legend
Half-story
Saved by the people
Comes to mind.
How house after house
Emptied horribly,
How families were tormented
By hunger
And the land from under the snow
Without strength
Strove for warmth, like black flesh.
But no matter how the shaman begged at the sky,
The warm rain did not fall
And only death stirred the ashes.
Great-grandfather remembers the bitter time . . .
How many were killed by hunger in September . . .
The raven survived
Side by side with the dwelling,
Fed by Eskimo food,
Miserable,
Accidental,
But it helped him last till summer.
The snow melted.
Rivers and buds opened.
The sun poured blossoming on the earth.
The raven flew, a black dot, into the sky.

My great-grandfather did not leave the dwelling.
But in his cares,
In his brief joys,
Taking his eyes from the land,
He followed the flock of birds,
And waited, maybe
The raven would come back.
Autumn. The colors say good-bye.
Hoarfrost. Ice and gray.
Winter lays down its snows
And it's long, oh so long!
And the raven, they say, came back
Years later, flew back
To his savior's yaranga
And his feathers were gray . . .
With hoarfrost or . . .
Who knows!

. . . The sable runs on the ice floes, and Zoya's gray raven circles above it. . . .

"Why are you so sad, Zoya?" I ask the Eskimo poet.

"Our language is dying," she replies. "And is there even one ugly language?"

"No, Zoya, there are no ugly languages," I reply.

"Then if even one language dies, there is less beauty in the world," says Zoya, and then stops to think. "And you know what else? They're destroying our children with warmth."

"How's that?"

"Like this. As soon as an Eskimo baby is born, they take it from the mother's *yaranga* and put it in the dormitory, where it's warm. The child gets used to the warmth, to the radiators, and he grows weak. . . . And later, when he grows up, he goes out in the cold again, with the herd. . . . What kind of a herder of reindeer can he be? He dies in the cold. . . . Warmth is poison for people from the North. . . .

"Oh, we've been talking so long. . . . Will you walk me home?"

"Of course."

We walk a long time, through the whole village. We reach the city council. Right in front of the building, by the bus stop, two suitcases sit in the snow. The locks are broken and the suitcases are wrapped with clothesline.

"Here's my luggage from the village," Zoya says.

I was astonished.

"Zoya, we've been talking a long time — about four hours. You don't mean you left your suitcases all that time here in the snow, just like that?"

"Just like that," she replied. "Why, isn't it done?"

... The sable runs over the ice floes, and suddenly it slips. The water sucks the sable in, but the animal does not submit, its tiny claws holding on to the edge of the ice, and it hauls itself up this time. ...

The 1979 census showed just 1,278 Eskimos in Chukotka, and only 144 Yukagirs. They're the last Mohicans of the North. Zoya Nenlyumkina was right: "hothouse" conditions are murderous for northern children, for it weakens them, and once they get used to the warmth, the children are helpless in the white desert, in the howling blizzards.

But the nation has not died out, because there are those who cling to survivalist traditions. The *yaranga* is the best cradle of courage in the North. The snow-covered cones of the *yarangas,* made of deerskin, look like the breasts of northern Mother Nature. The tents are intelligently divided inside by skin walls. There is the entry, where most of the cold brought in by people is left; the dining room, where only a little cold penetrates; and the bedroom, where human breathing creates a trembling fortress of warmth. The oil lamps look like the mystically alive eyes of killed whales. And there are still those who know how to sew waterproof coats out of fish bladders. They make the children's union suits with a flap on the rear end out of the pelts of wolverines — because, the experts say, the wolverine's fur grows in such a way that it will keep frost from forming.

It is practically impossible to meet Eskimos dressed in the way they used to dress a century or two ago. You'll see Wrangler jeans under a sealskin coat, or moon boots on their feet, or earphones of a Japanese cassette player under a fox hat, or a calculator in the hands of the director of an animal-breeding sovkhoz.

But once our helicopter landed right in the middle of a reindeer herd, and out of the herd, as if out of the condensed fog of time, came a man dressed the way people must have dressed in the Stone Age. He had the face of a warrior armored against the cold, against gigantic snowy expanses, against the vanishing of his people. The face was hewn out of rock by an ax. Civilization had not touched that face, but in the depths of the eyes, hidden beneath an almost Neanderthal brow, lived the highly civilized instinct of survival, the civilization of interrelationship with nature, which had whispered so many of her secrets in his ear.

When I photographed him, I had the feeling that my Nikon and I were transported so far back in man's past that a still-not-extinct woolly mammoth would appear through the snow and trumpet a song of premonition of its death.

There still exist corners of the earth that are preserves of our prehistory, and there are still people who live as if there were no philosophy — just the philosophy of instinct — and no technology except the technology of survival. Most often these people have a greater moral purity. Lack of sophistication makes them more honest; lack of education more wise. I had a strange sensation before this human relic who came out of a herd of reindeer toward the enormous metal dragonfly that landed unexpectedly on the snow — I simultaneously pitied him and felt ashamed before him.

When the helicopter tore away from the ground, the relic man went back into the sea of reindeer, gray with frost, and dissolved in that sea, a ghost of mankind's childhood. He wasn't wearing a single modern article, not a single modern button, not a single modern thread. But there were threads connecting us, and we looked at each other like animals of the same species but of different periods.

. . . The sable miraculously scrambled out of the water back on the ice and shook itself. But the water had turned to ice on its sides and made it heavier. Now running was no longer just movement,

it was salvation — it was the only way to keep from freezing. Its little heart must have been beating wildly, forcing the blood beneath the fringe of its hoar-frosted fur, melting it with its desperate warmth. . . .

Now, about the Yukagirs — for that relic man might have been a Yukagir, judging by his features. Once they were a mighty tribe. But the tribe gradually weakened and thinned out, primarily because they were so kind. They say that the Yukagirs used to ask an animal's forgiveness before killing it. I recorded one such prayer, told to me by an old woman: "I know that you are as hungry as me, bear. I know that you have children, like me, bear. I know that you want to live, like me, bear. I know that my fire stick is longer than your claws, bear, and that our battle is unfair. Forgive me for all this, bear, and help me to kill you, bear." But the bears and other animals managed to get away during the long prayers of the Yukagir hunters, and the tribe began to die out.

. . . The sable warmed up running, realized it was saved, and recalled its dead companion, whose leg had been caught in a trap. She would have been proud of him. The sable thought that it would find itself another mate on the other shore, the American shore, and she should bear him a litter of tiny squeaking sables, and it ran even faster, as if it heard the call of an American female sable in the snowy wind. Her mate had been shot by an unsentimental hunter in the eye, so as not to spoil the pelt. . . .

Children of most of the peoples of the North — Chukchi, Eskimos, Kereks, Evens — surrounded me in the boarding school in the old Cossack settlement of Markovo. Markovo is an oasis in the tundra where humpbacked elk wander in forests filled with black currants and where the locals grow their own potatoes. You couldn't think of a better place for a boarding school, but it still reminded me a bit of an orphanage. As soon as the children hear a car outside, they all press their noses against the windows in the hope that it's their parents coming to take them home.

The children were dressed nicely in sweaters, scarves, stretch tights — city clothes — but as they looked at me their eyes glowed with the curiosity of baby sables regarding a large unfamiliar animal. When I asked the teacher if I could take the children outside for a picture, she clucked like a mother hen, concerned about the cold. "The children might catch cold, and our duty is to safeguard their health." But when she finally let them out, the children relished being in their natural element. I think their pleasure is captured in my photograph.

... The sable was gone from the ice floes spinning in the Bering Strait — only its footprints, like pearls flung into the snow, continued to float on the crumbling remnants of icebergs, far from the one who made the prints. ...

"What could have happened to the sable?" I thought aloud.

"He's in the States!" shouted the pilot over the noise of the engine, not having heard my question, but sensing my concerns. . . .

Bukhta Provideniia was preparing to celebrate the seventieth anniversary of the October Revolution, the Soviet Fourth of July. Near the town hall, where the Eskimo poet Zoya Nenlyumkina had calmly left her suitcases in the snow for four hours, carpenters were hammering a small wooden tribunal. Border guards with machine guns were drilling for the next day's parade, marching to the music of their band. The musicians looked so intent and solemn, you would think all of America was on tiptoe, listening to them across the Bering Strait. This was the very first parade on Soviet territory — seven hours before the parade in Red Square.

I celebrated in Sireniki — a Chukchi Eskimo village that was not so easy to reach. First we went by cutter from Bukhta Provideniia, then changed to military jeep. The jeep was so crowded with people that it reminded me of my life, where sometimes there isn't enough room for me. I was jammed, hemmed in from all sides, and my air was replaced with people's breath — vodka, onion, garlic, tobacco, and, occasionally, a child's gently milky breath. The jeep had turned into a cocktail shaker of human flesh, a steamy sauna, slowly crawling through the thirty-below air and snowy hills.

The passengers included two Eskimo beauties clutching their treasures to their chests — rock-and-roll records; a moon-faced

Chukchi bureaucrat with a jangling case of beer, the envy of everyone, on his lap; three drunken workmen with saws and axes wrapped in rags; new recruits, who looked like angels shoved into soldiers' uniforms; a specialist in the development of the North, nose buried in a book on Chinese economics, who kept nudging me with his elbow, "Wow!"; an elderly Chukchi woman with a fringed lampshade on her head, because there was no place else to put it; a faithful-looking officer's wife with four children tugging at her; a less-faithful-looking officer's wife with blue eye shadow, fire-extinguisher red lipstick, and so highly perfumed that the workmen next to her were beginning to get an alcoholic high; and last but not least, a militiaman sent to Sireniki to make sure people stayed sober during the celebrations and, for now, literally crucified by the crowd in the jeep.

I believe it was Pablo Neruda who said, "To become a first-class person, you must travel in third-class railway cars." If he had ever taken the northern jeep from Bukhta Provideniia to Sireniki, he would have sung the praises of this embodiment of democracy.

The celebration took place at the local club, and the agenda called for an official speech followed by a concert. To tell the truth, I had planned to skip the speech and tactfully had asked its author — the still very young director of the animal sovkhoz, who had a dashingly curled mustache like a prerevolutionary Cossack — how long the speech would last.

"About five minutes," he replied. "So be sure you're not late for the concert."

I thought he was kidding, but a miracle happened. The director, with bulletlike speed, noted the outstanding successes of perestroika. With an invisible scalpel he bravely cut open its failures so that their pus practically spurted into the audience. He launched a counterattack against the enemies of socialism abroad, and hailed the bastion of friendship of the peoples of the Soviet Union: the animal sovkhoz in Sireniki, where even though they had not met the quota for pelts, they were busily undergoing moral perestroika, in particular a struggle with alcoholism, as a result of which the radiant horizons of our future were rapidly moving closer. And all in five minutes!

After that volcanic eruption of information and enthusiasm, the young director heaved a sigh of relief and a minute later reappeared on stage as a member of the amateur choir, a role he clearly preferred to official speechmaker.

The parade in Sireniki was unique — almost the entire town took part, including the old people and the children. A column of marchers bearing red banners and colorful balloons went around the entire settlement, flanked by skinny sled dogs who howled to the marching band's music.

That night young Eskimos and Chukchis danced to rock music, and their cheeks were sprinkled with silver and gold, as if they were in some New York disco.

. . . With careful steps the Soviet sable approached an American sable and sniffed — it was a female. . . .

There is a monument in the city of Anadyr to the members of the revolutionary committee executed during the White Guards' takeover in 1920. When they were reburied in 1969, the pickaxes and shovels revealed bodies that had lain in permafrost for forty-nine years. The skin on their faces had miraculously survived, retaining the freshness of youth, as if they had fallen asleep the night before and were just waking up. But the miracle did not last long, and contact with the air made the skin shrivel, wrinkle, and decay. It was a tragically accelerated transition from youth to old age to death. . . .

. . . The female sable also sniffed the male. He had many smells about him that she had never known, but, most of all, he smelled of sable. . . .

On the Komandor Islands I came to observe the love games of sea lions. Their rookery is bounded by a wooden fence because, as opposed to walruses, they can get very angry and attack a human who shows tactless prurient interest. Of course, you can move around inside the rookery along a wall that resembles a fortress wall. But the sea lions are no fools and try to stay as far away as possible from the wall that reeks of the not-very-pleasant animals — humans. There is a way of getting inside — you climb into a huge wooden crate (called a tank) and move along, lugging the crate on your back. But it is dangerous, and there have been cases of the sea lions turning the tanks over and biting and beating the occupants with their flippers, almost killing them.

We should not be offended. After all, humans have been killing sea lions and seals for years in the most savage way, clubbing the babies to death. I decided against both the observation wall and the tank. I chose a third way — a precipitous cliff that overlooked the rookery. I scrambled to its edge and took pictures with my zoom lens.

Males were fighting each other in the sand for the right to love. The flirtatious females looked like wet shimmering question marks — who will win? The males, just recently fearless and ruthless with their rivals, suddenly turned shy and respectful, awkwardly poking their salty mustaches quivering with desire at the black button noses of their sweethearts.

The attitude toward the lone, old bulls, the former Don Juans of the ocean, was cruel. When they crawled over to push their way into someone else's lovemaking, they were harshly expelled from the invisible circle of love and pleasure, just desserts for the way they had treated the old bulls when they were in their prime.

In their sexual thrashing on the sand, covered with sea foam, sperm, and blood, the adults sometimes did not notice that they were crushing their calves to death. These little creatures killed by their parents' mating are called "crushlings" here. What a horrible and accurate word for our children, too, who sometimes are the victims of the unruly drives that can destroy our families. . . .

The most impressive part was not in watching the sea lions, but in listening to them. Their voices — tenderly purring, muttering sounds of love, rasping in growing passion, sighing in satisfaction afterward, grumbling at mates, angry with rivals, calling others into battle, trumpeting victory — blended with the pounding of the surf and the hiss of the lacy foam on the gravel into a symphony of the beginning of the world. . . .

. . . The Russian sable and his sleek American lady tumbled in the snow, squealing like children, and the Siberian snowflakes from his pelt moved onto hers, sparkling with the joy of not being alone. . . .

Red salmon were spawning in the Komandors, paying with their lives for the roe, a descendant hidden in each egg as if in a tiny lantern. The shores were scattered with dead fish — still red, but gradually turning dull, from pale pink to lead. Against the background of this cemetery, life danced wildly. Battalions of salmon, bursting with roe, were rushing upstream from Lake Saran into a tiny river that could not hold them all. The salmon dragged their bellies against rocks, crawled along the sand, jumped over obstacles.

The driver of our jeep picked up a salmon in his bare hands and squeezed ruthlessly. A red stream of roe gushed right into his outstretched hand.

The whole lake was being whipped up by the fins of other salmon, waiting their turn to break out. I ran into the water in my sneakers to the biggest concentration of fish and began taking pictures. The water around my stiffening feet seethed with fish, which looked like red-hot pig iron thrown into the water to cool off.

Old-timers told me I was lucky with the weather — it's usually rainy when salmon spawn, and today the sun showed through the clouds now and then.

I threw a coin into Lake Saran, so that I would return. That copper coin was my red egg.

. . . The Russian sable, tired after mating, rubbed against his American love, and his instinct told him their child was within her. . . .

I was not only born in Siberia, but I was reborn there each time I returned.

With my geologist and journalist friends, I have traveled five Siberian rivers — the Lena, Vilui, Aldan, Selenga, and Vitim — by motorboat, catamaran, and flat-bottomed *karbass*.

Once we ran aground on a rock in the middle of the Vitim, which was foaming like boiling water, and we were stuck there all night. Our little vessel creaked along the seams and threatened to fall apart every second. We drank, turned on the radio, and learned that Apollo had just landed on the moon. We sat in our falling-apart boat on a rock and stared into the starry cosmos above the Siberian taiga, and the Milky Way was like a heavenly Elba River across which the Americans, as they had during World War II, were offering us a fraternal hand.

In the early morning, the strongest man among us, the geophysicist Valerii Chernykh (146 kilograms soaking wet), managed to carry a rope to shore in waist-deep water that kept sweeping him off his feet. He tied the rope to a tree trunk and the rest of us came ashore holding on to the rope. Then we dragged our boat, the *Chaldon*, from the damned rock. So the Apollo, by keeping our spirits up, helped out the *Chaldon* back then without even knowing it. . . .

. . . It wasn't that the Russian sable didn't like America, but there were too many unfamiliar smells, too many unfamiliar paths, and too many traps with unfamiliar systems. At home, even though the traps were hateful, they were his own. That is, at the same time, more horrible and less horrible. . . .

We started our river trip along the Selenga in Mongolian territory and as we approached the Soviet border we politely radioed our border guards. They were very happy to have us and promised to meet us at the border, where they would grill shashlik on the shore for us and then hold a poetry reading for the garrison. Our boats, as if smelling the promised barbecue, surged ahead with inspiration, but a suspiciously long time passed without the sight of border guards with flowers in the muzzles of their rifles. At last our captain pulled out a map and determined that we were about forty kilometers inside Soviet territory. We turned back, against the current, and began looking for our courageous border patrol. The meat had to be reheated, but the poetry reading went very well.

Listing the local sights, an officer told us, "We have a war veteran here who has a personal letter from Stalin."

We permitted ourselves to express doubt. Then the officer took us to a hut with a glass-covered portrait of Stalin over the log gate. I have never seen anything like that anywhere in Siberia.

An elderly war veteran came out of the gate reluctantly.

"You really have a personal letter from Stalin?" I asked, trying to give my voice a neutral, semi-indifferent interest.

"I do," replied the man. "In gratitude for taking Orel. It's got my name, patronymic, and surname — all exactly correct. That's the way Stalin was — he knew all his soldiers by name. He was a respectful man. He signed it personally."

The man brought out his relic and showed it to me. He had been fooling himself, of course. Stalin's signature was rubber-stamped. I didn't bother to disillusion the old man with the truth — the truth would not help him. . . .

. . . The Russian sable said good-bye to his American girlfriend without much whimpering from either of them. She knew that if he did not leave with a farewell, sooner or later he would leave without one — that's how much he missed the other side, where he was born. She did not want to go with him because the land that was home to him might turn out to be frighteningly alien to her. And she did not have the right to endanger nature's seed growing inside her. . . .

I have often spoken of how much I hate borders. But I hate prisons even more. I don't think anyone hates prisons the way Siberians do. Beautiful Siberia was raped to turn it into a prison for all peoples. One of the happiest memories of my youth was the day when young people who had come to Siberia to work on construction sites after Stalin's death bulldozed the barbed-wire fortifications around former camps.

Once, in my hometown of Zima Junction, I asked for permission to see the inside of a strict-regimen camp. It was a prison for the most dangerous criminals, some of whom had committed several murders. Every one of them, however, told me that he was innocent, slandered, and asked me to help. It's a horrible thought if even one in a hundred men there was innocent, and that's possible through a miscarriage of justice and not even out of malicious intent.

Something else shook me up there, too. I was astonished by the amount of talent in the camp. There was an art show by the inmates. In one of the halls I saw a huge mural with a portrait of, arguably, Russia's favorite poet, Sergei Esenin, who hanged himself in 1930. Mayakovsky had once criticized him for weakness this way: "It's not hard to die in this life; making something of your life is significantly harder." Mayakovsky shot himself not long after. His line of poetry was a response to Esenin's eight lines below, written in blood:

> *Farewell, my friend, farewell.*
> *My dear, you are in my breast.*
> *The coming separation*
> *Promises a meeting.*
>
> *Farewell, my friend, not a hand, not a word.*
> *Neither grief nor sadness of your brows.*
> *Dying in this life is not new,*
> *But living, of course, is no newer.*

. . . The sable was lucky. In getting home over the floes, which were getting smaller and smaller, he managed one night to sneak aboard a fishing motorboat and hide behind a bucket of salted fish, listening to Chukotka Eskimo instead of Alaskan Eskimo, which was sprinkled with Russian words instead of English ones. . . .

Once when John Steinbeck was visiting me in Moscow, there was an unexpected knock at the door, and Uncle Andrei appeared, on his way south for a vacation with a plywood suitcase secured with ropes. Steinbeck, like a real writer, instantly forgot about me and concentrated on my uncle — for meetings between a Siberian truck driver and an American writer are still rare, unfortunately.

He asked my uncle if he had read his books. To my surprise, Uncle Andrei replied that he had read *The Grapes of Wrath* before the war, but it seemed to him that in the author's photo Steinbeck had a mustache but no beard. Steinbeck did not think this was enough. He demanded a plot synopsis. To my greater surprise, my uncle supplied it. Then Steinbeck asked him to name his favorite writer in the world. And my uncle floored me by naming Miguel de Unamuno. Steinbeck shed a tear, because it turned out that he had known Unamuno well and had loved him.

After Uncle Andrei's funeral, all the cars in Zima Junction sounded their horns for five minutes, united in a drivers' requiem.

Aunt Klanya is the grandmother of the husband of Aunt Zhen-ya's [widow of Uncle Andrei] granddaughter, Irina. She is the school watchwoman.

Aunt Galya is Aunt Klanya's daughter, the mother of Aunt Zhenya's granddaughter's husband. She is a pediatrician.

Elvira is Aunt Klanya's daughter. She works in the Party's regional committee.

Kolya is Aunt Zhenya's son, an electronics engineer.

Vova is Aunt Zhenya's granddaughter's husband, an engineer.

They are all my relatives, or my roots, or my branches. I will not chop off my roots, because then the branches will die.

A man's roots should be as deep as possible in his native soil, for only then can he embrace the sky with his branches.

My unrelated relatives who also brought me up are represented by the eighteen portraits of old Siberian women that I took during the filming of *Kindergarten,* the story of my Siberian childhood. The war was a harsh kindergarten for my generation.

I spent only a couple of hours with the conservator of Geyser Valley on Kamchatka. He led me, like Virgil, through the dangerously bubbling waters spewing from the center of the earth, which had scalded many a careless tourist. But I will remember him always for his devotion to nature. People like him are the personification of nature defending itself.

There were two marvelous men, road builders, who burst into my hotel room on the Selenga River, pulled off their shirts, and demanded that I photograph the artwork on their chests.

"Let all of America see us now!" one of them proclaimed. Well, I bow to their wishes.

I had wanted to photograph the Kamchatka women working in the fields. They agreed on one condition — that I first read my poetry to them. They came weary from the potato fields, bashful, flowers in their hands — after all, I was a visiting poet, defender of women, as Russian tradition demands. They sat on plywood crates and listened in a way that contained more poetry than all my poems. It was impossible to both read poetry and photograph my listeners. When I finished I asked them to "hold the mood," as movie directors put it, and they understood, and helped me take their pictures.

. . . Just as quietly and stealthily as he had gotten abroad, the sable jumped from the motorboat as it docked on Soviet soil and whizzed between the hawsers and barrels of oil, rushing toward his native, white, untracked haunts.

But as it ran past the whale cemetery, the sable stopped on its tiny pedestal — whale vertebra — and stared at the narrow strip of water between the two worlds. Suddenly it was drawn once more across the strait, even though that would mean a lot of leaping among the slippery and dangerously deteriorating ice floes. . . .

The Lotus Floats
to the Horizon *(1987)*

IN THE USSR, in the Urals, there stands a striped pole, with a sign on one side reading Europe and one on the other side reading Asia. I was born in Siberia, that is, I am an Asian. My psychology, like that of all Russians, is apparently half European, half Asian. Russia was under the Mongol-Tatar yoke for three hundred years and that had to have an effect on our national character. Historically, Russia's fate was to be a shield protecting the rest of Europe from invasions. Russia fell behind in development as a result and was the last country in Europe to emancipate serfs. Russian nationalists, who tend to be chauvinistic, always spoke up against the "Westernizers" and simultaneously raised a warning finger when speaking of the "yellow peril" from Asia. But Asia always attracted Russians as a mysterious, unknown world. The Russian artist and researcher Roerich even moved to India and converted to Buddhism. Prerevolutionary Russians had an enormous interest in Buddhist philosophy and it has grown again among contemporary young people, despite their profoundly materialistic education, or perhaps because of it.

Western activists against pragmatism also turn in their spiritual seeking to Asia — the British Beatles and the American Beat-generation poets, for example. Young men and women in Wrangler jeans and backpacks have become part of the Asian landscape.

After so many disillusionments — political and religious — they are drawn by Buddhism's tolerance and peace. The Buddha's embrace is wide. The fad for Mao jackets was a manifestation of left-wing snobbism, and passed quickly, but the pull of the East will not pass.

And not only is the West moving toward Asia, but Asia is taking steps to the West. Kipling once wrote:

Oh, East is East, and West is West, and never the twain shall meet

But his poetry (called imperialistic only by cheap interpreters), filled with love and lively curiosity about Asia, is a sign that the West is moving toward the East.

Japan, along with noticeably increasing militarization, is also the home of perhaps the most powerful peace movement on the earth. It was this country, which experienced the horrors of the atom bomb, that developed the brilliant metaphor with children making hundreds of thousands of paper cranes, ready to fly and protect humanity with their defenseless breasts against deadly missiles.

One of the best contemporary writers lives in Japan — Kobo Abe, who writes Kafkaesque descriptions of the dangers of standardization. The phenomenal growth of technology in Japan coexists with tiny apartments, with professional pushers stationed on platforms to squeeze people into crowded trains. Cattle is fed beer to make its flesh tender for sukiyaki. This Asian America is simultaneously superconservative and supercontemporary.

Even China, which used to seem as immobile as a gigantic dinosaur, is moving away from its traditional closedness and dogmatism. In 1985 in Shanghai I saw about thirty thousand people in line to see an exhibition of French Impressionists. Young Chinese artists, who had never seen a Van Gogh or Monet — even in reproductions — were scrupulously sketching the compositions into their notebooks. A Chinese biker carrying a Japanese color TV set on his back is an ordinary part of street life. Back from corrective labor camps, writers describe the horrible truths of the Cultural Revolution. Chinese translators, who had spent years shoveling manure on farms, secretly translated the best of European literature, hiding it from the Maoist police in their mattresses, and now China probably publishes more foreign literature than any other country.

When I visited Vietnam in 1986, after fifteen years, one of the writers who met me at Hanoi Airport said, "Fifteen years ago you recommended that we publish Gabriel García Márquez. We were a bit slow, that's true. . . . But here's his book. . . . And we're publishing Pasternak now, too."

Fifteen years ago the publication of those books would have been unthinkable, for militant propagandistic literature reigned. Art has changed, too. Vietnamese artists paint pictures that incorporate the ancient lacquer technique into surrealistic themes. However, as if under a bad spell, Vietnam still can't get rid of war — there are border skirmishes with China, battles with Pol Pot troops from Cambodia, and the eternal war with economic problems in the country.

Laos and Cambodia are the two countries most torn up by the never-ending jungle warfare, but they also strive for a peacetime culture, despite their isolation, and are gradually developing a new intelligentsia to replace those who were killed and those who left.

Burma, whose government holds probably the most openly isolationist position, declining both Soviet and American aid, also suffers from internecine partisan wars, and even on the tourist track once sung by Kipling — the road to Mandalay — the occasional bullets whizz by. This isolationism has its lovely rewards — Burma has saved its ancient cultural monuments like no other country, it has the most beautiful pagodas. When the restoration of one of the pagodas was announced, the people collected, I was told, fifteen tons of gold, gram by gram, piece by piece. But at the same time this isolation is a burden on the Burmese — it hinders their development, both industrial and spiritual.

Thailand with its Asiatic Venice — Bangkok — holds a unique place in Asia. Here is one of the freest presses in Asia (only the royal family may not be criticized) and one of the most economically open markets for the West. There is a sign at the airport claiming that everything in Thailand is 100 percent cheaper than in Europe. That is an understatement. For $30–$35 you can have a suit of pure wool, or silk, made in twenty-four hours; or, for

$50, superfashionable shoes of crocodile or iguana. Precious stones, polished brilliantly — especially rubies and sapphires — are not 100 percent but 300 percent cheaper than in Europe. The prices in Asia (with the exception of Japan) are generally astonishingly low, but only for tourists, for the average monthly salary is also astonishingly low. (In Vietnam it's 400 dong [$50], in Thailand, approximately $40, and in Laos and Cambodia, around $10–$12.)

Thailand has many good writers, who write in charming Thai, and Bangkok wants to become the literary center of Asia, holding writers' symposia. At one such gathering, where the Australian Morris West and I were guests of honor, it was clear that even writers from neighboring countries in Asia had a tragically poor knowledge of one another. Asia is not only striving to learn more about Europe, it is striving to learn more about itself. And when it discovers itself, when it takes stock of its strength and its talent, it will make a great leap forward, and who knows if Asia, today backward in many areas and torn by contradictions, won't be tomorrow's world leader?

The United States of Asia — the idea seems fantastic now, but who knows, who knows. . . . After all, even now over half the world's population is Asian. Wealth and affluence often weaken, decay, and self-destruct — just think of the Egyptian Pharaohs or the Roman Empire. But why look so far for examples — just recently the British Empire, having swallowed a fourth of Asia, was blown up from inside, like a frog trying to swallow an ox, and is once more confined to its island. The color of that island's inhabitants is getting darker from the influx of Indians, Pakistanis, and Africans, like a spontaneous colonization following the laws of historical revenge.

Crafts are phenomenally well developed in Asia — carving on wood and ivory, fabric and embroidery; while Europe and America are losing the talent of their hands, relying too much on machines. If today's backward Asian countries utilize the natural talent of their hands, which they have not lost, to master modern technology, the prospects of their development are enormous.

I was in Vientiane, in Laos, at a boat race. Afterward, in the twilight, the Laotians followed an ancient tradition and set paper lotuses carrying lit candles to sail in the waters of the Mekong. You had to make a wish and then watch anxiously how far your wish would sail.

I made a wish and lowered my lotus into the water.

Like a white star twinkling in the dark, it floated off, rocking uncertainly among hundreds of equally uncertainly glowing wishes. Some lotuses capsized on their own before they got very far from shore. Some went down under a big wave in the wake of a motorboat. Some were knocked over by rocks thrown from land by mean boys. My lotus kept sailing. I almost cried out when it was pushed up against the side of an anchored boat and then sucked under by the current. But it got out of it, as if imbued with a secret reason and will to live, pushed off from the boat and went on. I watched it a long time, as it grew smaller and smaller, until it looked like a tiny lightning bug and then dissolved on the fog-shrouded horizon.

Asia's fate is like that lotus with the fragile candle of hope burning in it. The lotus floats on the murky river of history amid so many corpses swaying in the waves. Bullets fly over that lotus, shells and bombs land around it, but it keeps sailing on. And if it manages to avoid all the obstacles or push away from them, it will reach the horizon.

Paintings Rolled into Tubes *(1981)*

IN THE SPRING of 1963 I was visiting Pablo Picasso at his house in the south of France.

The small, quick man, with the wrinkled face of an old, wise lizard who had left its tails many times in the hands of those who tried to catch it and train it, showed me his works. He didn't look at them, he watched me. His sly, curious eyes were taking me apart into my component elements and then putting me back in a different way, subject to his imagination. The frame of the *Rape of the Sabine Women*, painted in dirty pink shades, swayed, resting on an Eskimo sealskin slipper with a rolled up toe, worn on his bare foot. His hands, covered with gray but somehow merry hairs, moved with the speed of a conjuror, showing me mythological compositions in oils, then illustrations of Dostoevsky in ink, then rough pencil sketches. The confident and casual relationship between Picasso's hands and his works reminded me of the relation of a puppeteer's hands with his characters, brought out on parade with the help of invisible strings. The works danced in his hands, bowed, and vanished. . . .

"Well, did you like anything? Be honest. . . . What you liked I'll give you." Picasso's eyes drilled into me. I muttered honestly that I preferred his Blue Period to these late works.

Two young men with tense olive faces of underground revolutionaries who had not been introduced by name, apparently for conspiratorial reasons (Picasso had asked the reporter from *L'Humanité* not to photograph them), exchanged an even more tense look. Unexpectedly Picasso burst out laughing, demanded champagne, which appeared immediately on a tray in his wife's hands, as if it had been created before our eyes out of the genius's imagination.

"Mother Russia lives! It does!" shouted Picasso, waving his glass. "The spirit of Nastasya Filippovna, who tossed money into the fire, is alive.[1] Every signature of mine, even under a bad drawing, is worth at least ten thousand dollars!"

Picasso embraced and kissed me. He smelled of fresh apples and fresh paint. The two young men with tense olive faces rolled up three canvases that had been indicated by a gesture of the owner and without saying good-bye vanished with the tubes into the enormous world filled with prison and conspiracies.

1. Nastasya Filippovna is the hysterical beauty in Dostoevsky's *Devils*.

Exhibit at a Train Station (1978)

I ATTENDED A SHOW of the Bulgarian artist Svetlin Rusev. It was held inside what may be the most beautiful train station in the world, in Sofia. At first it seemed that the paintings were simply *above*. Above the Bulgarian peasant women waiting for a train, exhausted by the big city noise, their baskets and bags filled with the holy rubbish of purchases in the capital. Above the laborers, in whose heavy eyes the gray river of the conveyor belt still flashes or in whose ears the lathes still whine. Above the fragile girl student, a red petal of Rose of Bulgar sticking to the fringe of her jeans. Above all those who are leaving, arriving, waiting, meeting, seeing off, dying and being born, in the marvelous and exhausting chaos of the *mobile perpetuum* of human life, on the canvases hang the victims of the terror in Chile, crucified on bloodied barbed wire — and the suffering of distant Santiago, reflected in the eyes of Bulgarian peasant women, becomes part of the crowded Sofia station, filled with human breathing. The most wonderful part is when the peasant women, forgetting the weight of their bags, look at themselves as painted on the canvases, look in surprise and a bit warily, and perhaps for the first time think about themselves: who are we? The paintings cease being above, they slowly descend into the depths of human eyes, get into the train with people, and travel into the unknown.

I do not believe in art above. Either above the station or above the fray. Great art should not be ashamed of being exhibited in a train station. The train station of our life, filled with suffering and hopes, was described by Pasternak: "station, the fireproof box of my partings, meetings and partings. . . ." The artist's role in the station of life must not turn into the station policeman, or the shoe-shine machine, which for coins will lick even blood off the shoes of a killer, or the loudspeaker, or the tourist ad, or the poster. Art as an exhibit at the train station is the only opportunity to stop, even for a minute, the hurrying, nervous world, to make people come to terms with a re-created self, to stop and think: who are we?

You can not teach people to ask this question. Didactic methods have never improved people. A pompous slogan cannot penetrate as deep inside a person as a great painting; and even if it does penetrate, that is not good. Only self-examination, prompted by great art, makes us better people. This thinking is sometimes unpleasant, scratchy, painful, but shame on those who expect only "pleasure and recreation" from art. The great artists are not decorators of the world's suffering, not clever musical arrangers of cries and groans; they are the suffering, they are the cries and groans. Anyone who puts aside a "hard book" and replaces it with an amusing humorous or mystery novel is potentially morally dangerous. A person who rejects other people's suffering in a book could as easily turn away from suffering in life. Dostoevsky said, "We either feel horror, or pretend to feel it, while actually enjoying the spectacle, like fanciers of powerful, eccentric feelings that move our cynical idleness, or like small children we wave away horrible visions and hide our heads in the pillow until the horrible vision is gone, so that we can forget it in our games and merriment."

Once the poet Boris Slutsky said to me that he divides all humanity into three categories: those who have read *The Brothers Karamazov*, those who haven't read it yet, and those who will never read it. I pointed out that unfortunately the largest category was those who had seen *The Brothers Karamazov* on TV. People only think that they watch TV. Actually, the TV watches them. A turned-on screen is the unsleeping eye described by George

Orwell. The illusion of being everywhere when you are actually nowhere is frightening: you can quietly munch your hot dogs and sauerkraut and playfully caress your wife while on the screen Othello is suffocating Desdemona or people are being shot. The real screen into the world is a great book, because you cannot turn books on and off, even though attempts have been made. Such attempts are doomed to failure, because a great book is turned on forever.

Creating great books is torment, and it is torment to read them, because only great pain is the mother of great literature. But God grant that people be tormented only by art. Ingmar Bergman said that when we solve everything that seems like problems now, the real problems will begin. But we're far from that. The suffering caused by love of art is necessary suffering, which makes a person a person. We are still living in a world of unnecessary suffering, which demeans human dignity, in a world of suffering created by force and violence, including its bloody concentrate — war. They say even a bad peace is better than a good war. That is sometimes questioned. I say it is better, because at least people are not killing each other with bullets and bombs, not burning peaceful villages with napalm, not crushing them with tanks. But I do not agree that such a peace remains bad indefinitely, since war goes on even during a bad peace. It is more subtle, more hypocritical, because false propaganda is war, because betrayal of the interests of our own people and exploiting them is also war, because cynical politicking is also war, because terrorizing by fear of losing your job is also war, because bureaucrats in civilian clothes but militaristic in their nature are also war, because racism is war, because all forms of chauvinism, including anti-Semitism, are also war.

A world without principles is war pretending to be peace. You do not have to declare war against other people, or cross the borders of other states, to still be in daily aggression against your own people, forcing your way across borders of conscience. But every nation is part of humanity, and aggression against our own nation is aggression against all of humanity.

Humanity must not stoop to the morality of mafias, who agree not to produce one or another weapon but still have the right to use knives of slander and mistrust. We need not only a semblance of peace, but permanent peace on principle — that is the will of all people. And the principle that could unite humanity exists. The principle is man himself. I do not believe that we must speak to one another only in compliments about our societies — all societies are imperfect to some degree, just as human psychology is imperfect. None of us lives in paradise, and if it exists in the next world, no one has returned to this one to tell us of his impressions. But even as we tell hard truths to each other, we must do it like doctor colleagues bent on saving our world and examining its wounded body, and we must not help by a single word those who wounded humanity. Even the truth said with gloating is better than a lie.

Political profiteering polemics, when each side showers the other with rhetorical accusations, reminds me of the trial of Mitya Karamazov, when the prosecutor and the defense attorney both try so hard to express themselves articulately and garner applause that they forget the object of their argument — Mitya. And humanity, forgotten in these polemics, can only whisper as Mitya Karamazov did, "My soul feels bad, gentlemen . . . take pity."

When we are dealing with a living creature — humanity — writers must not become manipulators of other people's suffering to get applause, which is sometimes the result of rather dirty hands clapping. Each of us has his own professional style, but in dealing with one another we must maintain a single style — propriety. We must not imitate the howls of third-rate coyotes from the newspaper jungles, who try to pit writers of the world against one another, like Yellowstone grizzlies against Siberian bears. Even through the newspaper jungles, we, the writers of the world, must toss each other Mowgli's saving lines: "We're of one blood, you and I!"

Sometimes we writers fall into professional pessimism, doubting the effectiveness of our words: if even Dante, Shakespeare, Cervantes, Goethe, Tolstoy, and Dostoevsky did not manage to improve mankind, then what can we do? But that pessimism is unfounded. If humanity has a conscience, it is thanks to the great power of art.

T. S. Eliot once wrote a grim prophecy:

This is the way the world ends
Not with a bang but a whimper.

We must do everything we can with our words to keep humanity from getting to the bang. But our words must also do everything possible to keep humanity from whimpering.

And when in the train station of life we must board our last train, may our works glow on the walls of that station, like our testament to the living.

PART VI

Russian Geniuses

Brief Essays

Pushkin

Pushkin is the sum of Russia's mastery of world culture.

Pushkin is the homeland not only of Russian poetry but of the Russian soul. Dostoevsky was right when he said, "Pushkin did not try to guess how to love the people, did not prepare himself, did not study. He suddenly found himself being the people." If I could resurrect only one person, I would resurrect Pushkin. . . .

Tutchev

He had poetic genius, but compared to Pushkin, he lacked the mischievous human genius. Tutchev was too often constrained in a proper suit and it is absolutely impossible to picture him, like Pushkin, in a red shirt untucked, at the Kishenev bazaar with gypsies and bears. . . . But, then again, why did he have to be like Pushkin?

Baratynsky

To remain yourself next to a unique personality like Pushkin is also unique. Baratynsky lit his own torch, not a borrowed one, and went down into his soul, looked around, and said, to no one in particular and to everyone at the same time: ". . . why there's a man here . . ."

Dostoevsky

There are suppositions that Dostoevsky's profound insights into the dark byways and pits of human psychology can be explained by his epileptic fits, which, like lightning in a storm, illuminated for an instant the hidden corners of the conscious and subconscious. But perhaps it was the other way around — his penetrating vision revealed such horrible secrets to him sometimes that it caused his fits?

Saltykov-Shchedrin

How kind fate was to Russian literature, sending such a clever spy into the bureaucrats' camp, who managed not only to write his charming reports, but also serve as provincial governor!

Chekhov

Chekhov was an antisupermanist. He held people who were weak, deprived of passions and only dreaming of them, higher than any "strong personality" or "powerful passions." Calling Chekhov's prose the "defense of the little man" is inaccurate. According to Chekhov there are no little people, because there are no little passions or torments.

Nekrasov

After Dostoevsky's speech at Nekrasov's funeral, the students, among them the young Plekhanov,[1] cried, "Higher, higher than Pushkin!" Nekrasov was not higher than Pushkin poetically, of course, but he was higher than Pushkin in terms of democracy. Nekrasov was the first who used his voice to give a voice to the Russian peasant. Nekrasov is the founder of the concept of "Russian intelligentsia."

Gorky

When Alyosha was being whipped, Tsyganok surreptitiously slipped his own hand under the whip, to ease the blows, which made his whole arm swell up. Gorky put his whole soul in

---

1. Georgy Valentinovich Plekhanov (1856–1918), revolutionary and critic.

the way when the Russian intelligentsia was being whipped so that his soul swelled up. It is fashionable now to blame Gorky for socialist realism and even for the Stalinist camps. In the last years of his life, Gorky was in a prison, too. He was neither bought nor blind. When he visited the Solovki camps, the inmates, dressed and cleaned up for his visit, held their newspapers upside down, to show that it was all a sham. Gorky took a newspaper from one man and turned it right-side up, showing that he understood their sign. I have my suspicions that Gorky had asked Stalin for permission to return to Capri in order to tell the world about the horrible truth of the camps, and that's why he went to Solovki and to the Belomorkanal. His silence and greetings there were payment for the opportunity to escape from the cage of gilded barbed wire that was his alone.[2]

Mandelstam

I often ask myself why it was Mandelstam, a totally apolitical poet, who was the first to write a poem about Stalin that was like a finger pointing at the murderer hiding under the friendly smile of the nation's father. Could it be because Mandelstam was only a poet and nothing more, that is, defenseless not only from the external world but from his own uncontrollable and risky thoughts? Mandelstam did not have the insurance of Akhmatova's haughty aristocracy nor Pasternak's flirtatious playing at aristocracy. Pasternak played at being a child. Mandelstam was one. He simply could not resist crying out like a child, "But the king has no clothes!" even though just as childishly, he hoped that he would not be killed, but forgiven for his prank. With a reputation for being weak-willed, Mandelstam unexpectedly turned out to be the strongest of all his poetic contemporaries in the face of history, thanks to his childlike spontaneity and inconsistency.

Alexei Tolstoy

A pen of genius. He lacked one thing — pangs of conscience. Without that no one has ever become a real Russian classic.

---

2. Gorky was denied permission to go to Capri. Stalin wrote, "The air of our Crimea is no less healthful than the air of Capri."

Bulgakov

In *The Master and Margarita*, the money Woland tosses from the stage and which then turns into meaningless pieces of paper — that is all the proclamations, and fluttering slogans, and resolutions of so many meetings, and the labor avowals to "catch up and surpass." This historical litter, which turns into fires, serves as the perfect smoke screen for all kinds of Archibald Archibaldoviches to bring out their smoked sturgeon safely wrapped in waxed paper. History should be more careful with cooking oil, so that it isn't spilled once again on railroad tracks.

Zoshchenko

Zoshchenko is the most gentle mocker of humanity in the history of literature. How loving those lampoons are!

Grossman

Life and Fate is the *War and Peace* of World War II.

Solzhenitsyn

Who has read all ninety volumes of Tolstoy's works? Shklovsky[3] confessed to me that he had not managed. But Tolstoy for us is primarily his *War and Peace, Anna Karenina, The Death of Ivan Ilyich, Kholstomer,* and *Hadji Murat,* and not his theorizing. . . . Our descendants are not likely to read all the volumes of Solzhenitsyn's works, or delve into all the nuances of his theories, some of which are dubious, and the polemics that surrounded him in his lifetime. But if in the future there is nothing like Stalin's tyranny and no one dares toss new Ivan Denisoviches into new camps, then our descendants must be grateful to Solzhenitsyn for that, for it was he who created the first manuscript memorial to the victims of Stalinism.

---

3. Viktor Borisovich Shklovsky (1893–1984), literary critic, specialist in Tolstoy.

Anna's Rebellion

NOTES ON *ANNA KARENINA* BY LEO TOLSTOY
(*1987*)

IN 1966 I visited Jacqueline Kennedy in her New York apartment. This woman, who achieved world fame during her husband's presidency, did not astound me with her beauty or intelligence, but she did touch me with her simplicity and naturalness, which miraculously survived in the paparazzi whirl of her life. In her bathroom, as if they belonged to a modest secretary, panty hose hung drying on the radiator.

"I would never have imagined you washing your own stockings," I said.

She smiled. "Well, what do you think I should do, throw them in the garbage? Every self-respecting woman must wash her own stockings."

I didn't ask about her husband's assassination. But suddenly, she brought it up herself. "Do you know, at that moment, in Dallas, I suddenly felt like Anna Karenina in front of the train. . . ."

There is a gigantic social distance between the former First Lady of the USA and a Chilean prostitute in a filthy brothel not far from Tierra del Fuego in the town of Punta Arenas. In 1968 my friend Francisco Coloane, the Chilean Jack London, brought me there. In his youth, when he was a sailor, Francisco fell in love with a girl from that house, had wanted to marry her, but she died of tuberculosis. The other prostitutes chipped in to put a marble angel over her grave, and every time he was in Patagonia, Francisco visited the cemetery and then the brothel. I accompanied him this time. The prostitutes greeted him not like a customer but as a relative. We had the local drink, Cola mono (Monkey's Tail), a monstrous mixture of milk and rum, wept, reminisced. . . . One of the prostitutes had a photograph over her bed, torn from a book. I couldn't believe my eyes; it was Leo Tolstoy, barefoot, in a white shirt, hands behind his back.

"Who is that?" I asked.

"My father," the woman replied briefly.

"But it seems to me that it's Leo Tolstoy," I insisted, as tactfully as I could.

"So what. Why can't he be my father, too?" she said, putting an end to the conversation.

That woman had not read *Anna Karenina*. But she had read another novel of Tolstoy's in Spanish, *Resurrection,* a present from a sailor, and she saw herself in the story of Katyusha Maslova. Katyusha Maslova is Anna Karenina in other social circumstances, and Nekhludov is a repentant Vronsky. That's a daughter of Tolstoy I found in Patagonia, so far from Russia.

Great art is always great fatherhood. Tolstoy spoke about it in one of his letters: ". . . don't say bad things about her [Anna — Y.Y.] to me, or if you must, do it with *ménagement* [discretion — Y.Y.], she's adopted after all." But in adopting Anna, he adopted many women present and future.

In 1872 Tolstoy was stunned by the suicide of one Anna Pirogova, who had thrown herself under a train not far from Yasnaya Polyana over a failed love affair. Tolstoy saw the woman's mutilated body and apparently that torment was the start of his adopting all similar tragedies. Tolstoy's torment over starting the book is stressed by all his attempts to hide that torment from friends: "I haven't dirtied my hands with ink or my heart with thoughts for two months, and now I'm starting on boring, trite Karenina with the single desire to quickly clear space and leisure for myself for other things . . ." (from a letter to [the poet Afanasy] Fet). "My God, if only someone else would finish A. Karenina for me! It's unbearably revolting" (from a letter to the critic

Nikolai Strakhov). But suddenly the intonation changes completely, even though it has the same self-mocking character in form: "How about instead of reading *Anna Karenina* you finish it and spare me from that sword of Damocles?" (from a letter to Strakhov). With his powerful hand Tolstoy bends the sword of Damocles hanging over him and shapes it into a train wheel.

A contemporary of Tolstoy's — Rusanov — recalls his conversation with the writer, when he asked him, "They say that you were very cruel with Anna Karenina, forcing her to die under the train." Tolstoy replied, "That opinion reminds me of what happened with Pushkin. He once said to a friend [about his heroine Tatyana — Y.Y.], 'I never expected that from her. . . .' "

But that was probably Tolstoy's way of fobbing off an immodest question. Anna Karenina appears in the novel with a train and dies under a train. The anxious musical theme of train wheels that comes in the beginning of the book could not have been accidental or random — it foreshadows the requiem development at the end. Shklovsky said it best: "Anna Karenina enters the novel as if through a steam engine wheel that is rolling along an old track, seeing nothing." The metaphor's knife slices to the essence deeper than many probing pokes with a scholar's scalpel.

"Whether she was crushed by love, dirt, or wheels — it all hurts," said Blok, and that metaphor, which does not allow us to primitivize the suicide with a single cause, is incredibly close to the triple nature of the real cause, which contains wheels, tears, and dirt.

When the novel was first published in chapters in the conservative journal *Russky vestnik* [*Russian Herald*], the monarchist critics rushed out with compliments, hailing Tolstoy for his "aristocratic" and "antinihilistic spirits" (in those days that meant antirevolutionary). However, when the novel was completed, the same journal rejected it: "The idea of the whole was not developed. . . . A broad river flowed but did not reach the sea, it was lost in the sands. . . ." The radical-left critics, who took the early praise of the right as an unwashable greasy kiss from reactionaries on Tolstoy's cheek, called the novel "salon art." Even the great satirist Saltykov-Shchedrin printed a mocking piece in his journal, treating the novel as something absurd.

Pasternak once wrote about Christ: "You will spread your arms out on the ends of the cross to embrace too many." The reason so many contemporaries did not understand the novel was that its arms were open for too many and at the same time. Naturally Ivan Ivanovich is flattered that someone wants to embrace him personally. But if at the same time someone wants to embrace Petr Petrovich, whom Ivan Ivanovich hates, he feels hurt. People who don't have the strength to be alone form groups, flocks, and herds and do not forgive those who live outside herds.

The loner Tolstoy was understood only by another great loner — Dostoevsky, who called *Anna Karenina* perfection. But the majority of humanity is made up of loners. And that is why Tolstoy took "too many" into his embrace — from the prostitute in Patagonia to Jacqueline Kennedy. What separates a great artist from a craftsman is that his art is a letter to everyone at once.

Flaubert said "Madame Bovary, c'est moi," and Tolstoy could say the same about Anna Karenina. The sybaritic side of his life is in Stiva Oblonsky, his former officer's charm in Vronsky, his semi-idealistic, semipractical truth-seeking is in Levin, but nevertheless, they are not Tolstoy, Anna is. The aristocrat Tolstoy developed the painful illness of guilt before everyone who was deprived of a piece of bread, a piece of happiness. A heavy partier, who had consumed more than a thousand single servings of English roast beef, he became a vegetarian, feeling spiritual hunger. The high-society beauty Anna felt hunger for love. The deeply religious Tolstoy became anticlerical and he was excommunicated from the church for "heresy." The religious Anna is choking on disgust for religious hypocrisy. Almost decided on committing suicide, she sees her traveling companion bless himself. " 'I'd like to ask him what he means by that,' Anna thought, glancing at him angrily."

Tolstoy had elevated the concept of "family" to a personal moral church, but became disillusioned in it, too, because under the scenery of so-called mutual respect he saw the death of love. Remember what Anna says about it, "They invented respect in order to hide the empty place where love used to be." Having paid his dues to the social chitchat in the capital, Tolstoy ran off to Yasnaya Polyana to seek "simplification," but there, among his family, among the peasants, he found not simplicity, but the false-hood he hated, complicating life. Almost all the faces that pass before her eyes irritate Anna before her suicide: "Why are they talking, why are they laughing? It's all not true, it's all lie, all deceit."

Tolstoy's fame turned into gossip, which wounded him and all his family, including his wife, Sofia Andreyevna. Anna's fame, as beauty and unfaithful wife, turned into gossip that became insult-ing. Tolstoy's flight from Yasnaya Polyana was a suicide in effect. His death took place at the Astapovo Station to the rhythm of the wheels that had crushed Anna. Both suicides were a rebellion of death after the failed attempt at rebellion in life. Tolstoy's rebel-lion began apparently right after the Crimean War, which trans-formed him. Anna's rebellion began with her love of Vronsky, which also transformed her. That love was Anna's personal Cri-mean War with the opinion of society, with her own position, which many envied, with her duties before her husband, with her love for her son, who was taken away from her.

Finally, her love for Vronsky turned into a war against Vron-sky himself. In horror, Anna found the egoist Karenin under Vronsky's cavalry charm. This is the eternal tragedy of a woman's love, because a woman gives everything to her lover and expects the same from him. Was this not Tolstoy's tragedy, who devoted himself to humanity and expected humanity to respond in kind? But humanity, like Vronsky, was too busy and could not give him the same love in his lifetime, for fame and curiosity are not love. "Genius is the train everyone misses," Marina Tsvetayeva said bitterly. Another train, more wheels. But were only Karenin, Vronsky, and Sofia Andreyevna egoists, and not Anna or Leo Tolstoy?

A woman's loving altruism in the desire to be completely one with the soul and body of her beloved also turns into owner-ship — that is, into egoism. The same thing happens to great art-ists, when altruism and self-sacrifice turn into the egoism of demanding no less sacrifice from everyone else. Anna's life had become unbearable. But in choosing a moment's pain over pain stretched over time she left behind pain for many years, and it is most unlikely that she improved the lives of those she left behind.

Tolstoy's life in Yasnaya Polyana had also become unbearable, but did his flight and his death improve the life of the survivors, who, yes, had tormented him, but whom he had tormented too?

The fates of Anna and Tolstoy intertwine and perhaps Tolstoy is more Anna than she is herself.

The novel begins with the sentence: "All happy families are alike, and each unhappy family is unhappy in its own way."

But what is a happy family? In many families, happy at first glance, there are hidden dramas, like cracks in the foundations of houses with beautiful facades. The complete conjoining of two personalities is impossible, and one of the two will always be trying to subjugate the other. Every family life is a struggle that sometimes turns into open warfare. Unclear relations are like a cold war. Tolstoy wrote:

"In order to undertake anything in family life, you need either total disagreement between spouses or loving harmony. But when the relations between spouses are unclear, and there is neither one nor the other, nothing can be undertaken. Many families remain for years in their old places, boring to both spouses, only because they have neither complete disagreement nor complete agreement. . . . "

It was these artificial relations that Anna saw in the train as she observed a couple: "Anna clearly saw how bored they were with each other and how they hated each other. And she couldn't help hating such pathetic monsters." With her temperament, Anna might have left Karenin even without meeting Vronsky. The love for Vronsky was one of the manifestations of her hatred for her husband, and if Vronsky had not existed, she would have invented him. By momentum her struggle for independence, which began with war against Karenin, turns into war with Vronsky. Even Anna's suicide is a military action. Here's what Anna thinks of Vronsky, her hatred approaching that for Karenin: "He has the right to go where and when he chooses. Not only to go, but to leave me. He has all the rights, and I have none." She uses that as an accusation of falsehood, not believing all of Vronsky's avowals of love. But just recently she had accused Karenin of lying: "I know that he swims in lies like a fish in water and enjoys it. But no, I won't give him that satisfaction. Anything is better than lies and deceit!" Anna doesn't want Vronsky to have satisfaction either. The train becomes a new Vronsky for her, with whom she betrays (with the price of her death) the old Vronsky, who had become almost Karenin for her.

Let's take another couple from the novel — apparently happy. Kitty and Levin love each other, but there is a constant struggle between them: either Kitty's open flirtation with Vasenka Veselovsky, or her jealousy of his business, or Levin's animal jealousy of Kitty. And yet they are almost the ideal couple. Once again we come across Levin's social altruism, which turns unwittingly into egoism vis-à-vis his own wife, and we see Kitty's maternal altruism, which turns into egoism vis-à-vis Levin. Even the most happy family life is always on the brink of disaster, according to Tolstoy.

Strangely enough, the most stable relationship for all its small but unhidden cataclysms is between Stiva and Dolly. Their unhappy family life is almost a textbook case: a tragedy with almost vaudevillian overtones. "I should have left my husband and started my life over. I could have loved and been really loved. Is this any better?" But Dolly stays with Stiva, calling him her "disgusting, pathetic, and dear husband." Stiva loves Dolly in his fashion, but it's more pity than love. Stiva is a coward. He is afraid of the slightest changes in his life, of Dolly's tears, of dividing up his small property, of being left unprotected before his mistresses, from whom he is protected by Dolly's existence, of disrupting the comfortable albeit rather confused status quo.

The fourth couple in the novel is Levin's down-at-the-heels brother, Nikolai, and the former prostitute Maria Nikolayevna with whom he lives. She has become the nanny for the man destroyed by alcohol and unbridled ambition. Nikolai pities her, if only because no one but the judge ever addressed her formally. Maria Nikolayevna pities him because his morbid pride is useless and eats away at him. An unhappy couple, where pity replaces love. And Nikolai's pity is pitiless, he takes out his frustration on Maria Nikolayevna, getting his revenge on the world for tossing him into the ditch on her pockmarked face. The real villains, against whom he rails, are far away. Maria Nikolayevna is nearby — and so she has to put up with the provincial Russian

Savonarola, whose only public tribune is his foul-smelling bed
that he can't even leave.

There is another couple in the novel — joined not by marriage
but by their joint care for a child — Countess Lydia Alexeyevna,
secretly in love with Karenin, and Karenin, who despises her but
needs her, and perhaps for that reason comes to hate her. "Alexei
Alexandrovich never thought about his woman friends, and the
greatest of them, Countess Lydia Alexeyevna. All women, as
women, were terrible and disgusting to him."

Yes, it is a sad picture of the union of men and women painted
by Tolstoy, who so wanted the union of two bodies, of two souls,
in his own life.

Genius is always a princess on a pea, and a family quarrel, even
a small one, can be turned into a world tragedy in a genius's
imagination. It seems to me that Tolstoy recognized in horror the
former charming Sonechka Bers he had loved and who was now
his wife, Sofia Andreyevna, in Lydia Alexeyevna, created by his
pen; and in some traits of Karenin, he recognized the Tolstoy he
hated in himself. When Tolstoy writes about Karenin, it sounds
like a confession:

"He experienced a feeling similar to the one a man might feel
after calmly crossing a bridge and suddenly seeing that the bridge
has been taken apart and there is an abyss there. The abyss was
life itself, and the bridge, the artificial life that he had lived."

Karenin liked to complain about certain higher spheres of society, calling them with the convenient word "they." "They could
not understand that, they were concerned only with personal interests." But for his subordinates Karenin was part of that "they."
Was Tolstoy parodying himself in Karenin's meditations? For all
his attempts to grow into peasant life and push a plow, the peasants could not accept him as one of their own, and for them he
was all "they."

Tolstoy saw two moral supports — the family and becoming
one with the peasantry — as a salvation, but he also subjected
those who choose these avenues to tormented doubts. That is
what *Anna Karenina* is about. But even more tragically, Tolstoy
doubted even the possibility of happiness. That is the most bitter

and most desperate part of Anna's rebellion and of Tolstoy's rebellion.

When he was completing *War and Peace*, Tolstoy quoted a French proverb in one of his letters: "Happy nations do not have a history." If Tolstoy does not believe in the possibility of happiness for individuals, how can there be entire happy nations?

I once read that, beginning with Sumerian times, there have been eighteen thousand wars on earth. If there is no peace in families of just a few people, how can there be peace in the multimillion family of man? Levin, who dreamed like Tolstoy of combining ideals with practice, thought:

"If I just stubbornly head for my goal, I will achieve it. The entire economy, and most important — the state of all the people — will change. Instead of poverty there will be general wealth, satisfaction, instead of hostility — harmony and mutual interest. Basically, a great bloodless revolution — beginning first in the small circle of our district, then the province, Russia, the world. Because a just idea cannot help being fruitful."

Levin thought that serfdom was one of the main causes of human alienation. Serfdom had been abolished in Europe by then, but if you read the European classics of that period, you will see that it is all a cry of alienation! "I know that people have invented many others to replace the chains of serfdom," Nekrasov said after the abolition of serfdom in Russia. The dream of American abolitionists seemed to have come true, and Harriet Beecher Stowe's Uncle Tom is no longer overseen by Simon Legree, and there are many black mayors in the United States, but has the race problem — in itself only a part of the gigantic problem of human alienation — disappeared?

As a genius, Tolstoy understood that the answer to alienation had to be sought in the primary cell of humanity — in the family. The great bloodless revolution had to be started not in "the small circle of the district," as Levin thought, but from the tiniest district of all, the family. It was much harder for Levin in that circle, despite his love for his wife and children, than in the district one. Levin in his family was like Don Quixote, who received his own

island to govern, even though he had not asked for it; Sancho
Panza had. Thank goodness that for all his quixotic nature, Levin
had a healthy dose of Sanchopanzism, too. All of Tolstoy's su-
perhuman efforts collapsed in the family circle, for no man is a
prophet in his own family. In Sofia Andreyevna's eyes, Tolstoy
was much more rigid than Karenin.

Tolstoy wrote that he loved the "national thought" in *War and
Peace* and the "family thought" in *Anna Karenina*. Here is Levin:
"That word 'people' is so vague. The rest . . . not only do not
express their will, but they don't have the slightest idea what they
should express their will about. What right do we have to say that
it is the will of the people?" But if Tolstoy was tormented by the
vagueness of the word *people,* wasn't he also tormented by the
vagueness of the word *family*? Tolstoy called marriage "the most
complicated thing in the world," "the hardest and most important
thing in life." For all his tendency to didactic recipes in his philosophical treatises, Tolstoy offers no recipes in *Anna Karenina,*
as if afraid of all the medicines in the world. Moreover, it sometimes seems that he does not believe at all in family happiness,
even though he does not force that disbelief on others — unwill-
ing to take that sin upon himself. It is not surprising that Tolstoy
dropped from the final version the following passage, far from
family optimism:

"We like to imagine unhappiness as something concentrated, a
fact of something completed, while . . . unhappiness is life, a long
unhappy life, that is, a life in which the setting of happiness remains, while happiness, the meaning of life, are lost."

Vronsky, who finally achieves his dream, having Anna, is not
too jolly: "Despite the complete realization of what he had wanted
for so long, he was not completely happy."

And here is Tolstoy on his favorite, Levin:

"Happy family man, a healthy man, Levin had been so close
to suicide that he hid the rope, so as not to hang himself with it,
and feared going out with his rifle, so as not to shoot himself."

And here is Tolstoy's own confession: "I wanted to get away
from life with all my being. The thought of suicide came to me
as naturally as previously I had had thoughts about improving my
life."

But let us stop and think, after these rather frightening lines, was Tolstoy such a hopeless pessimist? Note that Tolstoy speaks only of the "naturalness" of thoughts of suicide, but you will never find a word about the naturalness of suicide itself. A sixteen-year-old teenager I know, usually taciturn and private, once asked me how I felt about suicide. I understood that he might have been thinking about suicide for the first time in his life and that he was horrified. Horror of thoughts of suicide can lead to suicide. As calmly as I could, I explained that everyone who thinks has thoughts about suicide, it's just that many people hide it. The teenager sighed in relief. But that persistent thought could have led to a dangerous sense of inadequacy or morbidness.

Some zealous teachers pound Korolenko's[1] line "Man is created for happiness the way birds are for flight" into the heads of their school charges. If you accept that, then unhappiness is somehow equated with winglessness. Being unhappy is somehow shameful. So many people hide their unhappiness, like a bad illness, covering it up with a false happy front.

Anna Karenina was the victim of "aristocratic society," which considered "unhappiness" just such an illness. Today's pseudo-aristocratic elite, which did not inherit a tenth of the culture of the old cream of the aristocracy, did inherit the hypocritical attitude toward "unhappiness."

"But I've been spoiled since rot touched the times, and sorrow has been turned to shame, making the bourgeoisie and optimists cringe," was Pasternak's take on that hypocrisy. Pushkin had a reason for setting the talent to think next to the talent to suffer: "I want to live, in order to think and suffer."

We must bring up our children with a readiness to suffer, with a readiness to be happy. The television salad of human suffering presented on the news teaches people not to suffer or feel compassion. A teenager whose ears are plugged into a Walkman of pop culture may not hear the cry for help of someone being killed on the street nearby. In this era of aggressive pop culture millions of teenagers know Michael Jackson better than Dante, Shakespeare, or Tolstoy. Pop culture is nothing more than bodybuild-

---

1. Vladimir Galaktionovich Korolenko (1853–1921), writer.

ing for the ears. The world's classics cultivate suffering and compassion.

Tolstoy's great lesson is that man's unhappiness is not his insignificance. Levin's sad thinking is: "In infinite time, in infinite matter, in infinite space a bubble surfaces — an organism, and that bubble will last, and then burst, and that bubble is me." But at the point where Levin's unhappiness begins, where he begins having thoughts of his own insignificance — that is where his insignificance ends.

Tolstoy confessed: "The content of what I wrote was as new for me as it is for those who read it."

A family novel grew into an encyclopedic book, because the author's suffering was not romantic but encyclopedic. The novel is not overloaded. Every character is alive, not dictated by the "general theme," and each of them is a person who does not fit the general theme. The almost caricatural configuration of Karenin in the early sketches disappears once Karenin begins moving and speaking. Compared to many contemporary "deceived" husbands, who sink to the level of injured property owners in their hatred, Karenin is almost the ideal deceived husband. The drier and more logical his own character, the more morally heroic is his behavior at the bedside of Anna giving birth to another man's child. In that scene Tolstoy became Karenin, gave him his soul, which had been in Anna before that. But Tolstoy's soul was so enormous that there was enough for Levin, and Vronsky, and Stiva, and Frou-Frou. Frou-Frou broke her back, like Anna.

Tolstoy was a great actor who played so many roles on the pages of his books — from Napoleon to Natasha Rostova, from Helene to Platon Karatayev — and who could transform himself even into a horse.

In rereading *Anna Karenina*, I had a sense of irritation at first. After the horrible experiences of the twentieth century — Big Bertha, poison gases, tanks, bombs, concentration camps, and Hiroshima — the torments of Tolstoy's characters seemed toylike to me. I even had the nasty thought, "I wish I had your problems, gentlemen." Levin's conversations with his friends on changing the world sometimes drove me crazy with their length and naïveté.

But it is most likely that our descendants in the twenty-first century will find our thoughts on changing the world naive, too. The concrete ideas on how to change it will become obsolete, perhaps even funny, but the desire to improve the world will remain unchanged.

Many theories and attempts to realize them will be cruelly devalued. But there is one thing that will never be devalued — the preciousness and uniqueness of human feelings, among them love. No matter how humanity changes, complete happiness in love will probably remain unattainable, a constantly receding horizon, and there will be a woman in the future who will repeat the words of Anna Karenina: "Love . . . The reason I don't like that word is that it means too much, much more than you can understand."

§ *Enormity and Vulnerability*

VLADIMIR MAYAKOVSKY

(1978)

THE FIRST THING that comes to mind when you hear the name "Mayakovsky" is a feeling of his enormity.

Once after his reading a breathless coed made her way backstage to see the tired, sweat-covered poet. He had seemed a giant on stage. And suddenly she saw that giant unwrap a tiny translucent candy and pop it into his mouth with childish glee. She gasped, "Vladimir Vladimirovich, you're so big and you're eating that candy?" Mayakovsky replied in a booming bass voice: "What do you want me to do, eat chairs?"

Mayakovsky hid his vulnerability behind his enormity, and most people did not see it at all — especially from the audience. But sometimes it showed: "What can a block like me want? A block wants many things. . . . It doesn't matter to yourself that you're bronze or that your heart is like a cold metal. At night you want to hide your ringing in something soft and female. . . ." Or "On what delirious and stormy night, by what Golgothas was I conceived, so big and so unneeded?" Sometimes the theme of the enormity unneeded by anyone reached self-mockery: "The sky weeps uncontrollably, and the little cloud has a grimace on its wrinkle of a mouth, as if a woman had expected a baby and God tossed her a crooked idiot."

Later Mayakovsky assiduously avoided the slightest reference to his vulnerability and even boasted that he had thrown away a brilliant quatrain on the pretext that "it's easy to do the aching":

> *I want to be understood by my native land*
> *And if I'm not, well then,*
> *I'll bypass my native land,*
> *Like driven rain.*

This must have been a ploy for getting this quatrain, which he obviously liked, into the readers' memory. But why did Mayakovsky fear revealing his vulnerability so much? Compare him to Yesenin, whose strength was that confessional tossing up of his own weaknesses and inner black ghosts. Sergei Esenin is a marvelous poet, but Mayakovsky is huger, and therefore his vulnerability is huger. The huger the vulnerability, the huger the defensiveness. Mayakovsky had to defend himself all his life from those who were smaller than he — from literary and political Lilliputians, trying to tie him up, like Gulliver, with thousands of threads, sometimes seemingly tender silk threads, but ones that dug deep into the flesh. The great Mayakovsky had a fear of injections — not only the memory of his father's death after accidental blood poisoning, but also the constant sensation of all those lilliputian needles jabbing his expansive but exhausted body.

As a child Mayakovsky used to climb into clay wine jugs — *churi* — and declaim inside them. The boy liked the powerful resonance. He seemed to be training his voice to project, to have a mighty echo that could cover up the beating of his heart, so that his enemies would not guess how fragile his heart was.

People who knew him personally recall how easily hurt he was. All giants are like that. Mayakovsky's giantness was not playacting; it was natural. The jugs belonged to other people, but the voice was his. Mayakovsky's poetry is an anthology of passions according to Mayakovsky — passions of the huge and vulnerable, like himself. There is no lyric narrative poem in world literature equal to *A Cloud in Trousers* in terms of frayed nerves per word. Mayakovsky's love of the Don Quixote image was not random.

Even if Mayakovsky's Dulcinea was not what she seemed, let us thank her for the "uplifting deceit" that is higher than "swarms of low verities," in Pushkin's words.

But Mayakovsky, in contrast to Don Quixote, did not tilt only against windmills and doll-like Saracens. Mayakovsky was a revolutionary not only in revolution but in love. Romance in love began for him with a scornful rejection of society where love was reduced to "pleasure," to being an integral part of comfort and personal property. The romanticism of the early Mayakovsky is special — it is sarcastic romance. Mambrin's helmet — actually the barber's basin — made people laugh at Don Quixote. But Mayakovsky's yellow shirt[1] was a mockery of society, into which he was breaking with his powerful shoulder, dragging in the tiny ships of the Futurist fleet, helpless without their good-natured Gulliver.

Prewar Russian poetry was rich in talent but poor in passion. Salons were busy with mediums and table turning. People adored reading Przybyszewski.[2] Even in the great Blok you can find lines of erotic mysticism, when he allowed his pen of genius to write such tasteless lines as "So stab my heart, yesterday's angel, with your sharp French high heel!" Poets tried nostalgia for Asargadon or the rosy Brabant lace cuffs of Corsairs, or they sang the praises of exotic pineapples in champagne,[3] even though they themselves preferred vodka and a pickle, or they sought salvation in Pushkin's classicism. Mayakovsky like no one else understood that "the street was writhing, tongueless, it had nothing with which to shout or speak." Mayakovsky tore love out of the alcoves and speeding carriages and carried it, like a weary, tricked child, in his enormous arms with strained sinews, toward his hated and familiar street.

The central line of civic poetry, Pushkin, Lermontov, Nekra-

---

1. Mayakovksy often wore a yellow shirt for his public readings. This was considered an affront to good taste and fit into his campaign to shock the middle class out of its complacency, to slap the bourgeoisie (*épater les bourgeois*).
2. Stanislaw Przybyszewski (1868–1927), Polish writer popular in Russia, a Decadent.
3. These are references to Valery Yakovlevich Bryusov (1873–1924), leader of the Symbolist poets; Nikolai Sergeyevich Gumilyov (1886–1921), Acmeist poet; and Igor Severyanin (1887–1941), Decadent poet.

sov, was blurred by the blood of Khodynka, Tsushima, January 9, 1905,[4] mixed with the punch served in literary salons. Mayakovsky's declaration that it was time to throw Pushkin from the ship of modernity seemed like blasphemy. Actually there was much more Pushkin in Mayakovsky than in all the classicists put together. In his final confession, "At the Top of My Voice," that direct line is inarguable. "At the Top of My Voice" is the "I have raised a monument to myself" of the prophet and bard of socialist revolution. Pushkin's intonations are clearly heard through the crude, choppy lines of his descendant, so unlike him superficially. But back in 1925 Mayakovsky said, "We ought to be learning from the masters who personally lived through the path from Pushkin to today's revolutionary October."

Pushkin's lines were, "I loved you so sincerely, so tenderly, as God grant you be loved by another" for his time was a rebellion against the concept of love as ownership. His descendant cried out: "So that there be no love that is servant of husbands, lust, or bread, damning beds, rising from sheets, so that love comes to the whole universe."

Mayakovsky had Lermontov in him, too — the harsh protest against so-called rules of so-called society. Lermontov's "Ah, you haughty descendants" was transformed into a form as crude as the era, "You, who live from orgy to orgy, with a bath and warm toilet." Lermontov and Mayakovsky were related by their hatred for everything that destroyed great passions in people, making them faceless and similar not only in social but in intimate relations. Mayakovsky has Pechorin's sardonic nature, and Arbenin's despair, and the gasping, stumbling voice of the badgered hero of *Mtsyri*. The scorn for what Pushkin and Lermontov called "the black [lower] orders" was in Mayakovsky's genetic code. His experience showed him that despite social cataclysms, those people were clever at mimicry and survival. Before the

---

4. Hundreds of people were crushed to death in the crowd at Khodynka Field during the coronation of Tsar Nicholas II.

On May 27–28, 1905, the Russian fleet was smashed by the Japanese in Tsushima Strait, in the decisive battle of the Russo-Japanese War.

January 9, 1905, was called Bloody Sunday, when soldiers fired on a peaceful protest march led by Father Gapon.

Revolution he called these people with their spiritual blackness bourgeois and after the Revolution the "newly appeared Soviet Pompadours."

The third powerful source of Mayakovsky's civic strength was Nekrasov. Mayakovsky tried to joke, when asked about Nekrasov's influence. "At one time I was interested in whether he was a cheater or not. But I dropped the case for lack of evidence." But that was a mere polemical pose. Listen to Nekrasov's lines: "Forgive me this brazen laughter. Your logic is a bit strange. Can Apollo Belvedere mean less to you than a chamber pot?" Not only the intonation, but the rhyme *derzkii/belvederskii* is pure Mayakovsky. And can there be a better epigraph for *A Cloud in Trousers* than Nekrasov's "From the gloating, gabbling, and bloodstained lead me to the camp of those who are dying for the greatness of love!"

And the rebel against tradition was actually the main heir of the great trinity of Russian classical poetry. Mayakovsky did not tear down the walls of the house of Russian poetry — he simply tore off the tasteless wallpaper, knocked down the partitions, and enlarged the rooms. Mayakovsky was the result of the traditions of Russian poetry and not their overthrow. It's no accident that he resembled so many literary heroes, a conglomerate of Dubrovsky, Bezukhov, Bazarov, and Raskolnikov.[5] Mayakovsky blasphemed desperately, "I thought you were an all-powerful god, but you're a failure, a tiny little god." But his relations with God were much more complex than appears at first glance. Mayakovsky's early poems are sprinkled with biblical images. The logical explanation is the simple one — when Mayakovsky was in prison in his youth, the Bible was one of the few permitted books. Of course, revolutionary ideas often used this ammunition to fight the hypocrisy of clericalism.

Mayakovsky's satires, without which he is unimaginable, show Pushkin's daring hand — as in *Fairy Tale about a Priest and His Laborer, Balda* — Krylov's colloquial ease, and Sasha Cherny's

---

5. Dubrovsky is the eponymous hero of Pushkin's tale about a gentleman robber. Bezukhov is the hero of Tolstoy's *War and Peace.* Bazarov is the nihilist hero of Turgenev's *Fathers and Sons.* Raskolnikov is the student who wants to be a superman in Dostoevsky's *Crime and Punishment.*

barbed sarcasm (especially in Mayakovsky's *New Satyricon* period).[6] However, the last's influence should not be exaggerated — there is too great a difference in the level of their gifts.

Mayakovsky called himself "the loud-mouthed Zarathustra of today." This must be taken with a grain of salt, like his intentionally shocking "I love to watch children die" or "I never want to read anything. Books are books!" A great writer has to be a great reader. He knew literature very well, or he would not have turned into a great poet. What attracted Mayakovsky to Nietzsche was not his philosophy, which was later expropriated and distorted by fascism, but the power of his poetic images. Before World War I, amid collapse and ruin, amid anemic occultism, Russians saw Nietzsche as a rebel against spiritual tininess, against moral chill, against the bourgeoisification of the spirit. But Nietzsche saw war as cleansing the stagnant blood of humanity. Mayakovsky, despite his brief burst of false patriotism at the beginning of World War I, became the first antiwar poet in Russia. Many poets were still partially enthralled with the Hussar romantic view of war. Mayakovsky, following the laws of the new historical inevitability, burst out of that prison.

When the Italian Futurist Emilio Marinetti came to Russia and tried to propagandize the beauty of war, he was rebuffed harshly by his seeming brothers — the Russian Futurists. Igor Severyanin's irresponsible "But if we must, well then, fine! My horse! Champagne! Dagger!" was countered by Mayakovsky's bleeding: "In the rotting railroad car 4 legs for 40 men." The numerical metaphor tore the bloom from the false romanticism of mass killings. Nietzscheanism was only a fleeting interest of the young Mayakovsky and it did not set deep roots in his heart. Mayakovsky's hero, tied by the hawsers of verse to a bridge over the river of time, is higher than a superman, he is a man.

In his global views and perception of the planet as a single whole, Mayakovsky is close to Whitman, whom he must have read in Konstantin Chukovsky's translation, which saved the great American from Balmont's sugary hands. Mayakovsky and

---

6. Ivan Andreyevich Krylov (1769–1844), Russian fabulist and translator of La Fontaine. Sasha Cherny, satirical poet, contributor to *New Satyricon*, a newspaper that flourished from 1906 to 1917. Mayakovsky was a contributor in 1915–16.

Whitman share a love for human energy and initiative, for physical and moral strength, and an understanding of the future as "the sole human dormitory." However, according to Mayakovsky, the right to enter that dormitory must not be given to exploiters, bureaucrats, the nouveaux riches of capitalism or socialism, careerists, brownnosers, or the bourgeoisie. There is no room for them in the future — except as educational exhibits. Whitman's entrance requirements to the future are rather blurry and vague. Mayakovsky's are harsher and stricter. The difference between these two poets comes from the difference between the two revolutions, American and Russian.

If we speak of the sources of Mayakovsky's poetic forms, the roots lie not only in folklore and Russian classics, of which I have spoken, but also in the innovations of the best painters of the early decades of the century. Let's not forget that Mayakovsky was a talented painter himself and had a professional understanding of art. "The black palms of gathered windows were dealt hot yellow cards" or "The grim rain squinted, and behind the black palings" is the language of the new painting. Kandinsky, Malevich, Goncharova, Larionov, Tatlin, Matisse, Delaunay, Braque, Léger, Picasso — their search for form on canvas moved along intersecting parallels with Mayakovsky's search in poetry. However, Mayakovsky was against form for its own sake: "If you take a violin apart into its planes a million times, the violin won't have any more planes and the artist won't have an unused point of view on that problem."

Mayakovsky's poetic genealogy is multibranched, and its roots can be found in other arts — the movies, for instance. Mayakovsky uses the method of montage. But only a minor poet can be born only of art. Mayakovsky's genealogy includes his most important parent — history. History determined his character, voice, images, and rhythms. A great poet is always inside history and history is inside him. Pushkin was that way and so was Mayakovsky. Everything that happened to the Revolution happened to him. ("That happened to the soldiers or the country or it was in my heart.") That is the complicated and by no means complete genesis of Mayakovsky — that gigantic child of history and world culture, who was born big and immediately walked the earth, leaving imprints in the cobblestones.

When the Revolution came, Mayakovsky, unlike many intellectuals, had no question about whether or not to accept it. He was its prophet, erring by only one year: "In revolutions' crown of thorns nineteen-sixteen will come." Snobs berated Mayakovsky for selling out to the Bolsheviks. But how could he sell out to them, when he was a Bolshevik himself! On the other hand, some dogmatic critics accused Mayakovsky of anarchy, individualism, formalism, and so on. His bolshevism was not enough for them. They tried to brand him a "fellow traveler" — Mayakovsky, who laid the tracks for socialism with his own hands! Mayakovsky's hugeness did not fit the Procrustean beds of snobbery or dogmatism — the feet in giant shoes victoriously stuck out in the air. They tried chopping them off — but they couldn't, the legs were too sturdy. Then they began using a two-handed band saw, pulling to the left and then to right, forgetting that the teeth were cutting into live flesh. But Mayakovsky didn't submit to being sawed, either — the teeth broke off, even though they made deep wounds.

The subtle master of lyric prose, Ivan Bunin,[7] who had sunk to profound bitterness, caricatured Mayakovsky as an unleashed oaf of the future in his diarylike book, *Cursed Years*. Esenin, whom intriguers in literary circles were always pitting against Mayakovsky, wrote heatedly, "And he, their chief house painter at headquarters, sings of corks at the Mosselprom."[8] Ilya Selvinsky compared Mayakovsky's departure from the group LEF[9] with Tolstoy's abandonment of his wife and was out-and-out insulting: "Tolstoy's departure was a blowing up of dams, and yours is merely a flight from drowning flotillas. He paid for his departure

7. Ivan Alexeyevich Bunin (1870–1953), poet and prose writer who rejected the Revolution and emigrated to Paris.
8. Esenin's reference is to the fact that Mayakovsky wrote advertising jingles; Mosselprom was the Moscow Agricultural Industry agency.
9. LEF (*Levyi front iskusstva*, Left Front of Art), founded in 1922, a group of revolutionary writers and artists, primarily past Futurists. Their goal was "to encompass the social theme by all the instruments of Futurism," as defined by Mayakovsky. He left LEF in 1928 and formed REF (Revolutionary Front of Art), which disbanded in 1930.

with his life, and you expect to be paid." Even Kirsanov,[10] whom
Mayakovsky led by the hand into literature, made an ugly reference to his teacher, in a period when they were arguing, in the
poem "The Price of a Hand," which he must have regretted the
rest of his life. G. Shengelya published a book-length mockery
called *Mayakovsky at Full Height.* The writers' boycott of Mayakovsky's exhibition, the removal of his picture from the magazine *Press and Revolution,* the ban against his travel abroad, the
fearless attacks at meetings — all that was difficult, and drop by
drop collected into the fatal drop of lead. Mayakovsky was not a
poet to leave life only because his "love boat was smashed against
daily life." The reason was complex. Besides his external difficulties there was his enormous, inhuman exhaustion caused not only
by the attacks but by the incredible burden Mayakovsky put on
his own shoulders. Mayakovsky strained himself. They said that
Blok "died of death." Mayakovsky died of life. There is no poet
in the history of literature who took so much upon himself. "The
Windows of ROST,"[11] advertising, daily work at a newspaper,
discussion, thousands of public appearances, editing the journal
LEF, travel abroad — all without a single day off. This was Mayakovsky's heroism and his death.

Russia came to the Revolution with 70 percent of the population illiterate. In order to be understood by the masses, Mayakovsky consciously simplified his verse, "standing on the throat
of my own song." A great lyric writer, a genius of metaphor, did
not feel superior to doing dirty work. He wrote: "In our strength
is our right. Where's the strength? In this cocoa." "Once you've
eaten macaroni, you will always be obedient." "Stop! Not another
step! Buy Prima cigarettes!" "Comrades, stop throwing nails on
the road. Nails have damaged many feet." "Marching in step, row
by row, the proletariat heads for victory!" "Weavers and laun-
dresses, it's time to stop believing foreign sheep!" "With the help
of the Rubber Trust, everywhere I step is dry!" Mayakovsky realized that these lines were ephemeral. "Die, my verse, die like
the rank and file soldier, like our nameless merles who die in the

---

10. Semyon Isaakiyevich Kirsanov (1906–1972), poet and member of LEF.
11. ROST (*Rossiiskyi Stenograf*), propaganda shop windows in Moscow to which Mayakovsky contributed.

storms." Those lines have bitterness and pride in equal measure —
and with full justification. No poet has sacrificed as much to
revolution as Mayakovsky — he even sacrificed his lyric poetry.
Therein lies his greatness and his tragedy.

Mayakovsky's agitprop work was never political opportunism
nor simple hackwork for money — frequent accusations. Mayakovsky was the first socialist poet of the first socialist society. The
status of the poet in that society had not yet been determined by
anyone. Mayakovsky wanted to join poetry to the state. He
wanted the new society to make the need for poetry equal with
the need for a bayonet defending the Revolution and the need for
a factory producing happiness. He wanted poetry to storm stages
and stadiums, to thunder on the radio, to shout from billboards,
to call out in slogans, to agitate in newspapers, and to inform even
on candy wrappers.

This call for combining poetry and state elicited doubts of the
purity of the poet's intentions not only among enemies of Soviet
power but among many intellectuals who welcomed the Revolution but who felt that poetry must be a state within a state. "I'll
give my whole heart to October and May, but I won't give up
my beloved lyre," wrote Esenin. Pasternak insisted on his special
position as poet in the era of social upheavals. But the work of
Esenin and Pasternak went beyond their own declarations —
Esenin did not spare his "beloved lyre" for the Revolution and
Pasternak found himself not a "guest" but a deeply engaged witness, who said through the lips of Lieutenant Schmidt,

> *I know that the stake where I will*
> *stand will be the border*
> *of two different eras of history,*
> *and I am glad to be chosen.*

But if this happened to Esenin and Pasternak against their
will, all of Mayakovsky's will was directed from the first days of
the Revolution to uniting with it. "I give you all my resounding
strength as a poet, attacking class!" His attitude toward poetry as
a state affair was historically unusual — for so many years Russia's best poets led the struggle against the state, even though they
longed for a time when civil society and state would be one. Some

people had the suspicion that what Mayakovsky was doing was court poetry for a red court. But the rhymed toadying of court poetry was always based on greedy flattery. There was never any of this in Mayakovsky, since the revolutionary spirit and toadying are incompatible. "And I, like the springtime of humanity, both in labor and battle, sing my homeland, my republic!" That is not flattery, it is love, and not accidental, but hard-won love.

Mayakovsky's patriotism was not only for the land, but the idea. For the sake of that idea, and not for profit, he waged a constant campaign for the total utilitarianism of poetry. He lost a lot with that — for any utilitarianism of art is doomed. The ephemeral Mayakovsky sometimes vanquished the eternal Mayakovsky. But even if only these lines survive all the agitprop work — "The poet licked away the tubercular sputum with a poster's rough tongue" — that justifies all the ephemera. Mayakovsky was the founder of a new, socialist civil sense. His mistakes must not be repeated, but his victories must not be forgotten, either. The eternal Mayakovsky vanquished the ephemeral Mayakovsky. But without the ephemeral Mayakovsky, the eternal would not have existed.

There is a primitive theory that is popular in the West: prerevolutionary Mayakovsky is a poet of protest, and the postrevolutionary Mayakovsky is a poet conformist. There is no prerevolutionary or postrevolutionary Mayakovsky, only the indivisible revolutionary Mayakovsky. He was always a protest poet. His assertion of the young socialist republic was also a protest against those who did not want to recognize it. Mayakovsky's poetry is a never-ending protest against the fact that "many scoundrels of all kinds are walking our earth." Mayakovsky won the moral right to struggle against foreign scoundrels by his constant struggle with domestic ones. Even in the twenties he wrote: "The threads of everyday life have bound the revolution. Quotidian life is worse than Wrangel.[12] Hurry, break the necks of canaries, before communism is defeated by canaries!" How can the author of

12. Baron Petr Nikolayevich Wrangel, commander of the White Army in the civil war that followed the Revolution.

Bureaucratiade, Factory of Bureaucrats, The Bedbug, and *The Bath* be considered a conformist?

Mayakovsky's production costs are great, but rebukes directed at the past are academic. Imitating Mayakovsky's poetic method is hopeless, because that method was dictated by history at a certain watershed period. Now we do not need primitive political slogans. We have outgrown many of Mayakovsky's poems, but we may not have grown enough for some of them, perhaps.

Sometimes it seems that his voice comes not from the past, but from the still foggy future, like the bass of a ship's horn breaking through to us: *"Listen, Comrade Descendants. . . ."*

Genius Is Beyond Genre

Dmitrii Shostakovich
(1976–1988)

A COMPOSER can be only a composer, an artist only an artist, a writer only a writer, and if they do not violate the laws of professionalism and morality — which to my mind are inseparable — at best they remain only private craftsmen. Genius is beyond craft. The works of private craftsmen can live for a long time, but only as part of a particular genre. Genius is beyond genre. The works of a genius grow over the framework of art in general and become part of the national and world treasure, including historical experience, along with the first attempts of subhumans to get up from all fours and become human, along with all the wars and revolutions, along with all the personal and public tragedies, along with all the threats, blood, all the tormented seeking of faith, hope, and love, along with all the great victories and losses. Ravel belongs only to music, Utrillo only to painting, Fet only to poetry, and glory and honor to them for their worthy service to their muses. But Pushkin, Beethoven, and Picasso belong not only to their muses but to history. Belonging to history does not mean betrayal of the muse, but symbolizes a higher level of fidelity.

The weeping of a veteran mutilated by war and the mighty echo of Shostakovich's tragic and victorious Ninth Symphony, which moved all of humanity, belong next to each other in history.

Shostakovich's symphony was not his personal victory, it became the victory of a nation that withstood and did not give up, and its sounds were invisibly woven into the victory banner hung over Berlin. Shostakovich lived a rare miracle — he was recognized in his lifetime as a genius. Shostakovich lived through difficult times, he had been insulted and injured. But the strength of genius lies in not transferring one's injuries onto one's entire nation, in knowing how to rise above injury, and even how to create music out of suffering.

Shostakovich's talent was Pushkinesque in its scope: he was a master of chamber lyricism, a subtle metaphysical philosopher (recall his Fourteenth Symphony, on the theme of death and immortality), a sharp satirist (his brilliant early improvisation on the denunciations of communal apartment neighbors or the music for the play *The Bedbug*), a resounding songwriter ("Don't weep, get up, curlyhead," a song which today is bitterly colored by our knowledge that the poet Boris Kornilov was killed in Stalin's camps), a powerful opera writer, and even tried his hand at sparkling operetta, his rare failure. This was all united by the strength of historical linkages, which makes creativity the property of history, not genre.

Civic spirit is not a declaration of love for the homeland, but that innate, inextinguishable feeling of time as part of eternity. That was Shostakovich's life. No insults nor world fame made him give up his civic spirit. A genius goes through trials by hot and cold water, but that is the process of hardening the spirit. Those who give in to difficulties or get hooked by the poisoned worm of fame die while still alive. Those who overcome this overcome death after death. Shostakovich managed not to notice his fame, and even if he enjoyed the success of his works, it was happiness not for himself but for his children who went out into life independently, separated from him.

When I met Shostakovich, I was stunned by his extraordinary modesty and natural shyness, which was not for show. I received a phone call in 1953. My wife answered the phone. "Excuse me, we are not acquainted. This is Shostakovich. Tell me, please, is Yevgeny Alexandrovich at home?"

"He is. He's working. I'll call him."

"Working? Don't disturb him. I can call whenever it's convenient."

That was Shostakovich all over. He knew what work meant. (The tact and politeness of a real genius are so different from the tactlessness of some so-called young geniuses, who burst into your apartment or dacha demanding you read their poems, paying no attention to the fact that someone is sick in your family or that you yourself are very busy.) I came to the telephone, agitated, of course. Shostakovich told me shyly that he wanted to write "one thing" to my poetry and asked for permission.

I don't need to say how happy I was that he had read my poetry. But despite my happiness, I still had doubts, and worried, when he invited me to his house a month later to hear what he had written. He was nervous too. His hand hurt by then, and it was hard for him to play. I was stunned that he was nervous, that he apologized beforehand for his hand and his bad voice. Shostakovich put a score on the piano that said Thirteenth Symphony and began playing and singing. Unfortunately, no one recorded it. He sang with genius, too — he didn't have a voice really, it had a funny rattle, as if something had broken inside the voice, but he performed exquisitely, with either an inner or an otherworldly strength. Shostakovich stopped playing, quickly led me to the set table, nervously knocked back two shots of vodka in a row, and only then asked, "Well, what do you think?"

What astonished me first of all in the Thirteenth Symphony was that if I (a total musical ignoramus) had suddenly developed an ear, that would be the music I would have written. Moreover, Shostakovich's reading of my poetry was so exact in intonation and sense that it felt as if he had been inside me when I was writing the poem and he had composed the music as the lines were born. I was also astonished by the fact that he combined in the symphony poems that seemed totally incompatible. The requiem quality of "Babi Yar" with the emotional expansiveness at the end and the touching simple poems about women in lines, the retrospective of all the memorable verses with the swaggering tones of "Humor" and "Career."

At the symphony's premiere, the audience experienced something rare: for fifty minutes they wept and laughed and smiled and grew pensive. I did make one remark to Shostakovich: the end seemed too neutral, going too far beyond the limits of the text. I was a fool and only later did I see how necessary that ending was, precisely because that's what the poetry lacked — an opening in ocean, eternal harmony, rising above the bustle and drama that came before.

Shostakovich wrote *The Execution of Stepan Razin*[1] in just that way — I simply cannot imagine other music for it. Once in the USA I even fought for the music with the composer Leonard Bernstein, who felt that Shostakovich's music was not as good as my poem. I think there was something too "composerly" in that judgment; he looked at the music from a professional point of view, which got in the way of experiencing it purely.

Incidentally, when I first read "Stepan Razin" in manuscript to such professionals as Andrei Voznesensky, Bella Akhmadulina, and Bulat Okudzhava, who had gathered at my apartment, Voznesensky's reaction was, "Well, it's not the worst thing you've written." Okudzhava expressed the outrage of a Georgian aristocrat: "How can you glorify that robber?" Bella was the most humane. She said, "Zhenya, I'd love you even if you didn't write poetry."

While working on *Stepan Razin* Shostakovich unexpectedly began suffering and called me several times: "What do you think, Yevgeny Alexandrovich, was Razin a good man? After all, he killed people, let a lot of innocent blood. . . ." Shostakovich really liked another chapter from *Bratsk Hydroelectric Station,* "Fair in Simbirsk"; he said that it is a pure oratorio and wanted to write it, but some doubts kept him from doing it. Incidentally, I would never have undertaken the composition of *Bratsk HES,* constructed on the principle of combining seemingly incompatible pieces, if not for the courage the Thirteenth Symphony gave me.

A rumor was spread in the West that under pressure from the government I allegedly wrote a second version of "Babi Yar" that was the complete opposite of the first. That never happened. I leave that rumor on the conscience of those who have become too

---

1. The peasant rebel Stepan Razin led a revolt of the Don Cossacks in 1670–71. He was executed just outside Red Square.

forgetful and today want to represent the past as if they were the
only honest ones. Raising yourself by lowering others is not the
best form of humanism. Here's what really happened. The performance of Shostakovich's Thirteenth Symphony was threatened
for two reasons. First of all, I was under fire from official critics,
and every line I wrote was scrutinized for flaws. Secondly, after
the publication of "Babi Yar," chauvinists accused me of not having any lines about Russians and Ukrainians, who were shot along
with the Jews. The ideological whisperers provoked Khrushchev
before the work was performed, reporting that I presented the
tragedy of the war as if the fascists killed only Jews and did not
touch Russians. I was accused of insulting my own people. The
poet Alexey Markov published his poetic response to "Babi Yar"
in the newspaper *Literaturnaya Rossia*, with the lines:

> *What sort of real Russian are you,*
> *When you've forgotten your own people?*
> *Your soul, like trousers, has gotten tight*
> *And as empty as a staircase landing.*

The situation was such that singers and conductors fled from
the Thirteenth Symphony like rats from a sinking ship. At the last
moment the Ukrainian singer Boris Gmyrya bowed out — he had
been threatened by anti-Semites. The Leningrad conductor Yevgeny Mravinsky, selected by Shostakovich, refused. Kirill Kondrashin took the baton, and the young singer Vitalii Gromadsky
agreed to perform. Many people came to the rehearsals at the
conservatory — everyone was sure that the official premiere
would be banned. On the eve Kondrashin was called "upstairs"
somewhere and told that they would not allow the performance
if there was no mention of Russian and Ukrainian victims in the
text. Those victims did exist and no one was forcing me to lie.
But it was crude and tactless interference, since it was a condition
for the performance and not simple advice. What could I do? I
wrote these four lines:

> *I stand here,*
>   *as if by a well,*
> *giving faith in our brotherhood.*
> *Here Russians lie*

                    and Ukrainians
            lie with Jews in the same earth.

I can't say that those lines added something poetically to the
poem. But they don't change anything in the poem, and the whole
story of the second "opposite version" falls apart. There is no
second version of "Babi Yar." I showed these four lines to Shostakovich and with his permission they were included in the symphony. Was I right then in making this compromise? I think so.
Otherwise, the world would not have heard Shostakovich's work
of genius for another twenty-five years — until today's glasnost.
Don't forget that this was the first poem against anti-Semitism
printed in the Soviet press after so many anti-Semitic campaigns
of the Stalinist times. The Thirteenth Symphony was one of the
first infant cries of glasnost from its cradle. Glasnost was almost
smothered in its cradle, but the infant lived and cries to this day.

Shostakovich suggested we create a new symphony on the
theme Pangs of Conscience. All that came out of it, unfortunately,
is my poem, dedicated to him. We planned an opera on the folk
hero Ivan the Fool, but there wasn't time. Shostakovich was at
the height of his creative powers when death cut short his life.

We lost not only a great composer but a great man. How
touchingly considerate he was, when he learned of someone's misfortune, illness, or lack of funds. He helped so many composers,
not only with his music but with his support. Genius is higher
than the less than wonderful genre of human behavior known as
envy. Speaking of a composer, Shostakovich sighed, "He's got a
rather vile soul. . . . Too bad. Such musical talent." He immediately added, "Genius and villainy are incompatible." Even a
scoundrel can be gifted, unfortunately, but he deprives himself of
genius.

Of modern foreign composers Shostakovich loved Benjamin
Britten and was his friend. Once we were listening together to
Britten's *War Requiem,* and Shostakovich kept wringing his
hands: that's how he wept, with his hands. Shostakovich was not
only a great composer, but a great listener, and a great reader. He
had a vast knowledge of classical and modern literature, followed
the important works in prose and poetry closely and somehow,

intuitively, he managed to find the important things in the flow of grayness and opportunism. He was inflexible in his personal conversation toward opportunism, cowardice, and toadying, just as openly as he was kind and tender toward everything talented. Unfortunately, as much as I liked his judgments in small circles, I disliked many of his articles and speeches. These were empty praise of the Party and socialist realism. They were not written by Shostakovich, just signed by him. I once rebuked Dmitrii Dmitriyevich for it. He was a conscientious man, very strict with himself, and he admitted that I was right, but explained sadly, "Once I signed under words that I did not think, and ever since then something happened to me — I became indifferent to words I signed. But in music I never signed a single note that I did not think. . . . Perhaps I will be forgiven for that at least. . . . "

In the spring of 1968 the following incident occurred. I was at Shostakovich's house talking about the Prague Spring — with hope and with anxiety. My anxiety was explained by the fact that our centralized newspapers began printing articles criticizing Czech "glasnost" as a "betrayal of socialism." Actions could follow words like that. Shostakovich was nervous, drank spasmodically, and then ran to the next room and showed me an open letter from Soviet cultural figures against the Prague Spring.

"I'm going to sign. Yes, I will. . . . I've signed all sorts of things in my life. . . . I'm a broken man, it's over for me," Shostakovich said, mocking himself.

"Dmitrii Dmitriyevich, for God's sake, don't sign that letter," I said. "You can set a dangerous example for young composers. They'll be able to tell themselves, 'Well, if even Shostakovich signs whatever they want, why shouldn't I sign? . . .' Dmitrii Dmitriyevich, at least don't sign this letter. . . . Other people's lives depend on it. The words you sign could later turn into tanks."

Shostakovich shook, and then crumpled the letter.

"All right, all right . . . I won't." He ran back to the next room. He was gone about five minutes. When he returned his face was ashen and immobile, like a mask. He didn't say another word that evening.

There are no people who never make mistakes, but you have to find the courage, like Shostakovich, to condemn your weaknesses at least to yourself. Some people not only can't look inside themselves with the eye of a just and stern judge, but try to pass off their weaknesses as convictions. Shostakovich told me that when he was working on the music for the play *The Bedbug*, he met Mayakovsky for the first time. Mayakovsky was in a bad, nerve-racked mood, and behaved with obnoxious hauteur and offered the young composer only two fingers instead of his hand. Shostakovich, despite all his piety before the great poet, did not give in and extended one finger in return. Then Mayakovsky laughed good-naturedly and gave him his whole hand. "You'll go far, Shostakovich." Mayakovsky was right.

Shostakovich is with us, in us, but he is no longer only with us, he is far away — in tomorrow's music, in tomorrow's history, in tomorrow's humanity.

Poetry Can't Be Homeless

Marina Tsvetayeva

(1987)

WHEN OUR MOTHERS' PREGNANCY with us ends, our houses' pregnancy with us begins. We are not yet completely born when we still rattle around in its wooden or stone womb, stretching our helpless but furious arms toward the exit from the house. Along with the sense of a roof over our heads, we develop a longing for the door. What's beyond it? While we learn to walk inside the house, we have not yet been born. Our first cry, when we trip on a rock outside the house, that is the real first cry of birth. Character is tested where the familiar walls of the house no longer protect. The longing to leave the house in no way means a hatred of home. That longing is the desire to test oneself against the huge, unknown world, and that desire is higher than mere curiosity: it is the basis of the rebellious human spirit, for a spirit is cramped in any walls. The motto "My home is my castle" is a symbol of weakness of spirit. The spirit is a castle on its own, even if there are no walls around it. There is no one who does not respect a home. But there is no one and no writer without the desire to leave the house. Life offers other houses, some pretending to be your own home, houses that suck you in like a swamp, houses that are like cradles lulling your conscience. But a real person, a real writer, strives and torments himself to get the only comfort — the cruel, impoverished comfort of freedom.

Didn't Leo Tolstoy love his estate, Yasnaya Polyana? But when he felt something shackling and emptying in his house, he raced for the door, beyond which lay the unknown and freedom even if only the freedom of death. Jack London artificially tried to create freedom within the "Wolf House" he was building in Moon Valley, but he may have set fire to it himself, feeling the stone walls pressing in and suffering from nostalgia for the hopelessness of his youth. Nostalgia for hopelessness is not an insult to the parental house — it is a longing to unite with all humanity, where people are homeless, where justice, conscience, equality, brotherhood, and freedom are homeless. Alexander Blok called on fate to attack him: "Let me die beneath a fence, like a cur!"

The lofty hopelessness of the spirit rising up against a beautifully furnished absence of spirituality — is this not our parental home of art? Hopelessness is the human sorrow; it is only in eyes half shut by fatty folds that sorrow is seen as shame.

A great woman, perhaps the greatest ever to live, wept with desperate fury:

Every house is alien to me, every church is empty for me. . . .

That woman was Marina Tsvetayeva.

A home hater? A church hater? Marina Tsvetayeva. . . . How can you say she did not love her paternal house, when she remembered every rough spot on the walls, every crack in the ceiling, until the day she died? But in that house, in her mother's bedroom, was a painting of Pushkin's duel.

> The first thing I learned about Pushkin was that he was killed. D'Anthes hated Pushkin because he could not write poetry and challenged him to a duel, that is lured him out in the snow and killed him with a pistol shot to the stomach. . . . So since the age of three I knew firmly that a poet had a stomach. . . . I became a sister with that duel. I'll say even more — there is something sacred in the word "stomach" for me, and even a simple "stomachache" engulfs me with a wave of trembling sympathy that excludes any humor. We were all wounded in the stomach by that shot.

So even inside her beloved paternal house, a sense of hopelessness arose in a three-year-old girl. Pushkin went off into death —

an irreversible, frightening eternal hopelessness — and in order to feel like his sister, she had to feel that hopelessness for herself. Later, abroad, suffering with loneliness for her homeland and even trying to mock that longing, Tsvetayeva rasped, like "a wounded animal, shot in the stomach,"

> *Longing for homeland! A hassle*
> *Long proved false!*
> *It's absolutely all the same to me*
> *Where I should be absolutely alone,*
> *Along which stones to wander home*
> *With my shopping bag*
> *To a house that doesn't even know*
> *It's mine, like a hospital or barracks.*

She even bares her teeth at her native tongue, which she adored, and which she could knead tenderly and furiously with her worker's hands, the hands of a potter of the word:

> *I won't be charmed by my*
> *Native tongue, its milky call.*
> *I don't care in which*
> *Language I am misunderstood!*

Then we come across those "home-hating" words:

> *Every house is alien to me, every church is empty for me. . . .*

Then comes even more alienation:

> *And everything is equal, and everything is the same. . . .*

And suddenly the attempt at mocking her homesickness breaks off helplessly, ending in an exhalation of genius, which turns the meaning of the poem into a heartbreaking tragedy of love for her homeland:

> *But if on my path appears a bush*
> *Especially — a rowanberry . . .*

That's all. Just an ellipsis. But those dots are a powerful and endless, mute admission of a mighty love that a thousand versifiers who write not with those great dots, each of which is a drop of blood, but with endless puny words to create pseudopatriotic drivel will never be able to express. Perhaps the greatest patriotism is always like that: in ellipses and not in empty words.

Thus love for her house — but through the exploit of hopelessness. That exploit was the life of Tsvetayeva. She didn't fit in too well in the house of Russian poetry, divided into living rooms, salons, corridors, and literary kitchens. Her first book, *Evening Album,* was praised by bards like Bryusov and Gumilyov, trendsetters then, but their praise had condescension, which hid their instinctive sense of danger. The very young Tsvetayeva gave off the dangerous smell of fire, which threatened the orderliness of that house and its partitions, which could easily go up in flames. Tsvetayeva compared her poetry with "little devils bursting into a shrine filled with sleep and incense." She did not go as far in shocking the bourgeoisie as the Futurists, who wanted to toss Pushkin off the ship of modernity. But lines like this from a twenty-year-old girl

> *Scattered in the dust of stores*
> *(Where no one bought them!)*
> *The time for my poems, as for*
> *Precious wines, will come.*

did not make poets, who were sure of the preciousness of the poems from their vineyard, very happy. There was something challenging in that girl.

All of Bryusov's poetry, for instance, was like a neatly furnished semimuseum living room in the House of Poetry. But Tsvetayeva's poetry could not be a thing in that house or even a room — she was a whirlwind bursting into houses and mixing up all the pages of the aesthete's poetry written in calligraphic hand. Later Tsvetayeva said, "There is a place for everything under the sun — the traitor, and the rapist, and the murderer, but not for the aesthete! He does not count, he is expelled from the universe, he is a zero."

Despite her schoolgirlish lace collar, Tsvetayeva appeared in the House of Poetry like a gypsy, like Pushkin's Mariula, with whom she liked to compare herself. And gypsies are the triumph of hopelessness over being settled.

In her earliest poems, there was a cruelty and harshness

heretofore unheard in Russian women's poetry, which was rare among male poets, too, come to think of it. The poems were astonishingly ungraceful. Karolina Pavlova and Mirra Lokhvitskaya looked like embroidery next to wrought iron. And the iron had been made by a girl's small hands! The aesthetes grimaced: a woman blacksmith — unnatural. Akhmatova's poetry at least was more feminine, with softer contours. But this was all sharp angles! Tsvetayeva's character was a tough nut — it had a frightening militancy, a teasing, prickly aggression. Tsvetayeva was recompensing for all the sentimental drivel of the many languorous lady poetesses, who filled the journal pages with their caramel treacle; she was rehabilitating the very concept of female character, showing by her example that it meant not only flirtatious infidelity and charming passivity, but a firmness of spirit and the strength of a master.

There was nothing of the bluestocking suffragette about Tsvetayeva — she was a woman from head to toe, reckless in love, but strong in the breaks. Rebelling, she sometimes admitted the "stone hopelessness of all my pranks." But through the independence of her art and her behavior in life, she fought like no other woman poet for the right of women to have a strong personality, rejecting the clichéd image of femininity, self-melting into the personality of the husband or lover. Mutual melting into each other, she accepted that as freedom and was capable of taking joy in even brief happiness:

> *Mine! — what other rewards.*
> *Heaven! — in his arms, his mouth.*
> *Life: unbridled happiness*
> *In saying good morning!*

Where is she, the rebel, the proud? What simple, loving words, under which any happy woman would sign. But Tsvetayeva had her own sacred commandment: "Even in my dying hiccups I will be a poet!" She did not give that up to anyone for so-called happiness. She not only knew how to be happy, but she knew how to suffer like the most ordinary woman.

> *Lovers are taken away by ships,*
> *Led away by the white road . . .*

> *And a moan rises above the earth:*
> *"Darling, what did I do wrong?"*

But she preferred the unhappiness of freedom to the happiness of subjugated love. The rebel awoke in her and the "gypsy passion for parting" threw her into the homeless "somewhere":

> *Like the right and left hand*
> *Your soul is close to mine.*
> *We are close blissfully and warm*
> *Like the right and left wing.*
> *But a whirlwind rises — and an abyss*
> *Lies from the right to the left wing.*

What was the whirlwind? Tsvetayeva herself. What keepers of morality call infidelity, she called faithfulness to herself, for that faithfulness lies not in subjugation but in freedom.

> *No one, digging through our letters,*
> *Understood to the fullest*
> *How unfaithful we are, that is,*
> *How faithful to ourselves.*

I don't know of any poet in the world who writes as much about parting as Tsvetayeva. She demanded dignity in love and demanded dignity in parting, proudly stifling her cry, only rarely unable to hold it back. The man and woman parting in "Poem of the End" speak like representatives of two equally great states, with the difference that the woman is still greater:

> *[He] "I didn't want this.*
> *Not this." [She] ("Silently: listen!*
> *Wanting is the affair of bodies,*
> *While you and I are souls for each other.")*

But how could men take offense from a woman poet who in an imagined meeting with the person she loved most of all in the whole world — Pushkin — refused to lean on his arm to go up a hill. "I'll go up myself!" the rebel said proudly, even though she was practically an idol worshiper inside. But I'm confusing and simplifying the situation here. Tsvetayeva's pride was such that she was certain: Pushkin would know right away with whom he was dealing and would not dare offer his arm. Of course, at the end of the poem Tsvetayeva softens and allows herself to run down the hill hand in hand with Pushkin. Her attitude toward Pushkin is amazing: she loves him, and is jealous of him, and argues with him as if he were alive.

Think of her incensed fury, which may be colored by her punitive harshness toward Pushkin's wife for marrying General Landsky after Pushkin. Pride like that is a self-defense and can be heard in her marvelous poem "An Attempt at Jealousy" ("After Carrara marble, how's life with a plaster cast?").

Mayakovsky worried that Pushkin might be covered with "an anthology glaze." In this Tsvetayeva joined Mayakovsky. "Pushkin in the role of a monument? Pushkin in the role of a mausoleum?"

But her pride stiffened her back: "I take Pushkin's hand, I don't lick it." With her great pride, Tsvetayeva compensated for all the "lack of pride" of women who lost their face in the face of men. Women all over the world must thank her for that. With the power of her talent Tsvetayeva showed that a woman's loving heart was not a fragile candle or a transparent brook created so that a man could be reflected in it. It was a fire that could leap from house to house. If we were to try to find the psychological formula for Tsvetayeva's poetry, it would be in juxtaposition with Pushkin's harmony, a breaking up of harmony by elemental forces. There are those who like to extract aphoristic lines from poems and base a conception of the poet upon them. Of course, we could make that experiment with Tsvetayeva's poetry, too. She has clear philosophical moments, such as "Genius is the train everyone misses." But her philosophy lies in the elemental forces of life that become the elemental forces of verse, of rhythm, and her concept is an elemental force.

The heart of a real poet is a house for the homeless. The poet is not afraid to let the elemental forces into himself and is not afraid of being torn apart by them. It happened to Blok when he let in the Revolution, which wrote his great poem, "The Twelve," for him. It happened to Tsvetayeva, also, when she let in the forces of her personal and civic feelings and the only thing they were ruled by — the elemental forces themselves. But you need strict professional discipline for the forces of life to become the elemental forces of poetry. Tsvetayeva did not allow the elements to rule in her craft — she was the master there.

Marina Ivanovna Tsvetayeva is an outstanding professional poet, who with Pasternak and Mayakovsky reformed Russian versification for many years hence. The great poet Akhmatova, who was so impressed by Tsvetayeva, was merely a keeper of traditions and not an innovator, and in that sense Tsvetayeva is greater than Akhmatova. "There's enough of me for 150 million lives," Tsvetayeva used to say.

Unfortunately, there wasn't enough for even one, her own.

V. Orlov, who wrote the introduction to the one-volume collection of Tsvetayeva published in the USSR in 1965, offensively reproaches the poet for "rejecting with hatred the loud-voiced populist element." Hatred approaches villainy, and as Pushkin said, "Genius and villainy are incompatible." Tsvetayeva never fell into political hatred — she was too great a poet for that. Her perception of the Revolution was complex, contradictory, but those contradictions reflected the confusion and search of a significant part of the Russian intelligentsia, which first hailed the fall of the tsarist regime but then recoiled from the Revolution when it saw the blood shed in the civil war.

> *Was white — became red:*
> *Blood crimsoned him.*
> *Was red — became white:*
> *Death whitened him.*

That wasn't hatred, it was a wail.

It was for this reason that Tsvetayeva had such difficulties in emigration, because she never participated in political hatred and stood aloof from all the groups and factions, for which the trendsetters of the day attacked her. They were irritated by her independence, both political and artistic. They clung to the past, and her verse shot into the future. That's why it was homeless in the world of the past.

Tsvetayeva could not stay away from Russia and she returned. She did not return only because she lived in horrible poverty in the West. (It's terrifying to read her letters to her Czech friend

Anna Teskova, asking her to send a decent dress to Paris so that she could make a rare, miraculous public reading, for she had nothing to wear.) Tsvetayeva came back not only because a great master of the language could not live without the language. Tsvetayeva returned not only because she despised the petit bourgeois world around her, which she denounced in *Newspaper Readers* and *Ratcatcher*, and not only because she hated fascism, against which she spoke so angrily in her Czech poems.

Once, before the Revolution, when she met her future husband, Sergei Efron, in the Crimea, Tsvetayeva vowed never to leave him. She had never made such vows to her homeland. But when Efron returned to the USSR, two longings, two innocent guilts plagued her, tormented her, for leaving, abandoning, something precious, defenseless, and her own. Tsvetayeva must have known about the bloody Bartholomew's nights her homeland had lived through in the mid-thirties. Nevertheless, she returned in 1939. She was not shot, she was not sent to the camps — they punished her slowly by indifference, not publishing her, and by arresting the people closest to her. Sergei Efron, her daughter, Alya, and her sister, Anastasia, were arrested in rapid succession. Strand by strand, this was spun into the noose that eventually killed Tsvetayeva. A meeting with Akhmatova excited her but then disappointed her because the hoped-for closeness did not develop. She had expected more warmth from Pasternak, too — he did what he could, but he couldn't do much. In a tragic coincidence, it was he who brought Tsvetayeva the rope to help pack her suitcases when she was being evacuated from Moscow. He had even joked, "You can hang yourself on a rope like this — it won't break."

Tsvetayeva was sent to Elabuga in Tataria with her son, Mur. She sent the unanswered letter to the Writers' Union of Tataria with a request for translation work. The fee she asked was soap and shag tobacco. But almost the entire Writers' Union of Tataria was under arrest then. Tsvetayeva helped the local policeman's wife do laundry and got a little extra food for that. Tsvetayeva went to Chistopol and wrote a letter to Nikolai Aseyev with a request for a job as dishwasher at the writers' dining room. Unable to take the "swarm of humiliations," Tsvetayeva sent her son off to the airport construction site where he was working, and then hanged herself in the low-ceilinged entryway, tying the rope to the heavy, textured nail used for yokes and fishing nets. "Everybody comes around and looks at it and touches it," the owner of the house told me glumly. "Maybe you'll take the nail away?"

It's unlikely that Tsvetayeva was hoping to find "domestic coziness" for herself — she was looking for a house for her son, not for herself, and for her many poem children, whose mother she was, and for all her sense of being doomed to hopelessness, knew that Russia was the home for her poems. Tsvetayeva's return was a mother's act on behalf of her children. A poet can be homeless, but not poetry.

The Proletariat Does Not Need Psychosis

Andrei Platonov

(1988)

Not Being Heard Is Not Being Too Late

A CHARACTER of Platonov's, the curious old capitalist Khoz, peacefully rotting in good health for 101 years and not lacking a certain sexual sentimentality, comes to the land of the Bolsheviks. With bitter compassionate sympathy, the American centenarian watches the inspired but criminally inept builders of socialism going about their work in the Artel of Fourteen Red Huts. Slightly romantic but mostly skeptical, Khoz warns the slightly skeptical but mostly romantic enthusiasts who are dangerously obsessed with building the World Economic and So Forth Mystery, "Karl Marx told me in the middle of the last century that the proletariat does not need psychosis."

Perhaps a similar thought occurred without Marx's help to the young Armand Hammer, when in the mystery land he saw astonishing reconstructive energy coupled with the destructive self-reliance of a utopian psychosis. The practical businessman must have noticed even then that too much Russian lumber was going for the poles of banners and slogans, for bureaucratic desks, and for the tribunes of orators. He must have wondered even then why a country so rich in resources had a line — that zoological phenomenon incomprehensible to corrupt capitalism — at every step.

A half century later, casting the gaze of an aging tiger of the world's jungles from the window of the Bolshevik limousines so ingratiatingly supplied, Dr. Hammer must have noticed that in a country of unstable political doctrines and reputations, the only unshakably stable thing is the line, the queue.

Today's line is the visual symbol of the punishment for utopian psychosis. Today's line signifies the glaring loss of the people. Economic profit can sometimes be immoral, but an entire nation's loss is always immoral.

The immorality begins with unfulfilled promises. The slogan "Land to the people!" was not fulfilled. The blacksmith in Platonov's *Chevengur* puts it clearly: "How clever: you give us the land, but you take the wheat down to the very last grain: you can go choke on land!" The slogan "All power to the Soviets!" was replaced with power to the bureaucracy, who speak proudly of themselves this way: "Without the bureaucracy, respected warriors of the state, the Soviet state would not last a minute. . . . Who are we? We are the re-pre-sen-ta-tives of the proletariat!" The forced politization of the economy was psychosis just as much as the politization of personal life.

Bureaucrats didn't worry about making a moral mistake — they were afraid of making political mistakes. They forgot what was profitable and not profitable in economics, but they remembered what was ideologically harmful. The utopian psychosis consisted of building socialism with methods that contradicted the ideas of socialism. The methods were the most unprofitable ones because they were immoral, and the most immoral because they were unprofitable.

The "free" labor of millions of prisoners did not balance the expenses for barbed wire, guards, guard dogs, camp towers with machine guns, and the bulky machinery of surveillance and illegality. Psychosis is not profitable.

There were no people who didn't see any illegality at all. Don't believe the lie, "We didn't know a thing." They may not have known everything, but they knew. They knew, but they didn't want to know. Don't believe that Stalin didn't know. He knew more than the rest. He wasn't afraid of those who knew but did not know. He was afraid of those who knew and wanted to know more. He destroyed them first.

Stalin scribbled "Bastard!" on Platonov's story "In Vain." In one of his letters, Alexander Fadeyev [first secretary of the Writers' Union] wrote, "I recently missed the ideologically ambiguous story by Platonov, 'Doubting Makar,' and I properly got hell from Stalin for it." Platonov was dangerous not only because he knew, but because he saw more. Why didn't Stalin simply destroy Platonov? Did he confuse all those millions of names or simply forget his? Maybe he considered him a holy fool and took squeamish pity on him — how could you have a Russian state without a holy fool on the ramparts? Perhaps it was an artistic error of Stalin's taste — he didn't realize that "this thing is stronger than Goethe's *Faust*" (as he valued Gorky's "The Girl and Death"), didn't understand that Platonov was a genius, and a dangerous genius at that, and just took him for a scribbler unworthy of arrest?

Perhaps he appreciated Platonov's caliber as a writer, but hoped that he would change his mind and tried to frighten him first by not allowing his publication, then allowing some things in print, first arresting his son, then releasing him already mortally ill after working in the lead mines, first allowing attacks on Platonov in the press, then permitting his appointment as a war correspondent for the journal *Red Star*? Was there something of long-distance cat-and-mouse in all this? History may give us the answer, it may not. But the fact remains: No writer ever exposed Stalinism from within as Platonov did, and yet Platonov miraculously did not die in a camp but of a natural death in 1951. But there is an even more mysterious riddle in the life of this great writer of the World Economic and So Forth Mystery.

How did Platonov understand, back in the 1920s, that which our society is only beginning to realize now, and with great difficulty at that? It was as much of an exploit as being inside a bonfire and analyzing the burning kindling and the people throwing it in and also pitying them for their "holy simplicity."

Platonov did not excuse them, he pitied them. But Platonov did not include inquisitors in the "holy simplicity." Even in "Che-Che-O" (1928), written with Pilnyak, there is a clear and markedly ironic hint at Stalin's personality and his mannerisms: "The majestic Muscovite, in whose honor they were drinking wine, judiciously and mysteriously taciturn, grew more animated. 'That's not quite it, comrades, not quite!' he said. 'We aren't getting used to equilibrium. I would make our main slogan now be equilibrium of enterprises. Otherwise instead of self-criticism, we get flogging . . .' In this part of his speech, which incidentally was not very understandable or clear, the Muscovite offered his interlocutors some Duchess Flore cigarettes."

A superficial reading of *Juvenile Sea* might give the impression that Platonov, unable to bear the torment of the sword of Damocles, was paying compliments to the Main Swordbearer: "Vermo found Stalin's 'Questions of Leninism' and began rereading that transparent book, in which the bottom of truth seemed so close, when it was really so deep." But who is Vermo, so delighted with Stalin? "Vermo was not so interested in a happy lot for humanity — he tried not to imagine it — as in the murder of all the enemies of creative and laboring people." Stalin's admirer is a rather frightening man. Here's more: "Vermo watched her walk away and wondered how many nails, candles, copper and minerals could be extracted chemically from Bostaloyeva's body: 'Why build crematoriums?' the engineer wondered daily. 'We need to build chemical plants to extract colored metals and gold, various construction materials and fixtures from the corpses.'"

Vermo's secret thoughts were realized by the Nazis, who made soap and lamp shades from humans. Reading Stalin, Vermo "felt peace and a happy confidence in the righteousness of his life, as if an old serious comrade, whose face he did not know [just a few years later, the country would be papered with that face, engineer Vermo! — Y.Y.], was supporting his strength." The direct link between Stalin's ideas and their executive, engineer Vermo, prepared to break people down into their chemical elements for the victory of those ideas, is a serious accusation of Stalin and perhaps the first, before Mandelstam.

But Platonov was less interested in the main inquisitors than in those tossing the kindling. In his everyday life Platonov was luckily removed from the main inquisitors, but he did spend his whole life with the kindling tossers. The kindling tossers are sincerely certain that the people writhing in the flames are not people like them — of flesh, bone, and pain — but evil witches and sorcerers. Their sincerity does not absolve their guilt nor keep the sincere kindling from burning people alive.

Safronov in *The Foundation Pit* brings up his little girl this way: " 'While we, according to the plenum, are required to liquidate them as a whole class, so that all the proletariat and the hired hands are orphaned from the enemies!'

" 'And who will you stay with?'

" 'With our goals, with a firm line for future works, understand that?'

" 'Yes,' the girl replied. 'That means you should kill all the bad people, since there are so few good people.' "

But how is the girl to know who's bad and who's good? Whoever is branded "bad" will be bad, that is, subject to liquidation, and the girl brings kindling to the bonfire with a skip. The little girls Stalin patted on the head at the Mausoleum [during Red Square parades] held bundles of kindling and not bouquets of flowers. You can't blame the children for that, but you can't justify the corrupting pedagogy of psychosis.

The phenomenon of Platonov is that through the slogan-waving, hat-tossing twenties he foresaw the bloody 1937 and the collision of two opposite troubling winds that became the sandstorm of World War II. The power of Platonov's historical foresight is equal to Dostoevsky's. *The Devils* was tragically unheard — some revolutionary democrats decided that it was a lampooning novel, not understanding that it was a warning novel. Platonov's prose is also a warning. *Chevengur* prophesies Yezhov [Beria's predecessor], and Beria, and Hun wei bin, Pol Pot, and the Red Brigades. But Platonov's warning was left unheard and misunderstood — even by Gorky, who on the whole had a high opinion of him. Here is what Gorky wrote to Platonov when he asked for his help in getting *Chevengur* published in 1929: "Whether you wanted this or not, you gave your perception of reality a lyrico-satirical character. For all the tenderness of your attitude toward people, they are colored by irony and appear before the reader not so much as revolutionaries as 'eccentrics' and half mad. This, naturally, is unacceptable for our censors."

Platonov's voice was not heard in time as an alarm. The social utopian psychosis turned into the disease of human deafness. But there are alarms that though unheard during fires of the present can still warn of potential fires of the future. Not being heard is not being too late. Now, when we belatedly learn about so many tragedies and crimes, I sometimes feel unbearably ashamed of our people and our history. But the belatedness of our knowledge of history fortunately has a positive side. We are learning belatedly but fortunately that even in the cruelest years there were people who withstood mass psychosis. National pride without national historical shame for crimes turns into chauvinism. Historical shame is a creative force when its faithful ally is national pride. Platonov's prose was preglasnost glasnost. An alarm not heard in time can become an alarm for all times.

Bureaucracy Is Petrified Psychosis

The history of humanity is the history of great ideals and great psychoses. The provenance of mass psychosis, perhaps, is first tied to the bewilderment of early, shaggy man in the face of the beautiful, but sometimes threatening, destructive force of nature. The fear of nature forced primitive man to huddle dependently around the leaders who allegedly knew The Secret. The power of some people over others began with psychosis.

Fear of the mysterious hewed idols out of stone and wood, replacing the lack of knowledge with the psychosis of blind faith. Man's struggle for freedom was the struggle for freedom from mass psychosis.

Ersatz ideals, like fascism, were totally based on psychosis and collapsed along with it. But psychosis stuck to humanistic ideals as well — for instance, to Christianity, giving birth to the Inquisition. During the great French Revolution the psychosis of enemyphobia appeared, and the revolutionaries began killing one another. It was those times that prompted the tragic aphorism: "The revolution is a monster that devours its own children."

The psychosis of our Soviet enemyphobia destroyed the bloom of our nation before the war, making Hitler's vicious goal that much easier. But even the war did not interfere with the psychosis of "clarifying" personalities. The SMERSH agents drove front-line soldiers crazy with their surveillance even under enemy fire, defense units shot their own troops in the back, and heroes who escaped from German POW camps were sent to our camps. The paranoid "clarifications"[1] continued. But it had started back in the 1920s.

"I'm unclarified here," said one of Platonov's heroes with a heavy sigh. Umrishev, the head of a state farm, belongs to that group of people whose identity is constantly being clarified by the bulky, rusty Machine of Clarification, consisting of "sectors, secretariats, groups of executive directors, directors, departments, subdepartments, board collegiality, meetings, and planning into the far future some thirty years ahead. . . . Establishments of such profound and multifaceted planning that their decisions needed an eternity."

It might have been a planned rustiness, some crossed wires, or a lack of spare parts, but the Machine of Clarification turned into the Machine of Confusion, the Machine of Casting a Shadow on the Fence. "About twice a month the unclarified came to the offices and asked, 'Well, have I been clarified yet?' " A true Kafkaesque picture, which unfortunately is disgustingly dear to every Russian heart.

Bureaucratism was not a hideous growth on a healthy tree. Bureaucratism was many wood borers eating the pulp.

The bureaucrats, like marauders, moved invisibly through the smoking fields of the civil war, grabbing up everything loose. The whole country was loose, deformed, destroyed, and staring, and they began taking it over. The old regime bureaucracy was replaced by the new with such speed that the real creators of the Revolution didn't have time to blink. Lenin wrote, "The state apparatus is in such sad shape, if not to say disgusting, that we must first think seriously how to fight its shortcomings, remembering

---

1. "Clarification" is Platonov's term for the checking done by the secret police.

that these shortcomings are rooted in the past, which is turned over but still persists."

In the story "Garbage Wind," written about fascist Germany but describing Russia in the classic method of Lermontov's "Farewell, Unwashed Turkey," Platonov painted a landscape of the bureaucracy's paper psychosis: "Millions could now not work, but merely hail; besides them, there were crowds, and tribes, who sat in offices and asserted in written, optical, musical, mental, and psychic forms the majesty of the savior genius, themselves remaining wordless and nameless." And this passage from the 1920s is a prophetic parody of jamming foreign broadcasts: " 'They say the white bourgeoisie sends signals by radio. Smell that burning odor. . . . The air burns from the wireless marks.' 'Wave your stick!' Kopenkin ordered immediately. 'Mix up their noise — no one will understand it.' "

The bureaucracy needed the fetishization of the state as Highest Being, Highest Reason, for its survival. Today's banner "Man does not exist for the state, but the state for man" would have landed someone in the camps for ten years in Platonov's time.

" 'Without the state, you wouldn't have milk from a cow!'

" 'Where would it go?'

" 'Who knows where! Maybe the grass wouldn't grow either . . . There's no state in the African Sahara, or in the Arctic Ocean, that's why nothing grows there — just sand, heat and deadly cold . . . '

" 'Shame on places like that!' Leonid replied firmly."

Platonov was the first Soviet writer to say with the power of Gogol or Saltykov-Shchedrin that bureaucracy was ossified psychosis.

Is There Anything More Material than Morality?

Platonov the meliorator built material socialism. Platonov the writer built moral socialism in his books. But is there anything more material than morality?

Mass psychosis, like an avalanche, fell on our country from the "heights" of state thought. This avalanche rolled over once-fruitful fields, villages with their ancient order, churches, the proletarian dignity of Russian workers, the freedom of thought of the intelligentsia. Caught up in the psychosis, people voluntarily or out of fear turned into unstoppable stones in the avalanche, ruthlessly breaking anyone who didn't want to be a stone. But those who turned into stones, including their hearts, met the same fate — they were also crushed and crumbled by the next stones.

Platonov had the courage to stand in front of the avalanche and express doubts. The avalanche knocked him off his feet and dragged him along, but inside it, rolling, scraping, and bruising, he continued doubting. Platonov's doubts did not come from a desire to seem wise through aloofness toward people and history. Platonov doubted like a man walking on a wooden path laid over a swamp, doubting each plank, testing it with his foot before other people follow. Platonov doubted like a doctor who tests a drug before prescribing it. Such doubts are precious. If there is anyone who keeps humanity on the brink of disaster, instead of falling in, it is a doubter. Those who have no doubts at all triumphantly march into the abyss. The march of people without any doubts is the march of psychosis.

Platonov did not march in step with his contemporaries because he marched in step with some of his descendants. But Platonov loved his contemporaries even more because he knew them. Even history, which tossed him from side to side, and struck him hard but for some reason spared his precious head, pitied Platonov like a lost creature. Platonov tried to convince history that it was not so bad, to persuade history to stop and not destroy everything that breathed and was warm and rational. But in those days direct action against psychosis and even attempts to talk anyone out of it were seen as betrayal or mental illness by those who were maddened by class hatred.

Peter brings the doubting Makar to the police station. " 'Comrade chief, I've caught a psycho and brought him in.' 'Why is he a psycho?' the man on duty asks. 'What disorder has he created in a public place?' 'Nothing,' Peter said openly. 'He's going around and worrying, and then he'll kill someone. I've just prevented a crime.' 'You're right!' the chief agreed. 'I'll send him to the institute for psychopaths — for tests.' "

The self-defense of psychosis is to declare everyone who is not part of it psychopathic. During the stagnation years Tvardovsky had to go to a mental hospital to rescue Zhores Medvedev. The diagnosis — paranoid dual personality — was hypocritically made because Medvedev, a biologist by profession, was exhibiting "abnormally active" interest in politics and writing protest letters. Tvardovsky managed to get Medvedev out, but others were put in. The psychosis of stagnation was not as cruel and all-encompassing as the psychosis of the Stalin period, but it was much more cowardly and cautious — and sometimes more sophisticated and cynical. Despite the harsh or more moderate modifications of the psychosis, its basis was the same old political and medical quackery in determining what was normal and what wasn't.

Platonov wrote, "If they recognized particularly self-reliant people, they destroyed them with the morbid frenzy of normal children beating freaks and animals: with fear and voluptuous pleasure. That was the ideal 'state resident' . . . 'He knew no will, feeling only obedience, as joyful as voluptuousness.' " Voluptuous obedience of those above combined wonderfully with the voluptuous commanding of those below: sadomasochism of slavery and power. Mass psychosis is a multitude of inferiority complexes combined into a curative psychocomplex where people are forcibly cured of normality.

Platonov annoyed the literary "psychiatrists" because he kept "going around and worrying" and even had doubts. Platonov's very presence in literature shamed those who had no shame. That seemingly quiet, peaceful man, who never attacked anyone personally, didn't covet anyone's place, who was poorly dressed, unnoticeable, and never recognized in person — this man elicited envy and wrath by his sense of worth and self-reliance.

Doubting Makar tries to reach the civil conscience of the residents of a flophouse, " 'Comrade workers of labor! You live in your native city of Moscow, the central power of the state, and there is disorder and waste of values here.'

"The proletariat shifted in its bunks. 'Mitrii!' someone's broad voice said deeply. 'Give him a smack, so that he becomes normal.' "

That was the general reaction of many of Platonov's contemporaries to his prose, refusing to hear his appeals to their conscience and reason. This was a time when moral disorder was created under the guise of creating order, and, under the guise of creating socialist values, national and universal values were destroyed. Leopold Averbakh[2] wrote this way in his published "diagnosis" of Platonov's civil abnormality: "He comes to us with propaganda of humanism, as if there were something in the world more truly humane than class hatred." From the lead of class hatred Averbakh made the bullet with which he was later shot.

Another member of RAPP, I. Makaryev, titled his article on Platonov "Slander" and was later slandered himself, spending seventeen years in the camps. He returned toothless and bald, and at night he would climb the fence of the dacha belonging to his former comrade in arms in RAPP, Fadeyev, throw rocks at his darkened windows, and shout: "Sashka, it's the camp ghosts who have come for you! You'll pay for everything yet, Sashka!" Makaryev drank himself to suicide.

Fadeyev, who had criticized Platonov, never put anyone in prison but was forced by his position to sign information on the arrests of writers. He shot himself, tormented by his conscience for his sins and those of others.

A. Gurvich, who constantly criticized Platonov in the thirties, was cruelly spat upon in the early fifties during the campaign against "cosmopolites." If Platonov had been recognized in his lifetime, he would not have gloated over the fate of his critics but would have felt sorry for these miserable people confused by history and therefore having to pay cruelly for the cruelty they performed when their reason was clouded.

Devoid of religious psychosis, the Christian principle is unquestionable in Platonov. The socialist principle is there, too, but without the antireligious psychosis. In a review of a play called

2. Leopold Leonidovich Averbakh (1903–1939), literary critic, founder of RAPP (Russian Association of Proletarian Writers), was a powerful ideologue of the Party line in literature. Class hatred was part of the Marxist dogma. He was executed in the Stalinist Terror.

The Idiot, in 1920, the very young Platonov unwittingly painted his future portrait in his description of Dostoevsky's character: "Prince Myshkin is a proletarian: he is knight of thought, he knows much; he has the soul of Christ — the king of consciousness and the enemy of mystery. He does not return a blow for a blow; he knows that hitting the evil is like hitting children." For Platonov, who valued the word "master" above all, Christ is a master, the master of conscience. Platonov's Christ is the enemy of mystery because a mystery for the master is a lack of knowledge. The mystic pretending to be the "king of the unconscious and the enemy of mystery" is incapable of going to Golgotha, or writing *War and Peace,* or creating the theory of relativity. Platonov understood conscience as daily work.

The idols created by mass psychosis eventually are broken by the masses. The paradox of history is that the masses recognize as great those who did not give in to mass psychosis.

Hope Without Preliminary Conditions

It's too bad that in the 1920s the young Hammer did not meet Platonov, the young land-reclamation engineer from Voronezh, who in four years as provincial land director supervised the creation of 763 ponds, 316 artesian and pipe wells, 800 dams, and 3 electric stations; the drainage of 7,600 *dessiatines* of land; and the formation of 240 melioration peasant groups. Those two young businessmen filled with wild energy from two different systems could have set aside ideological chatter, made friends, united, and come up with something that would have made the world gasp! But the political psychosis was more important than the country's good. Mutual benefit from relations with the capitalist world was considered a dangerous heresy — what is good for them cannot be good for us. The same political psychosis existed and exists on the other side of the globe. The reactionaries of the world unite much more quickly than the proletariat.

Stalin, who was industrializing, hoped for favorable parallels with Peter the Great. However, as opposed to Peter, who had overdone Westernizing, he was mortally afraid of the "corrupting influence of the West" and put bars on the window to Europe

that Peter had cut. Peter personally cut the beards of boyars, while
Stalin began planting a new caste of boyars, the *nomenklatura,*
through fear and bribes with "blue packets" (the second, unofficial salary). Stalin did not imitate Peter the builder but Peter the
executioner. The great Russian historian Klyuchevsky character-
ized Peter's negative aspects this way: "Introducing everything by
force, even self-reliance, he built lawful order on general lack of
rights, and therefore in his lawful state alongside power and law
the all animating element was missing — the free person, the citizen."

Without free thought the Soviet economy could not develop,
either. Feverish purchases of foreign technology, like the Marion
excavators that Platonov studied, did not help. An old journalist
once told me that before the war Tass, the Soviet news agency,
bought four Leica cameras with Stalin's personal permission. Iso-
lated from the world's development, Stalin's industry alternately
made progress because of inhumanely intense labor or got stuck
in puddles of blood flowing under the excavators' Caterpillar
treads.

In his autobiography, Platonov wrote about why he had gone
into technology and not literature: "The drought of 1921 had a
profound effect on me and as a technologist, I could not be involved in contemplative work, literature." But Platonov's faith in
technology alone was undermined because it was often in the
hands of romantic ignoramuses or indifferent cynics. A social
utopian in his youth, Platonov quickly was cured from the temp-
tation of social utopias by bitter reality, the way a dog hit by a
car heals itself instinctively by eating unnamed plants. Platonov
did not replace unwise optimism with the seemingly wise pessimism of disbelief. But he did experience moments of pessimism:
"Sometimes it seems to me that I have no public future, but only
a future valuable to me alone." "Without me, the nation is incomplete," Platonov said once. But he was incomplete without the
nation. When Platonov devoted himself fully to literature, it
turned out not to be contemplative at all, more like hard labor.
There were intrigues, squabbles, and cretins to deal with. But
literature has one superior trait over technology: technological
projects that are not realized become obsolete, while great banned

manuscripts grow in significance. That is what happened with *The Foundation Pit, Chevengur,* and *Juvenile Sea,* which reached us over fifty years later. What kept up Platonov's spirits?

The hope that he would be published in his lifetime or that he would be published posthumously?

Hope without conditions. Hope without negotiating with life or death.

In his article on Pushkin, Platonov placed the living breathing man above the cold bronze image of state power. Platonov was also a builder of love for fellow man.

Brontosaurs That Give Milk

When you love a person, you have to warn him about all threats to him, even if they are already in his character, his soul, his habits. The same holds for nations. People lie to nations and play up to the people only out of indifference. They speak in the name of the people in order to use the people. When a real writer tells his people the bitter truth, the people should not take offense, because through such a writer the people can talk to themselves. In *The Foundation Pit* this question is posed: "What do you need with the truth? You'll only feel good inside your mind, but it will be nasty on the outside."

Really, what do people need with the truth? It can make things feel nasty not only outside, but inside your mind. Why are so many people insisting on finding out the exact numbers of the arrested and the killed in Stalin's time, the exact number of prisoners today, the exact number of crimes and suicides? Mere curiosity? Or the desire to understand the philosophical truth with the help of factual truth? Will we feel any better when we learn all those numbers? No, worse. But it will be harder to make new mistakes: being horrified by the truth is a good guarantee that there will be no repetition of the horrors. Have we been horrified enough by Stalinism, by Chernobyl to prevent their repetition?

Back to Armand Hammer, who has outlived Platonov by forty years so far. He helped us with medical aid after Chernobyl. How did that catastrophe happen? Platonov had given us the answer, but we did not want to hear it. Here it is: in a dream Makar saw a mountain, and on that mountain stood a man of science. Makar lay at the foot of that mountain like a sleepy fool, waiting for a word or a deed from the man of science. But the man stood in silence, thinking in terms of global scale and not about the individual Makar.

For Platonov the global scale was made up of individual Makars, as opposed to his bureaucrat who felt that "you must sympathize not with people who come but with their cases, which have been solidified in the person of the state." Idealizing the state and raising it above the person — that is as dangerously silly as raising a hotel's administrative staff and the *dezhurnayas* [floor ladies] above the hotel's guests, whom they are supposed to serve. But this is exactly what happened in our country both with the government and with hotels. And now imagine that the floor ladies begin dictating to the writers living in the hotels what they may write and what they may not. They may not write about the problems and tragic incidents that take place in the hotels. Anyplace where they begin to fear tragedies described in print is the place where new tragedies begin in reality.

People are creatures with dangerously short memories. We are not always impressed by retrospectives of crimes. Hitler, theatrically pressing his hands to his heart and with his eyes bulging like a toad's, today in a television documentary looks like a parody of the Chaplin prototype; Stalin on the same screen, hefting a sniper's rifle, is scary, but still a now-harmless parody. You ask yourself: how could so many millions of people have believed such obviously parodic, bloody personages?

Many of Platonov's personages and their ideas can seem parodic and unreal today. Take engineer Vermo: "Wasn't it time to forsake the ancient forms of animals and begin breeding socialist giants such as brontosaurs, who would give a whole cistern of milk at one milking?" Parody? But is this funnier than the fairly recent corn fixation? Utopias are more dangerous than reality, because they are more tempting. Thomas More, Campanella, and other Platonic utopians manipulated only their fantasies. But utopians who manipulate entire nations for the sake of forcing them into Procrustean beds, even if they have to wield an ax to do it, betray the pure, chaste desire for universal happiness that was the origin of utopias in the first place. These utopians could be people without dreams of executions but if they lack culture and responsibility for their actions, sooner or later they inexorably turn into people who "know not what they do." But do people have the right to act without knowing what it is they are doing?

Where Can Cultured Leadership Come from When There Is No Culture?

Engineer Vermo with his crackpot idea in the twenties to cover the whole steppe, "all of Central Asia with lakes of juvenile water," found takers in the Brezhnev era, who approved a plan to turn the course of Siberian rivers. That belongs in the Guinness Book of World Records under "Melioration Psychosis." You can't undertake the reorganization of a country like Russia without elementary culture. You can't start social experiments without having read Dostoevsky's *Devils* — there are many warnings there. Reading Platonov's *Juvenile Sea* would be good, too. It depicts Engineer Vermo, a social psychopath with a child's innocent eyes.

If you only knew, Engineer Vermo, how deprived of creative and proletarian rights was the "creative proletarian man" promised by Stalin! You should read Dudintsev's early novel *Not By Bread Alone*, about inventors who hit an impassable wall with their technological ideas. Our people's invincible inventive talent continued working even in the *sharashkas,* special scientific prisons within the Gulag camp system — just think of Tupolev, who created plans for Soviet military airplanes while behind barbed wire. But that was in spite of, not thanks to. Cybernetics was called a false science in the dictionaries of Stalin's time. They tried to separate Sakharov from science simply because the word "convergence" scared them more than the hydrogen bomb. Khrushchev might have liked solving the housing problem by growing giant pumpkins that could be hollowed out and turned into rooms for milkmaids and farm workers.

Platonov's character Peter became a big boss. He found an excuse for his thirst for power in Lenin: "We need more workers and peasants in our institutions. Socialism should be built with the hands of the mass man." But seventy years of practice has shown that many peasants and workers, once they become bosses, forget their own class. Counting on the mass man to be a leader was a mistake. In order to lead the masses, you have to be more than simply a "mass man." You must have culture per se and the culture of leadership. But where do you get the culture of leadership if there is no culture?

Bostaloyeva, another Platonov character, has a romantic approach to revolution. It sours to cynicism when the technical wonders of socialism fail for lack of minor spare parts. Bostaloyeva asked a boss for a ton and a half of wire she plans to use for making nails, which are in short supply at that period in the life of socialism. The boss, ready to help her with wire for a simple barter of her body, carefully asks, "You won't be insulted?" Bostaloyeva replies, "I won't be, because I'm used to it. Last year I had to get sheet metal for roofs, and I had to have an abortion. But I trust you're not a bastard like that."

Engineer Vermo, you thought even nastier things about Bostaloyeva. You wanted to turn her into her essential chemical elements. And you were the discoverer of the bureaucratic game of "cutting back" staff. Yet the bureaucracy keeps getting bigger, doesn't it? All you've cut back in fifty years is the number of talented, independent people.

You must be a pensioner by now, Engineer Vermo. You grumble about all the lines and that perestroika is moving slowly. But it was people like you in the first place who began slowing up perestroika back in the twenties. The best way to slow progress is by irresponsible acceleration of history. You are a dissident from the right. It was your thoughts in Nina Andreyeva's article, admit it. The humanistic thesis of the new thinking is alien to you; you do not accept that with the real threat to the whole world, human interests take on more significance than class interests. You keep harping that international politics must be determined only by class struggle and that people should be expelled from the Party for taking part in demonstrations.

You speak about Gorbachev with such condescending familiarity, as if you and your pals instead of history had brought him to power. You have such a sour look on your face, as if you had an abscessed tooth on both sides and it was impossible for you to smile normally. It's a good thing you're a helpless pensioner.

When the potential enemies of perestroika are politely sent out to retirement, it is a step toward national safety. Good-bye, Engineer Vermo. Enjoy your retirement.

Recount One More Time

Platonov wrote with awe of the provenance of masters. Were he alive today, he would be writing about the disappearance of masters.

Platonov's war comrades recall that whenever they spent the night in some manless village hut, Platonov always tried to repair the roof and chop some firewood.

Around 1950 I was "shown" Platonov in the backyard of the Literary Institute. He was clearing snow from a walk with a wooden shovel with metal trim. He was wearing a worn coat and a worn rabbit-fur hat with the earflaps down, and he moved the shovel so smoothly and habitually that he resembled an ordinary janitor. He did even this work with respect for the snow and the shovel. Platonov was not being published then, he was not written about, he was only shown, and from a distance at that. V. Barlas, an older friend, a geophysicist who later became a critic, let me read an extremely rare copy of Platonov's *River Potudan* without letting it out of his sight. It stunned me, confused me, and enchanted me. I had the feeling that I had been led into a secret underground passage where marvels were hidden from evil eyes and hands. Platonov's words in the flickering candlelight shimmered, sparkled, and glowed like precious stones that I had never heard of. That is how our country was living, donning cheap and pathetic fake jewelry for special occasions and hiding real treasures underground from itself and others. When the bloody psychosis ends, the psychosis of hiding remains by inertia for a long time.

The main miracle of Platonov's prose is that it was written, despite everything, and that it exists. Platonov left us, his descendants, who are poisoned by false history, his priceless testimony of a "self-made man." Platonov was one of the few chosen, like Vavilov, Chayanov, Voino-Yasenetsky, and Likhachev,[3] who

---

3. Vavilov and Chayanov, *see* note p. 104. Voino-Yasenetsky, *see* note p. 74. Dmitri Sergeyevich Likhachev (born 1906), literary critic and cultural historian, spent time in the Stalinist camps. Widely recognized for his moral authority, he is now chairman of the Cultural Foundation USSR.

miraculously survived. But being chosen hardly could have pleased Platonov, since he wanted his firm convictions generously sprinkled over the entire nation, without skipping a single doubting Makar. Platonov did not blame all the national disasters on the leaders and bureaucrats. Bureaucracy, according to Platonov, is merely a manifestation of a sociohistorical psychosis that affects all layers of the population, including the intelligentsia, and temporarily, Platonov himself. Platonov was the nation condemning itself not only for what it allowed to be done to it but also for what it did to itself. Bureaucracy is a neglect of the people for which the people pay.

Platonov's nomadic profession of meliorator tired him out, but it let him feel the sore points of the country's body, exhausted by the civil war, and which was wounded, crumpled, and gouged by the dilettantish, illiterate political and economic quacks. The countryside was the first victim of the utopian psychosis. And there are almost no defenders of the peasantry left in literature either. For all my love of Sholokhov's *Quiet Don,* I find this reasoning awful: "We tolerated the kulak out of need: he gave more grain than the kolkhozes. But now it's the reverse. Comrade Stalin added up the arithmetic and said, 'Get rid of the kulak.' " But nowadays we know that they got rid of the ordinary, average-income peasants who were the backbone of Russian farming. Comrade Stalin's arithmetic was way off. We are still paying for Stalin's bad accounting. Khoz, who became an accountant, suddenly tossed away his abacus: "Let them be approximately happy. . . . It doesn't matter — any count and account will need recounting anyway."

Perestroika is a time of great recounting. Not all writers can withstand the test. But Platonov does — both as a master craftsman and as a citizen. As a master, because he hated approximate words. As a citizen, because he disdained approximate happiness.

This Man Was Humanity

The fate of Platonov's prose resembled the fate of Pushkin's heroine Tatyana, as Platonov described it. "Here she is like a mysterious creature from an old fairy tale which crawled along the ground all its life, and its legs were broken so that the creature would die — and then it found its wings and flew up above the low place where it was supposed to die."

There are two diametrically opposed points of view of the Stalin period. One is that the appearance of a dictator, the forced collectivization, and the killing industrialization were a historical inevitability.

The other is that there was a humanistic alternative — the development of cooperatives, glasnost, democracy, and voluntary collectivization (the Bukharin version). The first version won, and everything followed Platonov's prophecy in *The Foundation Pit:* "Well, all right, you'll turn the republic into a kolkhoz, but the whole republic will be one man's farm!"

Besides the Bukharin version, there were others, of course. As far as I know, Platonov did not support any of them openly and was not involved in direct professional politics. But it is clear now that in his sociopolitical analysis Platonov was ahead of Stalin, and Bukharin, and many others.

The writer Andrei Platonov did not want to clamber up the mountain ranges of history tied to a group of climbers. He preferred the free-fall. But he flew so that he could see both the global scale and each individual Makar. Platonov's prose is brilliant Russian thought soaring above its times.

Platonov teaches us that the "proletariat does not need psychosis," it needs love — you can't survive without it. There is no writer of the Soviet period of Russian literature who is purer or more loving. What Platonov's character Fro said about the musician applies to Platonov: "That man, probably, was humanity." In the foreword to an early book of poetry, *Light Blue Depths,* Platonov wrote: "We hate our mediocrity, we stubbornly try to climb out of the mud. . . . Out of our ugliness grows the soul of the world." A person who did not lie about the past would not lie about the future.

Handwriting Resembling Cranes

BORIS PASTERNAK

(1962–1988)

AKHMATOVA wrote this about Pasternak:

> *He is endowed with an eternal childhood*
> *with the vision and generosity of stars,*
> *and the whole earth was his inheritance,*
> *and he shared it with everyone.*

That is the way a great artist comes into the world — inheritor of the whole world, its nature, its history, its culture. But real greatness lies not only in inheriting but in sharing it with everyone. For an educated mediocrity, possessing knowledge and hiding it is a pleasure. For a genius, possessing knowledge that he has not yet shared with others is torture. Pasternak often compared poetry to a sponge that soaks up life only to be squeezed out "for the health of greedy paper." As opposed to Mayakovsky, whom he nevertheless loved in a complex but loyal way, Pasternak felt that a poet must not force his poems and his name into the reader's consciousness through manifestos and self-promotion. Pasternak wrote about the poet's role in a different way: "Being famous is unattractive," "Life is only an instant, the dissolving of ourselves in everyone else, a gift for them," "With me are people without names, trees, roofs, the housebound. I am vanquished by them all and that is my only victory."

Nevertheless Pasternak, despite singing the praises of being "unnoticed," became probably the most famous Russian poet of the twentieth century, surpassing even Mayakovsky. How did that happen? The apologia for modesty was not a calculated attempt to use self-debasement as a way of finally getting recognition from humanity. Geniuses have no time for modesty — they are too busy with more important things. Pasternak always knew his own worth, as a master of poetry, but he was more interested in the mastery than in mass applause for it. The Nobel Prize Committee deigned to notice Pasternak only during the raging political scandal, yet Pasternak deserved the highest prize for poetry back in the thirties.

The novel *Doctor Zhivago* is far from the best thing Pasternak ever wrote, even though the novel is a landmark in the history of Russian and world literature. The complex, convoluted relationship between Lara and Yuri Zhivago, with the Revolution and civil war separating them and bringing them together, resembles in some ways the relationship of Katya and Roshchin in Alexei Tolstoy's trilogy *Road to Calvary*, completed in the thirties, long before *Zhivago*. Tolstoy put history first and Pasternak put the love story first, and that is the principal difference between the two novels and the two concepts. The French composer Maurice Jarré, who did the film score, understood the point and intertwined revolutionary march melodies with the love theme, Lara's theme, the theme of harmony that overcomes the storm. For a good fifteen years that theme was very popular, requested by customers in restaurants all over the world, including the Soviet Union, where the novel was not published. Once, during the European figure-skating championships, a skater began his routine to Lara's theme, and the Yugoslav commentator, who knew that he was being heard in the Soviet Union, exclaimed joyfully: "The melody is from the film *Doctor Zhivago*, based on the Boris Pasternak novel!" Soviet TV immediately cut off the sound. The skater twirled in complete silence on the screen. It was rather funny, but much more embarrassing and sad.

Something paradoxical had happened. Pasternak, who had never participated in a single political battle, had ended up in the middle of one, to his own surprise. But was it unexpected? He had predicted a lot about himself, and in the name of the bird had even called on the hunter to shoot: "Hit me in flight." He predicted, "When feeling dictates the line, it sends a slave onto the stage, and here art ends and soul and fate begin to breathe." I suppose most prophetic is the monologue of Lieutenant Schmidt from the poem of the same name:

> *I know — you feel you will not flinch,*
> *mowing down a man.*
> *Well, martyrs of dogma,*
> *you too are the victims of the age.*
>
> *I know that the stake where I will*
> *stand will be the border*
> *of two different eras of history,*
> *and I am glad to be chosen.*

There it is — the greatest Christianity — to understand even as you are being crucified that your executioners are also victims. Pasternak did become history's chosen, putting a love story ahead of history per se. The martyrs of dogma considered that counter-revolutionary. They were used to the theory and practice of turning people into cogs in a state machine. This apologia not of the state but of the human soul had to seem alien and heretical to them. They did not have the tolerance, the precious ability to understand that the original ideals of socialism did put the interests of a person above the interests of the state as a machine. History is fair only when it does not interfere in love stories. What Pasternak had to say in the late fifties seemed a dangerous heresy then. Today, when even government officials put the "human factor" higher than the interests of the state in their speeches, the former heresy is on the path to canonization. But it is too soon to speak of results, since there are enough examples in history of moral postulates being violated daily by those who preach them. Pasternak, without being a politician, instinctively sensed the inevitability of the coming political break and did become a border post on the boundary between two different eras in history. The scandal around the novel — aside from the terrible moral and physical blow to Pasternak — turned out to be marvelous advertising in the West, an ironic twist of fate, and made the long-existing great poet visible at last in the myopic eyes of the Nobel Committee and in the eyes of "mass readers."

But does that mean that Pasternak was understood in the West as a great poet? Sensed, perhaps, but understood, most unlikely. Even the novel was misunderstood by many — it was allegedly too complex. And the film version, for all the fine music and lovely acting by Julie Christie, was sentimentalized and simplified. The Oriental pretty boy Omar Sharif is too Turkish-delightful to be a Russian prerevolutionary intellectual, brought up on Tolstoy, Chekhov, and Dostoevsky. Pasternak's poetry, like all poetry, is almost untranslatable, but we still have that saving tiny "almost." In order to understand the irony of Pasternak's poetics, we must turn to his biography — family and literary.

Boris Pasternak was born into the family of Leonid Pasternak, a close friend of such major figures of the Russian intelligentsia as Tolstoy, Rachmaninoff, and Mendeleyev. Intellectuality was the very air the family breathed. Boris Pasternak had to choose between music and poetry in his youth. He decided, to our great fortune, on the latter, when his idol, Alexander Scriabin, listened to his composition and gave him a very left-handed compliment — that he had a good ear. Pasternak selected philosophy for his education and literature for his profession and studied in Marburg. The poetry of Rainer Maria Rilke had an enormous influence on Pasternak. This is easy to understand when you read the few poems Rilke wrote in Russian, with charming grammatical and lexical errors, but nevertheless very talented and with a clear, almost Pasternakian accent. It is easy to guess that much of Rilke in German became Pasternak's. But for all the Western culture Pasternak had imbibed, he was never a Westernizer. He once wrote much too categorically, "The soul is leaving the West — it has nothing to do there." Pasternak, like Pushkin, was simultaneously a Westernizer and in some sense a Slavophile, cool toward both a parroting imitation of Western culture and a limiting Russian nationalism. Pasternak criticized his own early poetic efforts, preferring his later poems, but I do not think he was right. Writers in general prefer their latest works, even if it requires a coquettish bashing of the earlier ones.

Pasternak lived a long time, and his poetics matured and

changed with him. The rebellion against academic classicism in
the early twentieth century was taking place everywhere in Russia — in painting, music, and poetry. Young Pasternak even
joined the Futurists, headed by Mayakovsky. Mayakovsky called
this quatrain by Pasternak a work of genius:

> *That day all of you from combs to toes,*
> *as a provincial tragedian does a Shakespearean drama,*
> *I carried you with me and knew you by heart,*
> *and wandered the city rehearsing.*

Mayakovsky must have liked this because it resembled Mayakovsky. The early period for both these great, though completely
opposite, poets had a certain similarity, but it later disappeared. In
Walt Whitman's expression, they joined for an instant like eagles
in flight and continued their path in complete isolation. Pasternak
said that he had provoked an argument just to cause a break,
something to which they were both doomed. But I don't think
anyone loved or pitied Mayakovsky more than Pasternak. It was
Pasternak who wrote these lines about Mayakovsky's suicide:

> *Your shot was like Aetna*
> *in the foothills of cowards.*

And much later, in his autobiographical notes, Pasternak gave a
precise analysis of Stalin's posthumous praise ("Mayakovsky was
and remains the best, most talented poet of the Soviet era") for
Mayakovsky. He said it was murderous for Mayakovsky's reputation rather than the salvation it had seemed at the time. "They
began forced planting of Mayakovsky, like potatoes. This was his
second death," wrote Pasternak. This coincided with the bitter
thought Pasternak had expressed on Lenin's death:

> *I thought about the provenance*
> *of the age of binding hardships.*
> *As a harbinger of privileges comes a genius*
> *and with a whip avenges his departure.*

Pasternak, who began with a rebellion of form against the classicists and who sometimes reached near incomprehensibility with
his concentration of metaphors, gradually grew clearer and with

the years achieved a crystal pure, filtered verse. This was true classicism, which is always higher than classicism based on reminiscence. Pasternak's verse is an astonishing combination of two principles — the physiological and the spiritual. The philosophy of his poetry is not thought out, but "muttered out." Of course, behind this seeming improvisational semidelirium there was enormous culture. The delirium of a highly educated and extremely sensitive man will be very different from that of a dictator or a bureaucrat.

Around 1950 Pasternak was supposed to read his translation of *Faust* at the Writers' Club. Poetry was muffled then, and there were no crowds of fans or mounted police to hold them back. The Oak Room was full, but not overly so, and I, a seventeen-year-old beginning poet, managed to squeeze in. The organizers were nervous. Pasternak was late. I put the envelope with my poems on my balcony seat and went downstairs to the vestibule with the secret hope of seeing Pasternak close up. For some reason, no one else was waiting for him there, and when the inner door was flung open and he came in, I was the only one he saw. He said in a singsongy voice and with a slightly guilty smile, "Tell me, please, where is the Pasternak evening taking place? I think I'm late. . . ."

I was bewildered and dumbstruck. Luckily one of the organizers popped up behind me and helped Pasternak with his coat. I was amazed by Pasternak's coat, because it was just like the coat — brown herringbone tweed, with a spare button on the inner pocket — bought by my mentor, a department head at the newspaper *Soviet Sport*. The coat was Italian, which was unusual for those times, but he had gotten it at a most ordinary Moscow store for 700 old rubles [under $100], and I had already seen several of those coats in the street. I don't know what I imagined Pasternak should wear, but it certainly wasn't something that anyone else could buy. Even more amazing was his cap — a gray cap with white nubbles, made of coarse printed fabric, which cost thirty rubles and was on tens of thousands of heads in Moscow, where people had not yet had time to dress up after the war. But despite the total ordinariness of his clothing, which in my silliness I could not accommodate with a real life genius, Pasternak was truly extraordinary in his every movement, as he gracefully kissed the ladies' hands, bowing with a playful courtesy that seemed his alone. This natural, innate lightness of motion, to which my rough childhood upbringing had never exposed me, had the aroma of a different era, miraculously preserved through social upheavals and wars. Only now, looking back through an ever-increasing distance, as I re-create the way he threw up his hands, the uninhibited turns, the mischievous sparkle in his joyful and cautious eyes, the unconstrained play of muscles in his dusky face, I think that Pushkin must have moved through life as easily and abruptly, surrounded by a special but comparable air.

When Pasternak began reading his translation of *Faust*, I was literally enchanted by his almost singing voice. Whenever he tore his eyes from the manuscript and looked up at the audience, I blushed like a maiden in the balcony, certain that Pasternak was looking at me. But Pasternak apparently did not like his own reading very much, and somewhere in the middle he suddenly slammed the manuscript shut and helplessly and piteously he said, "Excuse me, for Heaven's sake, I can't read at all. It's all some sort of nonsense."

It must have been some of the coquetry that Pasternak was given to, because the audience applauded, asking him to continue. In the hall, wrapped in a white down-and-wool scarf, was the beauty Olga Ivinskaya, Pasternak's mistress, and the model for Lara. I knew her well, because I had started coming to her in 1947 for literary consultations at the journal *Novy mir*, and her good friend Lusya Popova ran the Pioneer Club literary course I was taking. But I did not learn of their affair until much later.

When Pasternak began reading, I memorized these lines from his translation:

> *An artificial man needs privacy.*
> *A natural one finds the universe confining.*

The numerous parodies of those years depicted Pasternak as a sphinx, wrapped in privacy, even though this contention was usually supported by only one quotation, early lines clearly written with a smile:

> *Tell me, dear,*
> *what millennium are we in?*

But from that moment on he seemed to me to be part of nature harmoniously moving inside itself. Several years passed. Two young poets — Ivan Kharabarov and Yuri Pankratov — from the Literary Institute, where I was then studying, were always visiting him at the dacha, reading him their work, getting fed, and several times they suggested that Bella Akhmadulina and I drop in. Bella was outraged that these two young poets often referred to Pasternak as "Boris" in our student gatherings and that, according to their stories, they were taking up so much of Pasternak's time. She had once run into Pasternak on a country path but did not speak to him.

I always felt that the best meetings were those that happened accidentally. But I got a call from the foreign commission of the Writers' Union and was asked to accompany the Italian professor Angelo Maria Rippelino to Pasternak's dacha. I replied that I did not know Pasternak and could not do it. I was told that it would not be proper for Rippelino to go outside of town without an escort. "But he speaks perfect Russian," I replied. I was told then that I did not understand the most obvious things. "Then get someone else, someone who knows Pasternak," I replied. "What can I do, Rippelino won't go without you," the long-suffering voice moaned.

We had to go without warning. From the back of the garden, from behind a tree, Pasternak unexpectedly came out, just as dusky-skinned as ever but now gray-haired, wearing a white linen jacket. "Hello," he said, in a singsongy voice, looking at me with his surprised and the same time unsurprisable eyes. Suddenly, without letting go of my hand, and smiling, he said, "I know who you are. You're Yevtushenko. Yes, yes, you're just as I had imagined you — thin, tall, and pretending not to be shy. . . . I know everything about you — even that you skip lectures at the institute, and so on. . . . Who's that behind you? A Georgian poet? I love Georgians."

I explained that it was no Georgian poet but an Italian professor and introduced Rippelino. "Fine. I love Italians, too. You've come just in time — we're having lunch. Come along, come along — you must be hungry."

It was so simple and easy, and we were soon sitting at the table together, eating chicken and drinking. Of the others at the meal I remember the actor Boris Livanov, who was slightly under the influence and spoke loudly and with great talent. Even though Pasternak was almost sixty, he looked no more than forty-seven or -eight. His entire being vibrated with an amazing sparkling freshness, like a just-picked bouquet of lilacs with garden dew on their petals. He seemed to be iridescent, in constant motion from his dancing hands to the toothless smile on his mobile face. He was playacting a bit. But as he wrote about Meyerhold once:

> *Even if you've gotten into the game,*
> *you are right. That's how it should be played.*

This referred to him, as well. And at the same time, I recall other lines by Pasternak:

> *How much courage is needed*
> *to play for the centuries*
> *the way valleys play,*
> *the way rivers play.*

Truly, how much natural spiritual courage it takes to be able to smile that way! And that ability must have been his defense. Pasternak affected people not as a person but as a scent, a light, a rustle. Laughing, he recounted, "What a story happened to me today. A roofer I know came to me, pulled out a pint of vodka and a ring of sausage from his pockets, and said, 'I did your roof and didn't know who you were. Some good people told me that you are for the truth. Let's drink to that!' We drank. Then the roofer said, 'Lead on!' I didn't understand. 'Where am I supposed to lead you?' 'Lead me after the truth!' But I never intended to lead anyone anywhere. The poet is simply a tree that makes noise but never means to lead anyone anywhere. . . ."

As he told the story, he glanced sideways at his listeners and slyly asked with his eyes, "Do you think it's true, that a poet is simply a tree that never means to lead anyone anywhere?" Someone once wrote that Pasternak resembled simultaneously an Arab and his steed. That is astonishingly precise.

Afterward Pasternak read poetry, shaking his head slightly from side to side and drawling the words. It was his recently written "Bacchanalia." At the lines

> *But for the first skirt he sees,*
> *He'll break the leash,*
> *and then what things*
> *he will do*

he shot a wicked look at his wife, who was fingering the tablecloth nervously, and sighed merrily at the recognition of his wild youth, still fermenting inside him.

Pasternak asked me to read my poetry. I read my best poem of that period, "Weddings." It left Pasternak cold; apparently he did not feel the second inner theme, and took it for Siberian ethnography. But Pasternak was a kindly man and he asked me to read something else. I read "Prologue," which even my closest friends had criticized:

> *I am various,*
> > *I am stiff and I am merry,*
> *I am serious*
> > *and silly,*
> *I am incompatible,*
> > *inconvenient,*
> *Shy and arrogant,*
> > *mean and kind....*

Unexpectedly, Pasternak was delighted, he leaped from his chair, embraced and kissed me. "You have so much strength, energy, youth!" He demanded that I read more. I think that it was only my strength, energy, and youth that he liked, and not the poem itself. But he gave me a chance — now he wanted to like me. Then I read "Loneliness," which I had just completed, and which began this way:

> *How shameful it is to go to the movies alone,*
> *without a friend, a girlfriend, a wife.*

Pasternak grew serious, and there were tears in his eyes: "That's about all of us — about you and about me. . . ."

Rippelino was gone, and so were the other guests, and it was late at night. Pasternak and I were alone and talked a long time, and — damn it! — I don't remember what about.

I've had an even worse experience, though. It was at the birthday party for Fira Markish, the widow of the executed Jewish poet. I spent the entire day at the side of a taciturn old woman, dressed in black, and I drank and prattled nonsense, certain that she was a provincial Jewish relative. I remember that the old woman got up and left, apparently tired of my nonsense.

"What did you discuss with Anna Andreyevna? I had put you next to her on purpose," Fira asked.

"What Anna Andreyevna?" I asked, turning cold and pale, as comprehension came to me.

"What do you mean? With Akhmatova," Fira replied.

Luckily, it wasn't that bad with Pasternak, but I've lost a major part of the conversation. I do remember that I was supposed to leave for Tbilisi in the morning and that around five Pasternak decided that he was going to fly with me. But Zinaida Nikolayevna, who was supposed to have gone off to bed long ago, appeared and said sternly,

"You are killing Boris Leonidovich. It's bad enough you keep him up drinking all night, now you want to whisk him away. . . . Don't forget the difference between your age and his."

I quietly fled her just wrath, surprised that I had spent eighteen hours in the house of the great poet — from 11 A.M. until 5 A.M. the next day!

Soon afterward he let me read the manuscript for *Doctor Zhivago*, but for a criminally brief time, just one night. The novel disappointed me then. We young post-Stalinist writers were crazy about the chopped, so-called masculine prose of Hemingway, Remarque's novel *Three Comrades*, and Salinger's *Catcher in the Rye*. *Doctor Zhivago* seemed too traditional and even boring then. I didn't read the novel, I leafed through it. In the morning when I returned it, Pasternak asked me, "Well?"

I replied as politely as possible, "I like your poetry better."

Pasternak was noticeably hurt and made me promise to one day read the novel without rushing.

In 1966, after Pasternak's death, I took a foreign edition of *Doctor Zhivago* on a trip down the Lena River and read it for the first time. I lay on a narrow sailor's berth and when my eyes moved from the pages to the Siberian landscape slowly floating past and then back to the pages, there was no border between nature and the book.

In 1972 in the USA, Lillian Hellman, John Cheever, and a few other friends were arguing about the most significant novel of the twentieth century and, in the end, we all agreed on *Doctor Zhivago*. Yes, it has flaws — the epilogue is weak and the author arranges the meetings of his protagonists too naively. But the novel is a novel of the moral breakdown of the twentieth century, a novel that puts human feelings above history. Yet when I first read it, it never occurred to me what might happen to it.

A tragic scandal broke out over the novel. It was banned in the USSR and they tried to stop its publication in Italy. Pasternak had foreseen the possibility. Feltrinelli, the publisher, later told me that by prior agreement with the author he was to believe only those telegrams and letters from Pasternak that were written in French. Pasternak sent a telegram asking him to halt publication, but the telegram was in transliterated Russian. The novel was published all over the world. A few Western newspapers printed reviews with provocative headlines like "A Bomb Against Communism." Naturally, helpful bureaucrats put these clippings with translation on Khrushchev's desk.

After the Nobel Prize, the scandal escalated. Soviet newspapers published "workers' letters" that began something like this: "I haven't read the novel *Doctor Zhivago* but I am extremely outraged by it." The secretary of the Central Committee of the Komsomol [the Communist Youth League] and future KGB Major Semichastny demanded that "the swine Pasternak be thrown out of the Soviet garden." I was called in by V. Sytin, secretary of the Party Committee, and asked to condemn Pasternak in the name of youth at the next meeting. I refused. Sytin forced me to go with him to the secretary of the Moscow Party Committee and tried to persuade me in his presence. I refused again and said that I considered Pasternak a great poet and that he was no counter-revolutionary. The secretary heard me out and unexpectedly told Sytin to leave me alone.

But the snowball kept growing. A terrible personal blow for me was the appearance against Pasternak [at the Writers' Union meeting convened for Pasternak's expulsion] by two major progressive poets, Leonid Martynov and Boris Slutsky, whom I loved and who had both suffered a long time from Stalinist censorship. I owed Slutsky a hundred rubles, and after the meeting I went up to him, handed over the money, and said loudly, "Here's your loan. . . . I still owe you thirty pieces of silver." After this, the only strangely treacherous act in his irreproachably pure life, Slutsky fell into a terrible depression and soon withdrew completely and then died. Both he and Martynov had a false idea of saving the progressive intelligentsia during the Thaw by separating the left intelligentsia from Pasternak. But the Pasternak case itself was a terrible blow to the Thaw. Having sacrificed Pasternak, they sacrificed the Thaw itself.

A few years later, after Pasternak's death, Khrushchev told Ilya Ehrenburg[1] that when he was visiting Marshal Tito on the island of Brioni, he read the complete text of *Doctor Zhivago* for the first time in Russian and was astonished not to find anything counterrevolutionary in it.

"I was tricked by Surkov and Polikarpov,"[2] Khrushchev said.

"Then why not publish the novel?" Ehrenburg asked anxiously.

"They set the whole propaganda machine against it," Khrushchev sighed. "It's all too fresh in people's minds. . . . Give us some time, and then we'll publish it." Khrushchev didn't have time to do it, and Brezhnev didn't dare.

The novel is being published at last, now in 1988, and in great

---

1. Ilya Grigoryevich Ehrenburg (1891–1967), journalist and prose writer, war correspondent. He was a public figure in good graces with the authorities throughout his career. His novel *The Thaw* gave name to the liberalized post-Stalin period.
2. Surkov was secretary of the Writers' Union, and Polikarpov headed the literary and cultural section of the Party's Central Committee.

part thanks to *Doctor Zhivago* the circulation of *Novy mir* has jumped from 400,000 to 1,100,000.

But let us return to the year of the scandal, to the time of my last meeting with Pasternak in 1960. I did not want to be a tactless condolence giver, coming by without an invitation. The poet Alexander Mezhirov told me that Pasternak would probably attend Genrich Neuhaus's concert. We went to the Conservatory, and sure enough, we saw Pasternak in the lobby. He saw us from afar, understood, came over, and trying to be his usual merry self, warmed us with kind words, undeserved compliments, and quotes from our works. He invited us to visit. I went to his dacha soon after. Pasternak still emitted light, but it was now an evening light rather than a morning one.

"Do you know," said Pasternak, "Vanya Kharabarov and Yura Pankratov were just here. They said that some people named Firsov and Sergovantsev, I believe, were collecting signatures on a petition of students from the Literary Institute demanding that I be exiled abroad. Vanya and Yura were threatened with expulsion from the Komsomol and the institute if they didn't sign. They said they had come for advice. Naturally, I said, 'Sign, what difference does it make? You can't help me anyway, and you will hurt yourselves.' I gave them permission to betray me.

"With that permission, they quickly left. I went to the window of my terrace and watched them go. And I saw that they were running like children, hand in hand and skipping with joy. You know, people of our generation were also often weak and sometimes, unfortunately, also betrayed others. . . . But still, we never leaped for joy. It was not done, it was considered improper. . . . I feel sorry for those boys. There was so much about them that was pure, provincial. . . . I'm afraid they'll never be poets now."

Pasternak was right — Ivan Kharabarov became an alcoholic and died on a park bench in his early thirties. Yuri Pankratov wrote all he had to say and is nothing as a writer.

Poetry is unforgiving. Betrayal of others becomes betrayal of yourself.

As we parted, Pasternak said, "I want to give you one piece of advice. Never predict your own tragic death in poetry, for the power of the word is such that autosuggestion will lead you to the prophesied death. Just think how careless Esenin and Mayakovsky were with self-predictions and how they ended up, killing themselves with noose and bullet. I've lived this long only because I avoided self-predictions."

This is how Pasternak inscribed the book he gave me on our first meeting, May 3, 1959:

> Dear Zhenya. Yevgeny Alexandrovich. Today you read for us and you touched me and many of the guests to tears with the proof of your talent. I am confident that you have a radiant future. I wish you more successes, may your ideas be realized in perfected, exhaustive forms that leave room for the next ideas. Grow and develop.
>
>   B. Pasternak.

I believe it was Tsvetayeva who noted that Pasternak's handwriting resembled cranes in flight.

The critic V. Barlas, who died young and who once revealed many things in Pasternak to me, wrote: "Many stay alive too long. . . . They gain only years of lies and fear." Pasternak was also afraid, and he did not always enter into direct battle with falsehood. But he stepped over his own fear, which could have turned into lies, and in dying, he gained many years of flight for his cranes.

Index

DATE DUE			

Evtushenko   234217